KW-482-642

ADVANCE AUSTRALIA ...WHERE?

HUGH MACKAY

HACHETTE AUSTRALIA

ARGYLL & BUTE LIBRARIES	
34115 00420201 2	
HJ	28-Apr-2009
306.099	£10.99

HACHETTE AUSTRALIA

First published in Australia and New Zealand in 2007
by Hachette Australia
(An imprint of Hachette Livre Australia Pty Limited)
Level 17, 207 Kent Street, Sydney NSW 2000
Website: www.hachette.com.au

Reprinted 2007 (four times), 2008

This edition published in 2008

Copyright © Hugh Mackay Pty Ltd 2007, 2008

This book is copyright. Apart from any fair dealing
for the purposes of private study, research, criticism
or review permitted under the *Copyright Act 1968*,
no part may be stored or reproduced by any process
without prior written permission. Enquiries should
be made to the publisher.

National Library of Australia
Cataloguing-in-Publication data

Mackay, Hugh, 1938- .
  Advance Australia...where?

  ISBN 978 0 7336 2362 2 (pbk.)

  1. Nationalism - Australia. 2. Self-determination,
  National - Australia. 3. Australia - Social conditions, -
  2001- . 4. Australia - Social life and customs, - 2001- .
  5. Australia - Politics and government, - 2001- . 6.
  Australia - History, - 2001- . I. Title.

306.0994

Digital production by Bookhouse, Sydney
Author photograph by Lorrie Graham
Printed in Australia by Griffin Press, Adelaide

Hachette Livre Australia's policy is to use papers
that are natural, renewable and recyclable products
and made from wood grown in sustainable forests.
The logging and manufacturing processes are expected
to conform to the environmental regulations
of the country of origin.

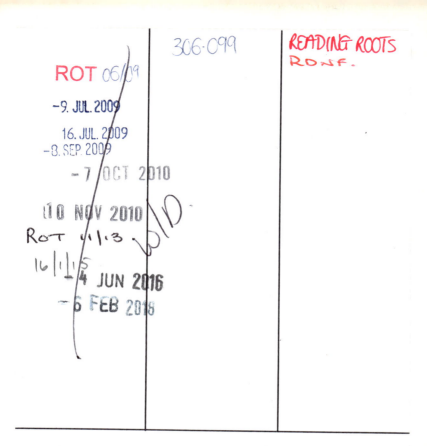

306·099

READING ROOTS
RONF.

ROT 06/09

−9. JUL. 2009

16. JUL. 2009

−8. SEP. 2009

−7 OCT 2010

10 NOV 2010

RoT 4.1.13.

16|1|15

4 JUN 2016

−6 FEB 2018

ARGYLL & BUTE COUNCIL
LIBRARY AND INFORMATION SERVICES

Books should be returned on or before the date above
Renewals may be made by personal application,
post or telephone, if not in demand

ARGYLL AND BUTE LIBRARIES

34115 00420201 2

Also by Hugh Mackay

NON-FICTION

Reinventing Australia

The Good Listener
(originally published as *Why Don't People Listen?*)

Generations

Turning Point

Media Mania

Right & Wrong

FICTION

Little Lies

House Guest

The Spin

Winter Close

To Sheila

Contents

Preface ix

Part One   How are the renovations going, Australia?   1
1   Project Australia: A work in progress   3
2   We haven't got everything right ... yet   18

Part Two   Kaleidoscope Nation   25
3   Ambiguity: The gender revolution   27
4   Uncertainty: The workplace revolution   61
5   Paradox: The IT revolution   99
6   Diversity: The identity revolution   137

Part Three Snapshots from the family album   161
7   The 'relationships' era: Reinventing
            marriage and divorce   163
8   Formula One prams: Wheeling out our
            smallest-ever generation   184
9   The mystery of the shrinking household   210

Part Four   The Dreamy Period   237
10   Turning away from The Big Picture   239

11	The quest for the perfect bathroom tile	263
12	Yearning for magic simplicities	269
13	The inward journey	278
14	A dream of 'the community'	285
15	Is the Dreamy Period coming to an end?	293
16	Re-engagement, or euphoria?	302

Part Five	**We need to talk about...**	**329**
17	Global warming: Are we serious about renewable energy?	331
18	Politics: Can we improve the system?	337
19	The Monarchy: Aren't we over it yet?	342
20	Public education: Do we really believe in it?	346
21	Poverty: A fact of life, or a problem to be solved?	354
22	Arts funding: Are we missing a golden opportunity?	361

One small step: What can an individual do?	**367**
Acknowledgments	371
Index	373

Preface

Attitudes are rather like banners fluttering in the breeze: they tell us which way the wind is blowing, but leave a lot of other questions unanswered.

As a social researcher, I'm acutely conscious of the hazards inherent in the study of attitudes. It's dangerous to assume too much from what people say: we are all very good at saying one thing and doing another. Asking questions is always risky, because most of us try too hard to give the 'right' answer. It's especially pointless to ask 'why?' (in personal relationships, by the way, as well as research) because that assumes there's a rational explanation, when there might not be. *Why did you marry that man, buy that car, take that job?* Who knows?

The other big trap is to assume attitudes predict behaviour when it's usually the other way around. Banners don't make the wind blow a certain way. Attitudes are an indicator of how we've reacted; they are not reliable predictors of how we might react to something that hasn't happened yet.

In spite of these shortcomings, attitude research is still a fruitful activity, especially when it's being used to try to explain what's going on. The birthrate is falling: *why?* The household is shrinking: *why?* Young Australians are reluctant to 'settle down' at the age their parents did: *why?* We won't find the answers to any of those questions by asking them explicitly, but there are ways of exploring people's attitudes without bludgeoning them with direct questions.

My primary source of information about attitudes is The Ipsos Mackay Report – a research project launched in 1979 as The Mackay Report and acquired by Ipsos Australia in 2003. It is based on two qualitative research techniques: non-directive group discussions and unstructured, conversational, personal interviews. All the fieldwork is done in private homes (or wherever respondents regard as their 'natural habitat') and adheres strictly to the principles of non-directive research: no questions; no predetermined structure; no restriction on the freedom of respondents to range widely over the topic.

Throughout the book, I quote respondents directly: their comments appear in italics, usually in indented paragraphs. I refer a number of times to *Mind & Mood* reports: these reports are based on freewheeling discussion about 'whatever's on your mind this week – whatever you've been thinking and talking about' and have proved, over the years, to be a valuable way of taking Australia's pulse.

My interpretation of attitudinal data is underpinned wherever possible by statistical data about Australian society. Almost all this material comes from the Australian Bureau of Statistics (ABS), one of our genuine national treasures. The ABS doesn't only conduct a world-class census; it also provides a continuous flow of information – regularly summarised in *Australian Social Trends* and *Year Book Australia* – about how Australian society is changing. *Advance Australia . . . Where?* is an attempt to analyse the reasons for these changes and examine how they are affecting our way of life. It also makes some predictions about where we're going: if you wish those predictions were bolder, try to imagine how well we could have anticipated, 20 years ago, what life would be like today.

That's the joy of contemporary Australia: it's a work in progress.

Hugh Mackay

PART ONE

How are the renovations going, Australia?

'Nice looking place you've got here'

1

Project Australia:
A work in progress

Attending a formal dinner a couple of years ago, I found myself seated beside a charming, articulate, professional woman who spent most of the evening telling me about her home renovations, including her new bathroom. I'd never met her before, had never been to her house and am never likely to. But I know more about that bathroom – especially the transforming effect of a new skylight – than I could possibly reproduce here. I know, too, that the new bi-fold doors in the living room have created a wonderfully flexible indoor/outdoor area.

It was a highly instructive conversation, and not just about the relative merits of granite and marble: it reinforced my conviction that home renovations had become the new focus of dinner-party conversation, replacing the previously fashionable exchange of cholesterol readings. It also struck me that our endless quest for the perfect bathroom tile might have become a way of distracting ourselves from some other, larger questions.

And then I had another thought: could the home renovation craze itself be a useful metaphor for the national project we've all been engaged in this past quarter-century?

Renovation is a good word for what's been happening to Australia. It suggests we're committed to improving our lot. Renovation is an optimistic activity that declares our belief in the future and our determination to make the most of it. When it comes to renovations, one thing usually leads to another: before you know where you are, you've decided to pull out the entire bathroom and install a Jacuzzi and then you realise the kitchen looks shabby, and if we tackle the rising damp in the spare room we could put in bigger windows while we're at it . . . a bit like raising education standards for women and finding the birthrate has gone through the floor, or deciding on tariff reform and then realising the labour market needs attention as well.

Renovations also create a lot of dust, debris and, occasionally, some casualties. They can drive us to distraction, too, right up there with divorce, bereavement and retrenchment on the list of things likely to adversely affect our mental health. 'Living with the renovations' is a term all home renovators understand: I once heard a woman, still recovering from the experience of having tradesmen-with-radios in her house for months, remark that even driving past a pallet of bricks outside someone else's house brought her out in a cold sweat.

Is it any wonder that, as a nation, we're a bit edgy? Who's surprised that we've established new records for consumption of tranquillisers and antidepressants? We have, after all, been transforming our society with more than a few skylights: in the past 25 years, hardly a stone has been left unturned in our relentless renovation of the way we live, the way we work, the way we marry (or not), the way we raise our children, the way we eat, the way we entertain and inform ourselves, even the way we communicate.

It's as if, on a vast national scale, we'd added a second storey to the house and taken a while to adjust to a light and airy top floor with a view we never had before. We hadn't anticipated the effort of going up and down the stairs, either, or the need to plan more carefully where to put things ('I've left my glasses upstairs again – I think I'd better get a second pair'). It also takes us a while to adapt to the new functions for some of the old downstairs rooms. Renovations change us, too.

Thirty years of work in progress

Just 30 years ago, it was a safe bet that almost everyone would get married, the vast majority of married couples would stay married, young couples would regard having children as a normal expectation and would probably start having them while the wife (never a 'partner') was in her early twenties. A career, at least for the husband, and a mortgage were stock-standard aspirations.

Those were the days when almost 90 percent of Australians were married by the age of 30, and 90 percent of births were to women under 30 (both figures having since dipped below 50 percent). Divorce was still stigmatised and no one would have predicted that 30 years later, more than 40 percent of marriages would be ending in divorce, or that about one million Aussie kids would be living with only one parent. The birthrate has fallen off a cliff: many couples now regard having children as an option rather than an expectation, and some simply leave it too late.

Even 20 years ago, only 57 percent of women in their twenties were in the workforce; today, it's 75 percent. Even more tellingly, 76 percent of women in their fifties are now in the workforce, compared with 52 percent in 1986.

Mortgages and careers? Renters now outnumber buyers in the under-35 segment of the housing market, and the straight-line/long-term career path is widely regarded by the young as a fate too tedious to contemplate.

Young people are harnessing the power of the information technology revolution in ways that leave their elders speechless. They are in continuous contact with each other and this has changed their attitudes to privacy (not very interested), planning (why settle on anything until the last minute?) and, courtesy of text messaging, language itself (btw tx 4 gr8 nite).

At work, we are still learning how to live with job insecurity and, as the distance between the top and bottom of the economic heap has grown, we have had to adapt to the prospect of a less egalitarian society than the one we used to dream of.

These aren't trends; they are fractures of trends. Trying to study changes like these is more like gazing into a kaleidoscope than a microscope.

Take the shrinking household: about 50 percent of all Australian households now contain only one or two people. Is this is a sign that we are becoming a nation of hermits? Of course not: the herd instinct is still alive and well in us. But it is a sign of how our living arrangements are affected by other societal changes. The low birthrate and high divorce rate (especially among older people) both contribute to smaller households, as does our increased longevity and the trend towards young people wanting to spend some time living alone before committing themselves to sharing a home with a partner. But even that is only one part of a more complex mosaic: some young people, as ever, choose to live in group households as a kind of surrogate extended family, while others are staying at home longer than any previous generation (about 45 percent of Australians in the 20–25 age-group are still living at home with at least one parent).

Considering the upheavals in the Australian way of life over the past 30 years, 'revolution' might be a better word than 'renovation'. Part Two explores the effects of the gender revolution, the workplace revolution wrought by the restructure of our economy, the IT revolution and even the revolution in our sense of who we are as Australians.

One obvious effect has been an overwhelming sense of busyness. Everyone is busy. Even people who aren't busy feel obliged to say they're busy. 'How are you going – *busy?*' has become our standard greeting, reflecting our hyped-up sense of constant movement, change and upheaval. In the midst of such comprehensive renovations, who's going to admit to being idle or unoccupied?

By the turn of the century, we were seeing the signs of the destabilising and sometimes debilitating effects of all this: continuing epidemics of anxiety and depression; disengagement from politics; an inward-looking focus and a loss of interest in big-picture issues; more prejudice and less tolerance in our attitudes to ethnic and other minorities.

We were also seeing the full flowering of capitalism, consumerism and materialism. We had a prime minister glowing with pride at the emergence of a nation of shareholders; politics seemed to be almost exclusively about 'the economy'; citizens were most often defined by their role as consumers, and our highly prized freedom was expressed, for most of us, as freedom to choose how to spend our money. The rise of consumerism, fuelled by the credit revolution, led us into record levels of personal and household debt.

Doubts and yearnings

Like anyone caught up in such revolutionary changes, Australians are given to moments of triumph, moments of despair and periods of re-evaluation. In the early years of the new century, the focus of our anxieties had shifted from the economy to society itself. Being no longer so concerned about unemployment, interest rates or the threat of inflation, we have had more time to reflect on some other aspects of our work in progress, and our assessments of how Australia is faring swing back and forth like an erratic pendulum.

Though we consistently assert that Australia is the best country in the world, we wonder whether our society is degenerating. 'Are our strengths becoming our weaknesses?' asked a participant in The Mackay Report's 2003 *Mind & Mood* survey, by which he meant that many of the things we are most proud of might contain the seeds of this degeneration.

We're proud of our prosperity, for instance, yet we know the gap between rich and poor is greater than ever. We believe we're all 'better off' but wonder if our very affluence causes stress. We're proud of our successful corporations, yet doubt whether the millions of dollars paid to their top executives can be justified in a society where the average annual personal income is $43 000.

You look at the Rich List they publish, and it's all terribly wonderful and glamorous but then you hear about the thousands of people who are homeless in our big cities.

I'm basically optimistic, but I do have reservations about the divisions between those who have enough and those who don't. The handouts to some of these executives would make you sick.

We're proud of our political stability, yet we regard our politicians as boring and uninspiring. Before he fell from favour prior to losing office, John Howard had been widely praised for his persistence, though few had ever been prepared to describe him as a charismatic or inspirational leader. His detractors came to regard him as a lackey of US President George W. Bush, and some believe he exerted a negative influence on the Australian psyche by reinforcing and exploiting fear and prejudice for political purposes. Labor leaders during the period of Howard's ascendancy similarly failed to ignite much enthusiasm, though Kevin Rudd's election as Labor leader at the end of 2006 generated a fresh spark of interest.

Maybe boring politicians are the price you pay for stability.

We're proud of our levels of tolerance and see ourselves as remarkably hospitable to immigrants and even refugees (apart from those we lock up in detention centres) but we sometimes wonder if we're *too* tolerant for our own good. 'Is multiculturalism working?' is a question still being canvassed by those who think of that word as having a narrow, exclusively ethnic meaning.

Australia isn't racist – we're the most welcoming country on earth. But I think we're starting to think that maybe we overdid it.

We're proud of our standards of health care, of Medicare and of the work done by medical researchers we regard as world class. But then we look at our public hospital system, stretched to capacity, and wonder why it doesn't match the quality of our health professionals. Are our hospitals top-heavy with administrators, we wonder, or are they simply starved of funds?

I hope we don't go the way of America. There, if you can't afford private health insurance, you're lucky to get the proper treatment.

We're proud of our brilliant technology, but wonder if it's contributing to the depersonalisation of society. We're proud of our efficiency and productivity, but wonder if we are putting ourselves under too much pressure. The effects of that pressure are felt not only in fatigue, but also in the perception that too many people are operating on a 'short fuse'.

Even in Byron Bay, people get into a hellish punch-up over a wave. So many people are so angry – people seem to be under more pressure, we're being pushed too hard. The mobile phone is a blessing but it means we're always on call, and the number of emails that come into my office would make you weep. When does the struggle stop? When do you get to sleep?

Australians typically offer three explanations for the belief that our society is 'degenerating': a lack of connectedness (*People won't even look you in the eye in the big cities*); a surrender to materialism (*I actually think we have too much, it makes you want more*); unbridled selfishness (*It's all me, me, me*).

But now, as we approach the end of the first decade of the new century, new directions are beginning to emerge in our thinking and dreaming. They sound like the yearnings of a society still struggling to adapt – still trying to find its bearings – in the age of discontinuity.

Recognising that so many things are beyond our control, we've shifted our focus to the things we *can* control, and that could be anything from home renovations or an obsession with body image to a world view, religious or otherwise, that helps us make sense of what's going on.

Many of us, having enthusiastically leapt onto the materialist treadmill, are starting to rethink our priorities and to wonder whether we are setting the best possible example to our children. One result of this is the surge of interest in 'values', as more Australians find themselves wondering how to restore some balance to their lives and find more time for family and friends.

Are we creating a new space for religion?

Another outcome of this period of reflection has been the return of religion to a prominent, unembarrassed place in the national conversation. Though attendance at Christian churches has declined to the point where only about 15 percent of Australians attend church at least once a month, the decline appears to have stopped and there are signs of growth, especially among young people, at the fundamentalist end of the religious spectrum. Many forms of non-traditional religious observance – Christian and non-Christian – are also emerging: home church or informal study groups, Buddhist meditation groups, inter-faith activities, faith-based rock concerts, new explorations of the meaning of God . . . even Anzac Day has taken on the character of a quasi-religious festival.

'Spirituality' may be back on the agenda, but if you fear a national outbreak of Puritanism, relax: there are more problem drinkers and serious gamblers than ever, an estimated 50 percent of under-thirties have experimented with illicit drugs, and sexual permissiveness still permeates the culture.

In *Australian Soul* (2006), Gary Bouma reports growth in what he describes as 'high-demand' religious groups such as the Catholics'

Opus Dei and the various forms of Protestant fundamentalism. (The Pentecostalist Hillsong church in Sydney, for example, claims 17 500 people participate in its weekly activities.) Such groups typically insist on narrow, prescriptive codes of dogma and religious practice, with an emphasis on separation from the world. Yet one strict fundamentalist sect, the Exclusive Brethren, has emerged as a rather improbable political pressure group: in 2004, it campaigned against Mark Latham and the Labor Party in an attempt, a spokesman later admitted to *The Sydney Morning Herald* writer David Marr, to protect federal funding for its schools – schools specifically designed to keep the sect's young people apart from Australian society.

The Family First political party, strongly supported by the Assemblies of God (another branch of Pentecostalism), similarly represents a more overt crossover between religion and politics than has been typical of Australian politics for the past quarter-century.

Growth in support for conservative religious groups such as these – whether Christian, Muslim or otherwise – might simply be a religious manifestation of a generally conservative political climate. Even so, their appeal to young people raised in a culture of gender equality is perhaps surprising, since they tend to assign secondary and even subservient roles to women. (Or is this part of the current rejection of hardline feminism by many of today's young women and in that way, paradoxically, linked to the contemporary 'raunch' culture which is itself a bizarre return to pre-feminist ideology? Chapter 3 explores this further.)

Another trigger for renewed debate about the link between religion and politics was Kevin Rudd's very public declaration of his religious convictions before he became Labor leader at the end of 2006. In media articles and interviews, Rudd claimed his religious faith was the source of his passion for social justice and that, for him, there was a natural link between Christianity and the policies of the Labor Party. That produced a flurry of reaction from religious believers on the conservative side of politics, including some unprecedented bragging about the number of Catholics on the Coalition's front bench – eight out of 18 in mid-2007 – all of which added heat to the issue. The question of politicians' religious inclinations had suddenly become a matter of interest.

The idea that religion could play a more prominent role in Australian politics is not universally welcome, especially by those who reflect on historical links between Christianity and fascism, or the bitter conflict, only recently resolved, between Catholics and Protestants in Northern Ireland, or contemporary examples of political and cultural extremism in some Islamic states. In his 2007 Manning Clark Lecture, 'Restoring the Primacy of Reason', Barry Jones noted several similarities between the religious motivations of US President George W. Bush and the leader of al-Qaeda, Osama bin Laden: 'Both are on a divine mission, fundamentalists, punitive, monocultural, prefer faith over evidence, believe in pre-emptive strikes and that necessity overrides the rule of law, manipulate fear, confuse revenge with justice . . .'

In May 2007, Andrew Denton marked his return to ABC TV with a program about religious fundamentalism in the US – just one example of a surge of interest in religion in journalism, politics and general conversation. This is partly driven by the increasing Muslim presence in Australia, drawing fresh attention to religion's potential as a strong element of cultural identity. It is also the result of more open discussion of atheism, stimulated by the popular writings of people like Richard Dawkins (*The Selfish Gene, The God Delusion*),

Sam Harris (*Letter to a Christian Nation*) and Christopher Hitchens (*God is Not Great*).

A heightened interest in the possible links between religion and moral values is reflected in growing support for church-based private schools, even among parents who may themselves have no particular religious faith but who believe such schools' religious culture may benefit their children's moral formation. Being confronted by new and challenging moral dilemmas – especially those arising from greater sexual permissiveness and others emerging from the frontiers of biotechnology that touch on the definition of life itself – some people searching for greater moral confidence are wondering whether it might be found in a religious context.

While many people express a yearning for clearer articulation of non-material values without resort to institutional religion, the whole idea of *spirituality* has acquired new currency. That may be an inevitable reaction to an overcooked materialism, but it has also arisen from our sustained epidemic of anxiety and an associated desire to find a still point in the midst of swirling uncertainty.

Our anxiety is fuelled by many things, from global issues like the threat of international terrorism, the grim scenario of global warming and the vaguely menacing rise of militant Islam, to more immediate, local issues like house prices, the burden of debt and the prospect of further interest-rate rises. Yet, being human, our deepest fear is of being cut off from the herd. Many of the changes to our way of life have had the effect of fragmenting and isolating us and, in response, there's a new craving for a sense of belonging. We like the idea of the small village, urban or otherwise – even the 'vertical villages' of apartment blocks. We want to reconnect; we want to feel part of an identifiable community.

Most people look to secular communities – including the neighbourhood itself – to satisfy their need to feel connected. But a growing number are turning to faith-based communities, formal or informal. The traditional parish church may be in decline, but new models are emerging to replace it.

The Great Australian Dream – where to now?

It's long been assumed that the Great Australian Dream was home ownership; in particular, owning a detached house with a front garden and a backyard, in a leafy suburb full of like-minded people living in similar houses. But we might have missed the point: the essence of that dream might not have been home ownership per se (though the belief that financial security depends on ownership of bricks and mortar has been planted deep in the Australian psyche). In today's jargon, it was always a *lifestyle* dream and most of us simply accepted that the house-and-garden package was the way to make it come true.

Everything's changing, including that conviction. The core dream is still about lifestyle, but our lifestyle aspirations are changing, too. So are our attitudes to the kinds of homes we might want to live in, and whether we should own or rent them. There's a new openness to apartment living, and not just among singles, childless couples or empty-nesters intent on downsizing, but even among some parents of young children who see both financial and social benefits in apartment living in inner-city communities.

The rising popularity of renting is partly a response to rising house prices that have put traditional home ownership beyond the reach of many young people in our major cities. But it's also a response to the values of a new generation who are more interested in flexibility and transience than stability and permanence. They want to keep their options open, and for longer than their parents did – especially when it comes to marriage and children. They want to create a particular lifestyle for now, but be open to other possibilities later.

With the postponement of parenthood happening on such a large scale, the urgency has gone out of the idea of establishing a conventional family home, at least for the under-35s. They are even starting to wonder whether home ownership makes as much economic sense as their parents thought it did. The Ipsos Mackay Report, *Living with Debt* (2007), found a sharp division of opinion among young adults between those who still aspire to home ownership and those who neither want nor can afford to own their own homes (or who may have tailored their aspirations to match their perception of reality).

> *For our parents' generation, buying a home was everything. It was what you wanted to do straight away. For us, it's not so important. I don't even know if I want a house. I just want to enjoy my life.*

For some, renting is a deliberate lifestyle choice; for others it's a kind of resignation to the idea that it's all too hard.

> *It's like the Australian dream is to own your own home but people are going, 'Well, that's not going to happen, so let's head off to Harvey Norman and buy a new couch instead.'*

Underlying the bravado, or the disappointment, implicit in such remarks is genuine confusion about whether home ownership is a good investment or not.

More and more people rent. They reckon they make more money doing that than buying houses. And some people put their money into a business rather than a house.

Of course, there are emotional factors at work here: particularly for the parents of young children, the 'nest' may seem more secure if it is owned. But there's a new openness to renting, and it's driven by more than economics.

2

We haven't got everything right ... yet

As with any renovation, we need to stroll around the project from time to time, checking on progress, correcting mistakes and, inevitably, discovering some neglected areas in need of attention.

Here are four to be going on with:

In April 2007, an Oxfam report on the health of Indigenous people in wealthy countries compared the situations in the US, Canada, Australia and New Zealand. Australia was rated the poorest of the four. The report was critical of the lack of political will in Australia to meet the growing crisis in Indigenous health, reflected in the fact that the life expectancy of Aborigines and Torres Strait Islanders is 17 years shorter than for non-Indigenous Australians. Oxfam noted that we spend $1.9 billion on confectionery each year, and that only a quarter of that amount spent on Aboriginal health programs would address the most pressing issues. Much of the disease among Indigenous Australians is preventable, being the result of poverty, overcrowding, poor sanitation, low levels of education, poor nutrition and poor access to accurate diagnosis and treatment.

Noel Pearson, perhaps the most widely esteemed Aboriginal leader in contemporary Australia, argues that we need to start with a determined attack on substance abuse and passive welfare. But none of this will happen without political will, and political will depends on political antennae: until politicians detect serious concern among non-Indigenous people, they are unlikely to feel obliged to tackle the problem with gusto, though the significant increase in funding for Aboriginal health in the 2007 federal budget looked like a big step in the right direction, carried further by the new Labor government in its 2008 budget.

In June 2007, in response to the latest in a series of thirteen official inquiries into sexual abuse of children in Aboriginal communities, the federal government suddenly announced it was taking control of all such communities in the Northern Territory, introducing bans on alcohol and pornography, monitoring children's school attendance and quarantining welfare payments to parents to ensure they were applied to the health and welfare of children. These proposals were described by critics as draconian, paternalistic and racist (as well as opportunistic, given an approaching federal election), but the very toughness of the measures – taken without consultation with Aboriginal leaders or the Northern Territory government – found widespread support in a society searching for the 'magic simplicities' described in Chapter 12.

Although the government's initiative was focused exclusively on the problem of child abuse, it may yet signal a summoning of the political will to tackle some broader Aboriginal health and welfare issues. When Kevin Rudd became prime minister in December 2007, he announced that reducing the gap in life expectancy between Indigenous and non-Indigenous Australians would be a high priority for his government and would be the subject of annual reports to the federal parliament.

In January 2007, while still Opposition leader, Kevin Rudd released some disturbing figures about education spending. We thought we were so smart about education: weren't we supposed to be up there with the world's best? Hadn't we once touted ourselves as the Knowledge Nation?

It turns out Australia only invests 5.8 percent of its gross domestic product (GDP) in education, which puts us eighteenth – close to the bottom – among countries in the Organisation for Economic Co-operation and Development (OECD). We're well below the OECD average for spending on early childhood education, and we have one of the lowest secondary-school retention rates in the OECD.

When we neglect one part of the renovation, others are affected. Rudd's announcement quoted statistics showing Australia's productivity has declined in line with education funding.

According to one of our foremost educationists, Professor Barry McGaw, public investment in universities has fallen by seven percent in the past decade, compared with an average *increase* of 48 percent in the OECD. Writing in *New Matilda* on 31 January 2007, McGaw noted that between 1995 and 2003, the public funding share of total tertiary education funding fell from 65 percent to 48 percent, which puts us twenty-fifth in the OECD. That reflects a shift to private funding of tertiary education, via HECS and a growing number of full-fee-paying students. Yet McGaw points out that only public funding makes a substantial contribution to the infrastructure that supports basic research, and private funding is inadequate to cover teaching and research (hence the rapid rise in student-to-staff ratios in our universities, from 14:1 in 1995 to 20:1 now).

In his 2007 budget, the federal treasurer, Peter Costello, addressed some of these concerns with the establishment of a $5 billion Education Fund whose investment earnings will be used to finance university infrastructure and research into the future, though teaching remains under-resourced. The Labor government extended this initiative in its 2008 budget by adding a further $5 billion and recasting the fund as the Education Investment Fund, designed to benefit TAFE, and possibly schools, as well as universities.

And here's a dark little corner, overlooked in our enthusiasm for some of the other renovations: a 2007 UNICEF report on the welfare of children in 20 economically advanced countries shows that nearly ten percent of Australian children live in households where no one is employed – and that's the highest rate of all the countries on the list except Hungary. The implications are significant for the health of those children: in *Inequality in Australia* (2003) Alastair Greig and his co-authors note that children who live in households where no one is employed have 27 percent more chronic sickness than other children.

Another worrying thing: while we've been preoccupied with the renovations, we've scarcely noticed our children putting on weight. Twenty-five percent of Australian children are either overweight or obese – double the proportion of 20 years ago. Given the greater risks of diabetes, heart and liver disease associated with obesity, this may be the first generation of children who won't live as long as their parents. With both parents working, more time spent sitting in front of computer screens, easy access to processed food and busy parents' growing inclination to use food as a treat or a reward, it's not surprising that children are getting fatter. (By the way, parental example might have something to do with it: 60 percent of Australian adults are now either overweight or obese.)

Like all renovators, we're jumpy about crime. While you're doing your renovations, you feel as if your property is less secure, you might be being ripped off and the very act of renovating might be drawing attention to your home as a target for burglars or vandals.

On a societal scale, there's a similar trend: our generalised sense of insecurity needs something to focus on, which is why our fear of crime greatly outstrips the reality. The past 15 years have seen most forms of crime either plateau or decline in Australia as in many other places, including the US.

But our fear is not entirely irrational: according to 2004 figures published by *The Economist*, Australia is the worst country in the world for serious assault (followed, a fair way back, by Sweden, and significantly worse than South Africa). The international economic forecaster IBIS*World* has 2006 data showing that one in two Australians are likely to be assaulted in their lifetime. Though average figures obviously conceal regional and other variations, and some groups (like young males) are disproportionately represented in the figures, IBIS*World* is right to warn that 'Australia is not a safe place to live, by developed world standards'. Still, the US's murder rate is more than three times higher than ours and Russia's more than ten times higher, so there's that to be thankful for.

'I'm so, like, over it?'

On a building site – including a home laid waste by renovations in progress – the mood is informal and bustling. The language is simple and direct. There's an air of impermanence. And that's a bit like Australia's current style: nothing too formal for a nation in the throes of redeveloping, redecorating and redefining itself.

We're keen to create a casual, relaxed ambience wherever possible, partly as an antidote to stress and partly as a symbol of our bravado in the face of a dark and daunting world. 'Don't stress!' we urge each other, even when a bit of stress might be appropriate.

Many of us go to work looking like people dressed for renovations (who'd wear a suit to knock down a wall or paint a cupboard?): by dressing more casually, perhaps we hope to make work seem less stressful. We look for casual dining experiences that will eliminate the risk of being intimidated by a snooty waiter in a formal setting. We strive for the casual look as evidence that we have achieved the cool lifestyle we aspire to.

The casualisation of language is part of the same culture shift: we favour the vernacular even in situations where a more formal approach would once have been expected. *G'day. How's it going? No worries. Have a good one. Catch you later.* When talking to an older person, for instance, or in a formal business setting, first names have largely replaced Mr or Ms, even when complete strangers are being addressed. 'Hold the line, James, I'll just see if Bill is available' where James, a 50-year-old, has announced himself to the switchboard operator as 'James Bond' and was half-expecting to be called 'Mr Bond' by the young-sounding telephonist, and Bill is the CEO whose status, James assumed, might also have warranted a respectful 'Mr'.

(James had forgotten to apply the building-site test: would the brickies call the builder 'Mr'?)

Formal letters – 'snail mail' – are now a rarity and even when they are written, they are taking on the informality of emails and text messages. 'Dear Jack' is now considered archaic if not prehistoric. You might get an unadorned 'Jack' or, if your correspondent is in a friendly mood, 'Good morning Jack' which can read oddly if you're opening your mail in the evening. 'Hi Jack' (already the gold standard for email salutations) is gaining ground too, in an attempt to blur the traditional distinction between written and oral language. And when was the last time you received a letter that ended with 'Yours sincerely'? 'Cheers', perhaps, or 'Regards' if you're over 50. 'Best wishes' is a current favourite, as long as your correspondent isn't in too much of a hurry; otherwise, you'll have to make do with 'Best'.

No doubt the cycle will turn, and formality will become the next big thing. We may never again receive letters signed 'Your humble servant' but fashions will stiffen; women will cover up (so tattoos will die a natural death); men will wear hats. But not yet: we're still a work in progress, and we need to keep our sleeves rolled up for that.

Renovations are an exhausting business. Who's surprised that, after 30 years of it, we decided it was time for a break? Is it any wonder we drifted off into the Dreamy Period (Part Four)? How that happened, why it happened and what will happen next, is the story of this book.

PART TWO

Kaleidoscope Nation

'I know we can't turn back the clock, but...'

3

Ambiguity: The gender revolution

Ask any woman under the age of 30, and she's likely to tell you she isn't a feminist. Doesn't like that label at all. Doesn't identify with it. For her, as for the unreconstructed male chauvinists of old, the very word conjures up images of overalls and hairy armpits. This can seem a bit puzzling at first: in so many ways, today's young woman seems like a feminist. You can see in her the attitudes and values of feminism; its signs and symbols are etched into her psyche. (Doesn't she know that about herself?) She may even think of herself as a counter-revolutionary and yet, like any counter-revolutionary, she is truly a daughter of the gender revolution.

Ask her, point-blank, about that magic word: liberation. *Ha!* She'll tell you the feminists got it wrong. She thinks hardline, old-style (i.e., pioneering) feminists defined liberation as a woman needing to achieve emotional and economic independence *in a certain approved way* that always included paid employment outside the home. If you were going to have a family, it meant having a family *and* a career. Ideally, it also meant accepting nothing less than a husband who believed passionately in the equality – indeed, the interchangeability – of men and women, was prepared to reveal his 'feminine side', and threw himself into housework and child-rearing with a zeal previously reserved for football, beer, meat pies and cars or, perhaps, paid work (that traditional bastion of male supremacy).

She'll tell you the old definitions of liberation were too narrow, too prescriptive, and based on just one idea: that a woman could not only have it all but *all at once*. Today's young women claim to be astonished that their mothers could have got it so wrong: *She said she was never going to be a doormat to the family like her own mother was, and then she became a slave to her so-called liberation. How stupid was that?*

They will sometimes acknowledge the long and often bitter culture wars fought by their mothers and grandmothers, but they refuse to be too impressed. After all, they say, how ridiculous that women ever put up with being treated as second-class citizens. How could anyone have ever thought men and women were anything other than equal? They talk of 'moving on' and they resent the criticism of some hardliners that they have sold out the feminist project, or turned back the clock by refusing to conform to the particular meanings of liberation that had currency 25 or 30 years ago – 'before we were born'.

For many young women, the meaning of liberation – if you're going to insist on using that word at all – is both simple and obvious. It means this: 'We're free to be whoever and whatever we want to be.' And this: 'We're free to change.' And this: 'We're free to have it all, but we're not going to fall for the trap of trying to have it all at once.' She may even tell you that truly liberated women are prepared to laugh at sexist jokes if they're funny.

Revolutions as fundamental and radical as this inevitably push beyond the agenda defined by the pioneers whose vision created its initial focus and whose energy – and anger – gave it momentum. The concessions won by one generation are taken for granted by the next, and changing circumstances and mores will either kill off or breathe new life into a well-worn term like 'liberation'. Ambiguity – multiple meanings, apparent contradictions, shifting ground, blurred focus – is the very essence of revolution. Each of us makes our own sense of what is going on: we tailor the messages of the revolution to our particular needs and circumstances.

In any case, it's not only free-spirited young women who challenge the ideals of the feminist pioneers: right from the beginning of the revolution, another group of women has clung defiantly to the idea of dependency on a man for no other reason than to provide themselves with a comfortable and prosperous lifestyle. The price such women pay is the knowledge that they are not being true to the ideals (possibly their own ideals) of equality: they accept a subservient role because, to be frank, they are not prepared to give up the comforts – the houses, the cars, the clothes, the travel – that go with the territory. Trapped in unfulfilling marriages, they find themselves living out one of the worst nightmares of feminism: staying, because they know how radically their circumstances would be altered if they were to leave. Here's their favourite joke: What's the four-letter word that keeps marriages together? Half.

What would the boiler-suited radicals of the 1970s say about the feisty, sceptical, sassy young women of today who wear sexy clothes and expensive make-up, and argue that the hallmark of feminism is not necessarily independence (economic or otherwise) but freedom of choice? What would they say about the proposition that freedom of choice includes the freedom to choose to be a dependent wife, at least for a while – 'as long as you love the guy' – or never to have children, or never to let a career get in the way of a lifestyle . . . or any other permutations of possibilities? What would they say about a generation that seems to revel in its ambiguities?

We know what they'd say, because they're saying it.

Some of them are affronted, offended and disappointed by what they see as a sell-out or repudiation of the messages of the women's movement, and a failure to respect its achievements and its heritage. 'How can you be a dependent wife and call yourself liberated?' they ask. 'How can you look like that – as if you're dressing up to attract men – and still call yourself a feminist?'

Part of the answer coming from the rising generation is, of course, that they may choose not to call themselves feminists at all, lest that label burden them with outmoded connotations. But the more complete answer, according to the new breed, is simple: liberation is meaningless if it doesn't imply freedom to be whatever kind of woman you want to be – and to be different kinds of women at different stages of your life, or even at different times of the day.

The older generation persists, trying not to sound too conservative or too prudish: 'How sure are you that you're equal? Don't you know working women still earn less, on average, than men? How can you associate yourselves with a religion that treats women as second-class citizens? How sure are you that you haven't fallen for the manipulators and seducers of the fashion industry and made yourselves into pawns and sex objects again? How smart was it to be prepared to give boys oral sex at 15? What were you getting out of that, if not some hollow popularity based on your willingness to subjugate yourself to second-class status in the relationship – if you can even call that sort of thing a relationship? Women's Lib was about dignity, you know, as well as independence.'

This debate will rage forever; it's partly about age versus youth. But the pioneering feminists are passionate in their concern about the implications of 'raunch' culture in fashion, music and advertising, the explosion of internet pornography that portrays women as sex toys or worse, and about the re-emergence of celebrities, from Paris Hilton to Victoria Beckham, who seem to undermine key messages of the women's movement. Is this a mere backlash? Does it represent a significant retreat from the gains of the movement? Is it just another face of modern commercialism? Or is it an attack on feminism more lethal than any mounted by men?

The life and death of Supermum

Not all older women are affronted by the new ambiguities in the approach of young women to gender issues. Some of those who struggled with the double or triple demands placed on them by the gender revolution are downright envious: while they believe Women's Lib was a necessary, long-overdue correction of inequality, injustice and unfairness, they ruefully admit that their own lives became unbalanced. They now wonder whether they sacrificed too much of their marriage and family life in their drive to establish a non-domestic identity and a measure of economic independence. Looking back they wonder whether it was ever really possible to have it all at once: *Something had to suffer – either your working life or your home life, and the choice was very painful: either you were letting down the sisterhood, or you were letting down your nearest and dearest.*

The holy grail of paid work outside the home came at a high price. Because paid work was not generally regarded as an alternative to marriage and children, or to the responsibilities of running a household, the 'have it all' mantra created a caricature of liberation: Supermum! Faster than a speeding 4WD on the way to childcare. More powerful than a man. Able to leap tall piles of dirty washing in a single bound.

This was the woman of theoretically boundless energy, who mixed it with the men at work and who fell for the idea that a woman actually had to outperform a man in order to be taken seriously in a blokey corporate culture.

But that was just the start. While she was inspired by the goals, the slogans and the spirit of the women's movement, there was another huge influence upon her: her own mother. Her mother had passed on to her a set of traditional expectations about marriage, home life and, in particular, the provision of grandchildren. So Supermum was torn. She had to be modern and traditional all at once: brilliance at work had to be matched by brilliance in the marriage, brilliance in parenting, brilliance in cooking and entertaining, and brilliance in housekeeping.

No wonder Supermum fell in a heap – emotionally if not physically. 'I can't be a workhorse all day and a show pony at night,' said one of my research respondents at the height of all this silliness, explaining why her sex life was in tatters and her marriage on the rocks.

Sanity finally prevailed for many of these women, but not before they had suffered unacceptable levels of stress, frustration and hardship. The myth of Supermum has been overwhelmed by reality, but it has destroyed many relationships and left many women – and men – bewildered by what happened. The dream, for many, became a nightmare; liberation did indeed come to feel like enslavement.

Watching all this were their daughters, wide-eyed with disbelief. *Some liberation – she's exhausted every night, she's permanently on a short fuse and all the fun seems to have gone out of her life. And for what?*

That searing question 'for what?' is the one that hurts. 'To change the world,' their mothers might want to answer. 'To pave the way for your generation. To prove to you that girls can do anything.'

Ah, say the daughters, but who was ever foolish enough *not* to think girls can do anything? Yes, we want it all, too, but we're not crazy enough to try to have it all at once. A career? Yes, or maybe several. Marriage? Not yet, but one day, possibly. Motherhood? Perhaps. But we're not rushing anything.

Their mothers are proud of this rising generation of young women – these new-wave feminists who don't even know they're feminists – though some tremble at their teenage daughters' nonchalance and confidence. *On the way to ballet in the car, she whips her pad off and puts another one on – I don't say anything. My mother never even called them periods.* That mother was quoted in The Ipsos Mackay Report, *Mothers & Daughters* (2002). Here's a 14-year-old from the same study: *I'm going to wear a black and red dress at my wedding.* (Perhaps the real surprise is that she's already contemplating a wedding.)

Mothers have encouraged all this liberation but they sometimes feel they are being drawn by their daughters into an even more open and communicative relationship than they had bargained for: 'She insists we talk about everything,' says one bemused mother. That kind of openness is hard to resist, but it can also be a challenge.

Today's young post-revolutionaries love being female and feel more in control of their lives than their mothers did at the same age.

They believe the world is their oyster; *choice* is the air they breathe. They sense that they and their mothers are on the same side, often united in their attempts to educate fathers and husbands who still seem a bit slow when it comes to grasping the full import of gender issues. They sometimes feel sorry for boys who 'don't get it', but have zero tolerance when it comes to older males who dare to patronise them or try to intimidate them because they are women.

The gender revolution at work

One of the most significant changes of the past 15 years has been the decline of mothers' guilt about the time they spend in paid work. Some mothers still agonise about whether their children are suffering because they are so busy, or so tired, as a consequence of trying to combine paid work with motherhood. But there's a new note of determination and even defiance in the attitudes of today's mothers. Many of them have passed the point of debating the issue: the pressure on their household budgets simply compels them to work. Even if they don't feel so compelled, women are more confident, more comfortable with the idea of combining paid work with motherhood, and they typically believe they are ordering their priorities fairly.

This is partly because the participation of mothers in the workforce has increased to the point where it now seems 'normal', and partly because mothers are more inclined to settle for a manageable level of part-time work while they are still juggling the demands of parenting. It's also partly because men are now expected to take more responsibility for the care of children. Fifteen years ago, male guilt about the competing demands of work and family was virtually nonexistent; today, any guilt about the amount of time available for parenting is being shared along with the childcare responsibilities.

In spite of the maturing of the gender revolution, it's still fair to say that, in Australian business at large, the rhetoric continues to outstrip the reality when it comes to an understanding of what women (and, increasingly, men) want from work. The women's movement might have redefined the institution of marriage and the character of family life and recast the political landscape, but many employers have failed to grasp what the revolution is really about, and have therefore failed to harness its power. In particular, there's a lingering male attitude in many organisations that assumes women are at work in a kind of 'amateur' capacity, especially if they are mothers, too; that it's 'nice' for a married woman with children to have a job; that the meaning of work doesn't have the same potency for women (especially if they are part-time employees) as for men.

About 45 percent of the workforce is female, and women hold roughly that same proportion of managerial and professional positions. But once you look a little higher up the corporate ladder, the picture changes radically. Among the Australian Stock Exchange's top 200 companies, women account for only ten percent of executive managers, 8.6 percent of board directors and 2.3 percent of CEOs. In the big law firms, women comprise 50 percent of new entrants but only 12 percent of partners.

Ah, yes, it's the glass ceiling, you may be thinking, and no doubt that's one factor limiting the accession of women to the top jobs. There are organisations, even today, where the culture is so unremittingly blokey and where male chauvinism is so rampant – often cleverly hidden behind inclusive-sounding corporate slogans – that women, feeling like aliens, prefer to leave rather than fight a battle for recognition that seems both unfair and undignified.

'This is the 21st century,' such women will say, 'why do we still have to convince men that we should be treated as equals?' Young women in particular are often appalled by the discovery that, at work, they are expected to tolerate older males who talk and act like unreconstructed chauvinists: 'Where have they been hiding? Who lets them get away with this? Haven't they got wives or daughters?'

But the blokiness of corporate culture is not only about gender prejudice; it's also about attitudes to work, and a belief that hard-driving, ruthless, competitive strategies are the only way to get to the top. Men in such a culture are often suspicious of the very notion of co-operation, and far more interested in outcomes than processes. 'They still play last-car-out-of-the-carpark-wins,' says one disillusioned female executive who has moved to a small firm where she can exert more influence on the culture. Another refugee from a large law firm describes 'wall-to-wall suits, slaving over their billable hours as if they have to put in all those hours to get the work done, when it's really only about money and status'.

That may be an unfairly jaundiced view, but it betrays a growing impatience with a corporate culture that doesn't so much create a glass ceiling as offer an unattractive glimpse of what lies in store for women who want to persist in the scramble up the traditional pyramid. To many women – especially those entertaining the idea of having children – life at the top looks either unreasonably onerous or just plain silly: 'Who'd want the boss's job? He's on his third marriage, never sees his kids, and goes home late with a bulging briefcase every night. Is he using the job to escape from something, is he inefficient, or is the workload really that absurd?'

Of course there's no one way of being a woman (or man) at work, and no single conclusion to be drawn about the ways women are subtly transforming the workplace. It's even simplistic to talk about the mere presence of more women at work having the effect of 'feminising' the workplace (though the workplace is being feminised in other ways, as we'll see later). Some women are clearly out to beat the blokes at their own game – dressing, talking and acting in ways that seem 'masculine', as if they still believe masculinity is one of the qualities required for success in management ranks. (Ironically, this represents a contradiction of one of the most fundamental themes of the women's movement.) The phenomenon of a female manager who is tougher than any male is well known in many organisations: 'I'd much rather work for a man than a woman,' is a typical sentiment expressed by women who report that female bosses – especially those who have elected not to have children – often seem to be trying too hard to outplay the men at their own game. Research conducted by the national recruitment firm Talent2 has found that 90 percent of the female workforce would prefer to work for a man.

I don't know whether she was jealous of my private life or just so determined to get ahead, but she was the most unsympathetic boss I've ever had. Men generally seem more sympathetic to the lot of the working mother, perhaps because they hear all about it from their own wives.

Among women who are trying to juggle their work and domestic responsibilities (and it's still true that mothers tend to take more responsibility than fathers for home and family), the thing they typically crave is a more balanced relationship between work and the rest of their lives.

They are looking for employment in organisations where there's more than empty rhetoric about gender issues, where the CEO understands the distinctive value women can bring to the organisation, and where that understanding is expressed in more flexibility in working arrangements – especially during the years of maximum responsibility for dependent children. We know that more highly educated women tend to have fewer children (discussed further in Chaper 8); what we still don't really know is whether that's simply because they favour careers over motherhood, or whether it's at least partly because employers make the combination too hard to manage.

Women are looking for jobs in places where it is accepted as fair and reasonable that people – male or female – should attach equal value to their work and family lives and where that conviction is reflected in the hours they are expected to work. Women who prefer to work part-time are also wanting to find employers who don't equate 'part-time' with 'half-hearted' and who recognise that an employee – man or woman – with a well-balanced life is likely to be a more valuable, more productive, more cheerful member of the workforce.

Liberated women had hoped to be able to liberate the corporate culture as well, rather than simply conforming to 'the way things have always been around here'. If their voices are not being heard in large, lumbering organisations, they will look for opportunities in smaller, more nimble enterprises where they might be taken more seriously.

As the rising generation enters the labour market, the push for more flexibility in working arrangements and a better work/family/leisure balance is unlikely to be confined to women. Young men are talking that language, too. They are, after all, members of the keep-your-options-open generation and their attitudes to work, like their attitudes to everything else, are more flexible and more assertive than most employers have been accustomed to. They are going to arrive on the employer's doorstep determined not only that work should take its proper place in their lives but also that the organisation they work for should reflect the values they believe in.

Women have been trying to develop a new way of thinking about work. But as the revolution matures, it may turn out to have been more about sanity – balance, values, clarifying the meaning and purpose of our lives – than about gender.

The granny backlash

One reason for the demise of Supermum was that her parents – especially her mother – came to the rescue. The current generation of grandparents has created one of the most formidable army of volunteers Australia has ever seen. In their teeming thousands, they are the unpaid helpers – nappy-changers, child-minders, unofficial playgroup leaders, homework supervisors, meal preparers – who make the lives of many of today's working mothers manageable. It's not a universal phenomenon, of course: many working mothers struggle without parental support and either have to pay for childcare or try to juggle their various responsibilities in ways reminiscent of the Supermum madness.

But those loving, supportive grandparents who have facilitated their daughters' liberation are themselves in danger of being cast in the role of Supergran. Daughters who have now produced a child or two and are determined to press on with their careers are inclined to assume that their mothers will step in whenever required to help with the children. It can be a tough call for the grandmothers: it's not that they don't want to help; it's not that they don't love their grandchildren (and feel themselves lucky to have them, when so many of their friends are still waiting); it's not that they don't have the time. The problem is that they are in danger of feeling as if they are being taken for granted.

They were half-hoping to have some kind of life of their own around about now, being relieved of the pressures of raising their own children, and with retirement or semi-retirement a reality. They had been dreaming of freedom, independence, flexibility – perhaps some extended travel. Instead, in many cases, they find themselves with an inflexible schedule of child-minding:

We pick up my daughter's children from school three days a week, and look after them until her partner gets back from work. It's often after dinner which means we feed them as well. Then we have the little one – my son's daughter – on Tuesdays and Thursdays. She's in childcare two days and with her other grandparents on Fridays. It means you have to plan everything around the times when you're responsible for the children. We love them dearly, of course, but it isn't what we expected...

Most of the grandparents involved in these arrangements do indeed love the kids and are pleased to be having this time with them. They are also conscious of having encouraged their daughters to maximise their potential in education and a career, and they acknowledge that this had to come at a price: 'We wanted her to do all this, so we can hardly complain when she needs help to make it happen.'

But a shadow lurks, and it is the shadow of resentment. Grandparents who feel they are simply 'on tap', with no thought given to their own needs or other activities, are understandably inclined to feel they are being put upon. And if the daughter says she's not going to work today because she's exhausted or unwell, or just 'needs some time', but still expects the grandparents to look after the children in the normal way, they may wonder if things have rather got out of hand.

In some cases, the grandparents ruefully acknowledge that this is merely an extension of their overindulgence of the children when they were younger: *We did everything for her then, so it's more of the same, really. We should have been tougher, but we weren't, so I guess we're partly to blame.*

The shadow darkens, though, when they hear their daughter airily saying to someone, 'I'm so lucky to have Mum around. I certainly won't be there for my grandkids – I'll still be working.' Translation: Mum was always a bit of a doormat, and nothing's changed. But I'm determined not to be like that if I ever have grandchildren. I'm a working mother and I'll be a working grandmother. (Possible additional subtext: even if I'm not working by then, I'll be valuing my freedom too much to be bound by the responsibilities of looking after grandchildren – one go at parenting will be enough for me.) Mothers who have been advised by their daughters to 'get a life' are sometimes driven to wonder what would happen to the grandchildren if they did. But the most charitable of them simply revel in grandparenthood and see this as the 'life' they've got.

In some reaches of the upper-middle socio-economic stratum, the expectation that grandparents will help out extends to financial support: the fees of many children at private schools are at least partly subsidised by their grandparents.

Will there be a grandparents' revolt? It's already happening – very gently – in some families: *I've told them one day a week is my limit next year. They'll have to make other arrangements. And we've made it clear that as soon as the kids are a bit older, we're going to take our long-promised trip, so something's got to give.*

Such grandparents are not reneging on their enthusiasm for the liberation of women; they are not retreating from the position of support and admiration of their daughters' achievements. They are simply drawing the line at exploitation.

Flashback: why a 'women's movement'?

You can still find women whose eyes fill with tears when they describe their encounter with Germaine Greer's first book, *The Female Eunuch*: 'I felt as if she had given me permission to express all my pent-up rage and resentment.'

Pent-up rage and resentment? How quickly we forget. The gender revolution in this country is barely 30 years old. As recently as 1977, a rising young female journalist on the Melbourne *Age* was told by her editor that she wouldn't be promoted to A Grade, because 'I don't give A Grades to women'. End of discussion. A few years previously, it had been explained to her that although she would put exactly the same contribution into superannuation as her male colleagues, she would only be able to receive two-thirds of the death and disablement benefits available to men. Why? Because she was a woman, of course. What other explanation was required?

A mere 30 years ago, married women were barred from holding permanent positions in the public service. If a woman married, she

had to resign from the permanent staff, since ~
to be reserved for breadwinners – mostly men
single women could just about qualify, as lon
to receive equal treatment. Lest we forget what ~
was all about, perhaps we need to remind ourselves that such attit~
were not only prevalent up to the mid-1970s but that, at the time,
most men didn't even acknowledge that there was an issue. That was
simply the way the world was. In the world of work, in particular,
women were simply regarded as inferior beings – they were worth
less money, less protection, less respect.

It was a time when a senior Australian public servant (male) could
get away with writing stuff like this:

> Even after some deliberation, it is difficult to find reasons to support
> the appointment of women Trade Commissioners.
>
> In countries where publicity media is well developed ... a relatively
> young, attractive woman could operate with some effectiveness, in
> a subordinate capacity. As she would probably be the only woman
> Assistant Trade Commissioner in the whole area ... she could attract
> a measure of interest and publicity.
>
> If we had an important trade in women's clothing and accessories,
> a woman might promote this more effectively than a man.
>
> Even conceding these points, such an appointee would not stay
> young and attractive for ever and later on could well become a
> problem.

And what might that 'problem' be, 'later on'? The author of this 1963
Australian government Minute Paper, Mr A.R. Taysom, was in no
doubt, and had no hesitation in spelling it out: 'A spinster lady can,
and very often does, turn into something of a battleaxe with the

ıg years. A man usually mellows.' (Yes, you read it correctly: ó3, not 1863.) Yet Mr Taysom's effort was consistent with the culture of the era. Even ten years later, such sentiments might have raised an eyebrow but they would not have been regarded as outrageous.

That document listed several difficulties associated with the appointment of female trade commissioners, all of which reflected, deadpan, the thinking of the time: men would be reserved in dealing with a woman, so she might not be as successful in obtaining information as a man would be; she would be unlikely 'to stand the fairly severe strains and stresses, mentally and physically, which are part of the life of a trade commissioner'; whereas a man 'normally has his household run efficiently by his wife, who also looks after much of the entertaining', a woman would have 'all this on top of her normal work'; most men's clubs do not allow women members, so they could not mix as freely with businessmen as men do. And the clincher: 'A woman would take the place of a man and preclude us giving practical experience to one male officer.'

Before you rush to judge Mr Taysom too harshly, hark to the words of a P.S. to his Minute Paper, penned by Mr N. Parkinson of the Department of External Affairs, concerning the employment of External Affairs trainees.

Since their recruitments of trainees are made under the Public Service Act, there is no way of precluding women from applying and in fact, many more applications are received from women than from men. Some are chosen and all appointments are made on the basis of the quality of their educational achievements.

About one woman is appointed to every twelve men. This year, one out of sixteen, last year one out of twelve and the previous year, none.

They have to be trained for 18 months before going to their first post. The average marries within five years.

It is a very expensive process, but External Affairs lack courage to slam the door because of parliamentary opinion, pressure groups and so on.

In 1963, those 'pressure groups' were like a faint, distant rumble from the revolution that was racing towards us, but only a few women and almost no men understood what was coming. The very year in which Messrs Taysom and Parkinson were articulating the reasons why women either shouldn't or couldn't rise to executive heights, Betty Friedan swept the world with her bestseller, *The Feminine Mystique,* in which she dared to name 'the problem with no name': the invisibility of women in societies that treated them as second-class citizens. The long-term effects of that treatment had become clear: ennui, emptiness and, all too often, a sense of worthlessness expressed in the common cry that 'I sometimes feel as if I don't exist'.

Friedan acknowledged her debt to Simone de Beauvoir's 1949 classic, *The Second Sex,* but it was Friedan herself who supplied the inspiration and the language to a generation of women who were about to become the revolutionaries of the Women's Liberation movement. Later, the fuel of anger and outrage was thrown on the revolutionary fire by Kate Millett's *Sexual Politics* and Greer's *The Female Eunuch* (both published in 1970). By the late 1970s, the revolution was in full swing.

And what a revolution is has turned out to be! Some ageing Australians may hanker after the peace and prosperity of the 1950s, but recollections of fabulous postwar economic growth and zero unemployment can blind us to the ugly realities of a period in our cultural history when many women were actually oppressed; when they knew their place was in the home whether they liked it or not; when many of them tried to take the edge off their boredom, their frustration, or their sullen resentment by the massive abuse of analgesics like Bex and Vincent's APC powders.

One of the most insidious forms of 1950s-style oppression was the strategy of claiming to value women highly, even putting them on a pedestal, as a way of never having to listen to their pleas for recognition. It was a clever strategy: while seeming to elevate women, it in fact kept them in their place and denied them equality with men.

Is it any wonder that in such a cultural climate, the birthrate went through the roof? What else were women to do but fulfil their destiny as mothers and homemakers? Why wouldn't it have been normal for girls to leave school at 15? Why wouldn't girls in their late teens have started accumulating a 'glory box', sometimes dubbed the 'hope chest', in anticipation of an early marriage that would rescue them from being, in the language of the time, left on the shelf?

Not all women welcomed the revolution, though, when it loomed up at them with its call to liberation. Some feared it; some ridiculed it; some felt genuine contentment with their lot and predicted nothing but trouble for a society that was foolishly trying to break down traditional gender stereotypes. Some fought back: the 'women who want to be women' movement was aimed at reinforcing the idea that women had a special place in society that was determined by their biology – a position that would be eroded if they tried to compete with men on their own terms. Many such women saw feminism as a challenge or even an affront to their femininity.

But gradually the message of liberation began to make sense, not just to the women who had gone to the barricades but to their more timid sisters as well. Once the window had been opened, there was no closing it. Light and air had streamed in, stimulating and nurturing the revolutionary spirit, and women began to respond to the promise of a new sense of identity, freedom and power. Here was the chance to throw off the yoke of second-class citizenship. Why wouldn't women have grabbed the opportunity to achieve a new-found sense of emotional and economic liberation that could only come from a sense of equality with men? This was not to deny the differences between the sexes, but simply to find ways of lowering the barriers of discrimination against women.

And why wouldn't they be outraged, all these years later, when they come across a relic, a dinosaur who doesn't get it? Many young women, born after the revolutionary dust had settled, have proceeded through primary and secondary school in a state of blithe acceptance of their equality with boys, only to encounter older men at university or in the workplace who think they are entitled to patronise them, harass them, touch them – or ignore them – *because they are women*. 'What planet do they come from?' is the response of young women who are usually more astonished than outraged at the discovery that some men still don't understand the meaning of 'equality'.

Many women will say the revolution is far from over. In her 2005 book, *The End of Equality,* Anne Summers notes that, on the latest available evidence, 1.1 million Australian women have experienced some form of violence in a domestic relationship. Summers also asserts that women's average earnings, across full- and part-time work, are still only 66 percent of men's. According to 2007 research conducted by the Australian Council of Trade Unions, women in full-time work earn an average of ten percent less than their male equivalents and ACTU president Sharan Burrow claims that women in the Australian workforce still suffer the same gender pay-gap they did in 1978.

Even so, it is arguable that of all the social, cultural, economic and technological revolutions that have swept our society in the last quarter-century, the greatest has been the gender revolution. By fundamentally redefining the role and status of half the population (and, in the process, calling on the other half to do some painful rethinking), the women's movement has transformed us, and is still transforming us.

As the evidence to be presented in Part Three demonstrates, the gender revolution has twirled the national kaleidoscope more vigorously than any of the other revolutions that are reshaping us. It has rewritten our marriage, divorce and birthrate statistics, changed the character of family life in controversial ways – partly through the rise of the one-parent family and partly through the emergence of the two-income family as the norm – and accelerated the shrinkage of the Australian household. It has helped to alter the character of many suburban neighbourhoods which are no longer populated by stay-at-home mums by day, nor linked so readily by the relationships formed between children on the school bus or in the street. It has also driven the transformation of the consumer marketplace and the retail environment, with its growing emphasis on prepared meals, single-serve food packages and high-speed self-service. It has transformed the workplace, the education system and the political landscape. (How many women, today, seek how-to-vote advice from their husbands?)

Whether they choose to call themselves feminists or not, today's women, young and old, are reaping the very reward anticipated by the revolutionary feminists: a new-found sense of identity *as women*, and an unprecedented degree of emotional and economic freedom and independence. If that bothers you, consider the alternative: women locked into unhappy, unfulfilling and subservient marriages by a *lack* of independence.

And what of Germaine Greer, these days? If some of her views – especially on life in Australia – sound increasingly bizarre, we need to remember her erudition and insights were always laced with some pretty bizarre assertions. 'If you think you are emancipated,' she wrote in *The Female Eunuch*, 'you might consider the idea of tasting your own menstrual blood – if it makes you sick, you've a long way to go, baby.' Perhaps even the most devoted of Greer's disciples have been wise to interpret feminism in their own way.

At last . . . The New Bloke

Only now are we beginning to see the long-term effects of the women's movement on the male of the species. (And let's be clear: it had to be a *women's* movement. Men were never entitled to a movement of their own; their job was to react to a legitimate revolution wrought by women.)

The male response has been slow, uneven and reluctant. And why not? As men gradually caught on to the idea that this was all about power-sharing – everywhere from the bedroom to the boardroom – they were hardly likely to give up any of their traditional power without a struggle. And since they had the example of their own fathers and grandfathers before them – to say nothing of the heritage of countless generations of a male supremacist culture – their nostalgia for the old way was understandable.

I know women are right to seek equality with men, but I can't help thinking my dad had it made. He was king of the castle and everyone accepted that's the way it was. Change a nappy? You've got to be kidding. If he wanted to read the paper in peace, that's exactly what he did. If he was away all day playing golf, we all accepted he was entitled to that.

In the early years of the gender revolution, legions of Australian males silently enlisted in a kind of underground resistance movement. They quickly learned how to adopt the camouflage of feminist slogans, but they rarely backed them up with behavioural change and they consoled each other, in low whispers, with the hopeful thought that this might all come horribly unstuck for women. There was a prevailing male view, right up until the mid-1990s, that women were biting off more than they could chew, and all men had to do was appear to encourage them but not offer enough support to help make their dreams come true. Even when men began to participate, in a limited and qualified way, in housekeeping and child-rearing duties, the trick was to see what you could get away with: help with the dishes, maybe, but then spoil it all by bragging about it; look after the kids while your wife went out, but then betray your fundamental lack of understanding by describing this as 'babysitting'. (What mother ever 'babysat' her own kids?) Encourage your wife's ambition to get a job, or undertake a course of study, but then make it clear that her domestic duties would still have to be done by her.

In *Reinventing Australia* (1993), I wrote that it was 'fair to characterise the typical Australian male response as being a dim awareness that something has gone wrong with his life. Recognising that his wife leads a different kind of life from the one she led 10 or 15 years ago (and a very different kind of life from the one his mother led), he clings to the hope that he might be able to maintain his existing pattern of living until the storm passes.' I also quoted the nastiest piece of silent resistance I have ever encountered, before or since: a man whose wife gave him her university assignments to post and who put them in the bin, instead.

The divorce rate had shot up in the late 1970s, but many men assumed this was merely a brief flurry of activity stimulated by the new Family Law Act. While it was true that the new Act was releasing a build-up of pressure from unhappy marriages that could now be ended with dignity and without having to blame anyone, it soon became clear that the high divorce rate was here to stay. Soon, the majority of divorces were being initiated by women: those who could not convince their husbands to take equality seriously were emboldened by the revolution to vote with their feet.

Once men realised that their marriages might be at stake, they started to pay more attention to the messages of the women's movement. But even then, it was hard for them to know how to respond, and women themselves were often unhelpful in giving guidance: 'He should just realise what's expected of him – I shouldn't have to spell it out for him.' Sharing in some of the housework was one thing; understanding how a relationship could be affected at every level by the very notion of equality was quite another.

Gradually, in response to a relentless barrage of feminist propaganda, the clear articulation of gender issues and the enactment of legislation that reflected the new approach to gender equality, men started to realise that the revolution was here to stay. As the epithet 'male chauvinist pig' came to feel less like a joke and more like a calculated insult it would be better not to deserve, many men quietly shelved their neckties decorated with cute little pigs.

Men even accepted that the language would have to change to acknowledge the new ways of thinking about gender equality. 'Ms' was to become the female equivalent of 'Mr'. 'Partner' became fashionable as a non-gender-specific alternative to 'husband' or 'wife' ('spouse' having gone the way of 'spinster') that also concealed whether partners were technically married or not. 'Actress' and 'waitress' were quietly dropped in favour of 'actor' and 'waiter' for everyone, though some linguistic vandals have tried to foist 'waitperson' on us.

The evolution of post-revolutionary language will proceed, though some distortions of our linguistic heritage are simply absurd: 'foreperson', for example, must be resisted: 'foreman' has never had gender connotations: the suffix '-man' in that word, as in many others, comes from the Latin *manu* for 'hand', as in 'manual', so 'foreman' has virtually the same meaning as 'leading hand'. And to talk of 'personning the phones' rather than 'manning the phones' shows just how silly this can get: 'manning', in that context, is all about hands, not blokes. The execrable 'chairperson' has largely evolved into a more sensible, and equally neutral, 'chair' or 'president', though some women are again opting to be called 'chairman', just as some senior male nurses are still called 'sister' and, in some private schools, female teachers are 'masters'.

But changes in the language of gender were important symbols, and they sent an unambiguous signal. Suddenly, *sensitivity* became the burning issue for men: sensitivity to the aims of the feminist project, sensitivity to the needs of women – at home, at work, in the wider community – and even a greater sensitivity to men's own 'feminine side'. Reversing the message of *My Fair Lady,* the cry coming from women in the 1990s seemed to be 'Why can't a man be more like a woman?' But things are rarely what they seem, and men who fell for that one were in for a nasty shock.

Not many men did fall for it, by the way: one classic male response to the phenomenon of the working wife was to remark how nice it was to have a more interesting and stimulating partner.

But the most absurd response to the call for greater sensitivity came from the men who took it to the max: the infamous SNAGs (Sensitive New Age Guys). This was a small subspecies of male, given to ponytails and Birkenstock sandals, crystals and incense, that appeared at first sight to be a welcome evolutionary leap – a rapid adaptation to the emerging independence of women and their insistence on equality with men. But celebration over the arrival of SNAGs on the scene soon gave way to doubt, and even to ridicule and contempt. Though feminists were assumed to have been responsible for their creation, the SNAGs were soon despised by liberated women, to the utter bewilderment of the SNAGs themselves and the relieved amusement of the rest of the male population who had elected to wait and see.

'I wish I could be pregnant so I'd know what it really feels like' was not the type of response liberated women were hoping for, and the SNAG was soon written off as being too limp for words. It turned out that the SNAG was an aberration: women wanted something more robust in the way of a response from men. They didn't want capitulation. They wanted engagement with the debate. They wanted a true revolution, not a hollow victory over men who had simply raised a pathetic little white flag (especially if they suspected, as some women did, that the cave-in mentality was a cunning strategy used by men to abdicate their responsibilities to a relationship).

The men who had been hanging back were rewarded. They had suspected women might find the new 'I-know-just-how-it-feels-to-be-a-woman' brand of sensitivity less attractive than a modified version of traditional masculinity. It now looked as if they were right. While some thought this might be an opportunity to slip back into old patterns, it was dawning on others that the process of adapting to the new world of gender equality was going to be a life's work – a gradual unfolding of insights and a continuous series of negotiations – a real relationship of equals, in fact, just as their wives (or ex-wives) had said it should be.

The death of the SNAG was inevitable (though there are still some about, looking as bewildered as ever, more SAG – Sensitive Ageing Guy – than SNAG). But an even more improbable male response made a brief, equally futile appearance on the cultural stage – the metrosexual, who came and went in a cloud of aftershave. Largely a figment of the imagination of a New York advertising executive (female, as it happens) looking for a new market to exploit, the metrosexual was supposed to be a more enlightened, more masculine response to feminism than the SNAG. This was the man who was prepared to adopt the sense of style, the flair traditionally associated with women – and to buy truckloads of cosmetics and cashmere to prove it – but who was distinctly masculine. For a while, there seemed to be a blurring of 'metrosexual' and 'homosexual' in people's minds, as if a metrosexual might be a straight man with gay style. Casting around for some Australian examples of the metrosexual, people seized on Ian Thorpe and, er, er . . . and gave up. The truth is there have only been about six confirmed sightings of Australian metrosexuals, so it's not a trend to which we should pay too much attention. To the extent that the word has survived (often in its abbreviated form, 'metro'), it seems to mean little more than 'a well-dressed man with a decent haircut'.

What women were really waiting for all this time was a proper engagement with gender issues by men who are both comfortable with their own masculinity and serious about the idea of equality with women. It was neither a cave-in nor a caveman that women wanted: what they wanted was the New Bloke and, 35 years after the revolution began, he's just beginning to arrive on the scene in serious numbers (though it's safest to regard him as a still-emerging subspecies).

The Mackay Report, *Mind & Mood* (2003), described him as vibrant, outspoken, optimistic, unselfconsciously masculine – and cheerfully reshaping the character of gender relations. The New Bloke is not the harbinger of some kind of latter-day 'men's movement', though; he is an authentic – if delayed – response to the women's movement. Along the way, he may have received conflicting messages from his mother and father, but the New Bloke has managed to combine the values of old-fashioned, blokey mateship with the new values of a more sensitive, more equitable, yet more relaxed approach to love and life.

Often posing as a traditional larrikin, the New Bloke wouldn't want you to know he's changing the world, but that's his agenda: he wants a world where people have more fun, are less inhibited, yet manage to be kinder and more respectful towards each other as well. He has a big heart and a strong sense of social justice. Nothing can dent his confidence that he has found the right balance between fun and responsibility. The 2003 *Mind & Mood* report also noted that 'if he has a worry about contemporary society it is that young women may have become a bit *too* feisty, a bit *too* independent, and – perhaps surprisingly – not as interested in parenthood as he is'.

> *I really like the thought of having a couple of kids I could grow up with. I thought I would be married by 28 but now it's obvious I won't be. The thought of kids is scary, but it's even more scary to think about not having them.*

At the same time, he 'knows where women are coming from' and understands they may have had to overcompensate for the injustices and inequalities of the past, which makes them more aggressive drivers, more assertive companions and more wary partners.

The New Bloke is no wimp, but he is no male chauvinist, either, though he gets a laugh out of pretending to be: mock chauvinism is one of his party tricks and he enjoys satirising his unenlightened comrades by telling outrageously sexist jokes designed to 'take the piss' out of his mates, not out of women. He's typically in his twenties, confident about his masculinity, attractively blokey in style. Try to get him talking about politics and he'll steer the conversation to girls, jobs, girls, sport, girls, the internet, girls, money, girls, movies, girls and drugs (legal and illegal).

He is as interested in having a good time as any bloke ever was, but the big difference is that he knows women are equal and he knows what that means. He accepts that a serious relationship with a woman involves taking her identity and her needs seriously, and he acknowledges that the woman's agenda is just as important as the man's. (Some of his best mates are women, by the way.)

The New Bloke despises 'old' blokes who pretend to be in love so they can get a woman to sleep with them. The New Bloke is prepared to be explicit about the difference between uncommitted and committed sex, and he knows plenty of women who are equally clear about that distinction. He is more respectful of the woman's attitude to sex than most members of his father's or grandfather's generation might have been: he may well have recreational sex with a woman who is similarly inclined, but he respects 'no'.

To borrow the key word from the women's movement, the New Bloke is *liberated*. He wants us all to lighten up and acknowledge that the pathway to good relationships between the sexes lies in an open, total acceptance of genuine equality. Any other way of operating strikes him as being unfair, unsustainable and just plain silly.

He is ambitious for 'the good life' even more than material prosperity. Symbols of material comfort, rather than material success, are important to him. He wants to be cool, and naked ambition is decidedly uncool. He wants to create and nurture a satisfying way of life in which women, and his mates, will play a big part.

And what does he do with his mates? *Drink. Play sport. Talk about women... what else?* The New Bloke claims to disapprove of drug abuse and addiction: characteristic of the rising generation of young adults, he describes his interest in drugs as 'recreational' and regards drugs like marijuana, ecstasy and cocaine as aids to the enjoyment of life.

His trademark is confidence, and he likes nothing better than a good laugh.

The main thing we do when we're together is try to make each other laugh. Your favourite mates are the ones that make you laugh the most. Life can be too bloody serious, if you ask me.

Nothing must appear to be taken too seriously (except in quiet, late-night asides), and it's his actions, rather than any speechifying, that reveal the New Bloke's attitudes to the world in general, and to women in particular. But his wild and self-mocking conversation with his mates will reveal occasional glimpses of a soft heart.

We all want to be successful, but we're not sure how the fuck to get there. Actually, my grand plan is to be a great Australian.

I sponsor two children in Africa and Brazil . . .
Is he serious? [asked a mate].
Yeah, believe it or not [said another].

The New Bloke is still an emerging species. There are plenty of male chauvinists still to be found among the young, as well as another subspecies: those who are cowed by the assertiveness of contemporary young women and cautious about approaching them.

And the New Bloke is not entirely new, either. Long before the gender revolution took shape, there were always men who understood that in spite of all the apparent differences between men and women, equality was not just possible, but essential. Such men were once regarded as either odd or exceptional: in everything from changing nappies to sacrificing their career in favour of a wife's career, they seemed to challenge the traditional stereotype of how a man – especially a married man – should behave. The difference is that, today, men are less likely to be mocked for their commitment to equality, or for their devotion to the idea of power-sharing, job-sharing and life-sharing with the women in their lives.

Once upon a time, a man wouldn't have dared interrupt a business meeting to say you had to pick the kids up from childcare, or get to the school concert on time. People would have thought your wife should have been doing all that. But it's a different world today.

Not everywhere, perhaps, but the world – including the world of work – is gradually adapting to the idea that equality means what it says. Some alleged gender differences are the subject of irreverent banter, especially among men: women prefer to visit the washroom in pairs, while men go alone; women tend to park used teabags at some intermediate point – a saucer, the sink – while men tend to put them straight into the bin. Other differences may have some scientific basis: men tend to be better than women at judging distances, though women are better at scanning the scene; women tend to be more intuitive, men more rational; most women enjoy sexual foreplay more, and are less orgasm-driven than most men. But the idea has finally taken hold that many alleged 'gender differences' are cultural rather than biological, and no greater than those that fall within the range of individual human differences, whether for men or women. *Vive la difference!* was never about superiority and inferiority; it was always about complementarity.

What women want; what men want

For women, *freedom* and *choice* have emerged as the tastiest fruits of the revolution. In the face of their new-found sense of freedom, women feel able to define their own goals in their own terms. Second-wave feminism may be less about 'having it all' and more about having the freedom to make 'the right choice for me, at this stage of my life', but the underlying drumbeat – *equality, equality, equality* – hasn't changed and women are marching to it with increasing confidence. 'Give me the freedom to be who I truly want to be, and I might even decide to marry you.'

For men, the goal is *authentic masculinity*. The New Bloke believes it's perfectly all right to be a 'bloke' – to acknowledge the legitimacy of masculine urges, masculine images and masculine culture – as long as you understand the real point about the gender revolution: men and women, for all their obvious differences, are equal. Thirty years after it began, the gender revolution has brought new life, new richness to the word 'person'.

4

Uncertainty: The workplace revolution

Gone are the days – ushered in by the 1950s and largely sustained through to the end of the 1980s – when people assumed they had a job for life if they wanted it. Gone are the days when stable employment was regarded as one of the twin pillars of a stable society (the other being stable family life). Gone, too, are the days when it was assumed that the job you were trained for would be the job you would do for the rest of your working life.

It's as true today as it ever was that people rely on their paid work to add an important dimension to their sense of identity, to give structure to their lives, and to supply them with the stimulation of colleagues and the sense of belonging that comes with being part of a work group. But the labour market has become less stable and, in response to that, there's a corresponding attitude shift, especially among young people who now typically expect their working lives to be more like a jigsaw than a straight line and who are as reluctant to use the word 'career' as they are to talk about 'marriage'. Switching between full-time and part-time, or cobbling together a couple of part-time jobs, or working flat out for a while and then 'kicking back' for a while – these are emerging possibilities, partly driven by the changing realities of the workplace and partly by changing attitudes to work. (Which comes first? It's not quite chicken-and-egg: attitude shifts are usually the product of a changing environment, as they appear to be in this case.)

The workplace is being transformed in three main ways:

The erosion of permanent, full-time work and, paradoxically, the rise of overwork. The past 20 years have seen stronger growth in part-time than full-time jobs, and a sharp increase in casual employment. About 27 percent of the workforce are now casual employees, and 28 percent are part-time workers, comprising 15 percent of all male workers and 46 percent of female workers. The steady redistribution of work over this period helps to explain why 1.8 million Australians are either unemployed or wish they could obtain more work while, at the other end of the spectrum, almost 40 percent of full-time workers wish they could work less, often citing the deleterious effects of long working hours on family life.

Our adaptation to job insecurity. The increasing casualisation of the workforce, jobs being gobbled up by technology, the impact of globalisation on the movement of jobs out of Australia and the bitter lessons learned from the era of corporate downsizing (with jobs seen as the first target for cost-cutting) have all contributed to a change in workplace attitudes and expectations. We now accept that no job is necessarily permanent, no industry is necessarily here to stay, and no assumptions can be made about the Australian workplace in isolation from the region and the rest of the world.

The increase in female participation in the workforce. In the 20 years from 1986 to 2006, workforce participation rates for women aged 25–54 have risen significantly. The greatest lift has occurred in the

45–54 age group, where participation has risen from 52 percent in 1986 to 76 percent in 2006. In the same period, participation has risen from 63 to 74 percent among 35–44-year-old women, and from 59 to 73 percent among 25–34-year-olds. The reasons for these changes are as complex as for any change in human behaviour: women's yearning for greater independence, both emotional and economic; the high divorce rate; the high cost of housing; increased expectations of economic prosperity and the perceived need for two incomes per family to achieve them; the rising education levels of women; the discovery by women of the previously well-kept male secret that work is therapeutic and that it is generally easier and more stimulating to be at work than at home.

The current mood in the workplace is optimistic about employment prospects. Even among those who, on the basis of past experience, know that 'permanent' no longer means what it once did, there's a general assumption that work is 'out there' and that a switch of jobs might not be unduly painful. Only the most vulnerable (especially unskilled) workers fear the impact of a possible recession; more generally, the workforce is clinging to the belief that the good times are here to stay. It's as if the mood of Donald Horne's 'lucky country' has returned. Horne's 1964 label was ironic and cautionary, not celebratory: he thought we were suffering from mediocre leadership, inadequate planning and a complacent population but that, thanks to the wool and wheat boom, we were lucky enough to get away with it. Today, it's a resources boom rather than a wool and wheat boom underpinning an economy that may otherwise be more fragile than it looks.

The direct threat of unemployment no longer hangs like a pall over the labour market as it did 15, ten or even five years ago, but there's a persistent undercurrent of uncertainty. In spite of the present rosy economic outlook for many Australians, the lessons about job insecurity were learned the hard way and they are not about to be forgotten. The recession of the early 1990s, the effects of corporate downsizing on the many thousands of Australians who have personally experienced the trauma of retrenchment, the virtual disappearance of many industries (especially in manufacturing), the pressures of competition from the global labour market and the steady growth of part-time and casual jobs at the expense of full-time, permanent jobs have all taken their toll on the psyche of the workforce. To this, in 2006, was added new industrial relations laws (repealed in 2008) that heightened the general sense of workplace insecurity. And when employees read that the average tenure for Australian chief executives is down to about three years, they acknowledge that the axe could fall anywhere, anytime, whether you're on the top rung or the bottom. The difference, compared with 15 years ago, is that they believe finding another job is likely to be easier.

A rougher, tougher environment

Even among employees who feel less insecure than they did a decade ago, there's a grim sense that time spent at work is not as pleasant or enjoyable as it used to be. The workplace is regarded as a tougher place. While some people acknowledge that 'we had to become more competitive', the human cost is thought to have been considerable, with employers widely regarded as more powerful and more ruthless; employees – especially casuals – more likely to be exploited; evening and weekend work taking an increasing toll on family life; economic imperatives overriding all others; and the 'stratospheric' salaries paid to top executives no longer bearing any conceivable relationship to average earnings.

In The Ipsos Mackay Report, *Australians At Work* (2006), it emerged that, in many organisations, employees feel they are more closely supervised and monitored than they used to be and that this doesn't necessarily make them more productive. In some cases, they simply learn to 'work the system'; more generally, they feel that morale suffers when each minute must be accounted for: 'What about time to chat? What about taking a break?' When, by contrast, an employee finds an employer with a more personal, flexible attitude (often in a small business or traditional family company) this is generally thought to create stronger feelings of involvement and loyalty than are typical of the workforce at large.

Shareholders are now regarded as the pre-eminent stakeholders in many organisations, and the need to 'prop up the share price' increases the risk of giving in to short-term thinking and a lack of proper strategic planning. In turn, this creates the feeling among employees that they are mere 'profit fodder', leading to resentment and a more guarded, reserved attitude towards corporate loyalty.

The 2006 repeal of the unfair dismissal laws for businesses with fewer than 100 employees and the introduction of individual workplace agreements provoked understandable anxiety, and published poll data suggested the moves were deeply unpopular among those who were aware of them. For those who regarded themselves as vulnerable to economic ups and downs, the new Work Choices legislation added to an existing sense of insecurity. For those who felt more secure, especially in the current period of a resources-led economic boom, the new legislation was initially assumed to have made little appreciable difference to their working lives or immediate prospects. But even they looked ahead with some trepidation – if not for themselves, then for their children:

I reckon things are going to get tougher, not easier. I wonder how kids just out of school or university are going to get on with these workplace agreements. Guess who will have all the power – not them.

In a 2006 interview with Margaret Throsby on ABC Classic FM, Professor Ron McCallum, dean of Sydney University's faculty of law and a distinguished industrial relations lawyer, said that the full effects of the new IR laws would not be felt for ten years and that he himself felt as if his life's work had been undone. Yet even when isolated stories of unfairness began to surface in the media, *Australians at Work* suggested that the mood in the workplace had been relatively calm in spite of increased uneasiness among casual and unskilled workers.

One reason for the contradiction implied by the lack of initial resistance to such an apparently unpopular move was the mood of the country at the time (see Part Four: The Dreamy Period). But another reason was that the union movement had itself become unpopular. Declining membership over the previous 15 years had been a symptom of declining respect for a movement that is still credited with having made a remarkable contribution to the wellbeing of Australian workers, but which had seemed to go too far in seeking conditions that were no longer perceived as fair or reasonable. Nevertheless, under the onslaught of a strong media campaign, resistance to Work Choices stiffened appreciably during 2007; the

Howard government even stopped using that label for its legislation, and Work Choices ultimately became a major issue in the 2007 election. It is conceivable that having been shocked by the Work Choices experience, more workers will again seek the support and protection of trade unions.

Perhaps the ugliest sign of lack of progress in the humanising of the workplace is the persistent phenomenon of *bullying*. Bullying is one of the most dramatic symptoms of a lack of respect for another person and, perhaps encouraged by a more generally ruthless commercial atmosphere, workplace bullies appear to be riding high. Bullying is sometimes disguised as 'tough' or 'realistic' management, and it sometimes hides behind the veil of new workplace laws that have made some employees feel more vulnerable to the possibility of dismissal if they appear to be causing trouble by 'blowing the whistle'.

No workplace phenomenon causes more tension, resentment and emotional distress than bullying, especially when, as is so often claimed, the bullies win: when complaints are made, the bully is often in a position of authority and is likely to be supported by more senior figures in the organisation.

Why is bullying such a widespread problem in the workplace?

One possible explanation is that many people seem capable of behaving quite differently at work from the way they behave with their families and friends: less open, less honest, more prepared to cut moral corners – sexually, financially and in other ways such as the pilfering of property – and more prepared to treat each other badly.

Perhaps it's the sense of the commercial imperative over-riding all others that brings out the worst in some of us. Since the primary purpose of business is to make a profit, the temptations to behave unethically are legion, and the pressures of the commercial marketplace can encourage recklessness in people who might otherwise be fair, kind and reasonable.

Or perhaps there's something about the nature of the workplace itself that encourages bad behaviour. The typical work environment is characterised by prolonged and sometimes quite intense personal relationships where, in a wide variety of testing circumstances, people are more transparently exposed to each other than in most other areas of their lives, including marriage. Workplaces are often like hothouses, generating pressure partly from the need to meet deadlines and goals (commercial and otherwise) and partly from the need to get along with all kinds of people you might not necessarily choose to spend so much time with.

Research conducted in 2003 by PricewaterhouseCoopers revealed that 47 percent of Australian businesses had suffered from some form of economic crime – theft, fraud, corruption, bribery – in the previous two years. The vast majority of those crimes were committed by employees against the companies they worked for. That's actual crime we're talking about, not merely morally dubious behaviour. But if that level of criminal activity goes on in our workplaces, it suggests there's something about the climate of many workplaces that loosens the moral constraints governing other aspects of our lives.

The phenomenon of overwork makes its own contribution to the problem of workplace bullying. In the May 2007 issue of *The Psychologist* (published by the British Psychological Society), Susan Cartwright and Cary Cooper summarise the extensive research into the problem. They report that a high incidence of bullying is associated with highly stressful work environments, and work overload. They describe the kind of workplace culture in which bullies are likely to flourish as characterised by a high level of competition, radical change, a climate of insecurity, a 'macho' management style, hierarchical structures, low levels of consultation, excessive work demands and a lack of procedures to tackle bullying and harassment issues.

In his 2003 book, *Dignity at Work*, P.R. Peyton argues that most people are capable of bullying. That potential can turn into reality when we are frustrated by others' behaviour or when we face excessive demands to meet performance targets. Many of us resort to 'micromanagement' and over-controlling behaviour in response to the stress of having to meet tough goals.

In an atmosphere where, according to many employees, there is a widespread reluctance to raise moral issues or question unethical behaviour, bullying can thrive and resistance to bullying can appear naive. But until the problem of workplace bullying is addressed on a large scale, and until employees who speak up – for themselves or on behalf of others – are protected and dealt with fairly, our workplaces will continue to offer dark places where bullies can hide.

The 'feminisation' of work?

In Chapter 3, the idea that workplaces are automatically 'feminised' by an increase in the number of women was challenged. But there's another sense in which many workplaces are indeed being feminised.

A high proportion of jobs in manufacturing, trades and unskilled manual work have traditionally been regarded as masculine in character and content, requiring physical strength, perhaps, and certainly operating within a work culture of 'blokiness' where personal style, presentation and grooming were low priorities. As the supply of such jobs gradually diminishes because of industry closures or contractions, increased mechanisation of manual work and the broader impact of technology, an increasing proportion of new jobs are becoming available in service industries – retailing, cafes, bars, restaurants, personal services – with an entirely different culture that fits more closely with stereotypical femininity. An emphasis on personal grooming, presentation skills, politeness, charm, a willingness to listen attentively and a general openness to the service mentality – qualities unlikely to be required in traditional men's work – are increasingly called for in service jobs.

Even a car servicing operation is likely to offer a 'customer interface' run by well-groomed 'meeters and greeters', male or female, who have no contact with the work of actually servicing cars. The mechanics will be hidden away, and there will be fewer of them than there used to be, as the servicing process is increasingly computerised and automated.

More emphasis is also being paid to health and hygiene in the workplace – again, an area traditionally associated more with women than men. In response, the wearing of rubber gloves, hairnets and other protective equipment all symbolise a change in workplace culture that is blurring the traditional distinctions between jobs and workplaces once thought more appropriate for one gender or the other.

As that culture shift proceeds, men begin to appear in positions once dominated by women. The male receptionist or telephonist is no longer uncommon. The male nurse now has an established place in the life of any hospital. The female doctor or lawyer will soon be as evident as the male of the species. Female pilots are gradually being accepted by our airlines; male flight attendants are a well-established fixture. Males and females are already regarded as interchangeable in most retail and restaurant roles: no longer need the *maître d* be a man, nor the cosmetician a woman.

We can assume that continued growth of the service and knowledge economies will result in fewer gender distinctions being drawn, and one longer-term effect of this shift will be that traditional, stereotypical distinctions drawn on the basis of gender will themselves be consigned to history. Work is not being feminised so much as 'neutered' and that will gradually turn out to have domestic implications as well. In everything from childcare and housework to the role of breadwinner, the longstanding tensions between men and women are more likely to be resolved through workplace conditioning than endless nagging at home.

At the other end of the spectrum – working from home – the workplace is not being feminised so much as domesticated, as many people struggle to establish the boundaries between paid and unpaid home-based work: 'It helps if I get dressed properly, at least by lunchtime, but I don't always manage it.'

Flexibility and control: the new buzzwords at work

This is Kaleidoscope Nation, and nowhere is that more obvious than in the workplace. In our ways of working and in our expectations of the future world of work, we are learning to adapt to increasing change, diversity, flexibility and transience. Though some employees feel wary and uncertain, others are revelling in a more sympathetic working environment. While some rail against the 'rougher' atmosphere at work, others report a more sensitive and enlightened approach to management by their superiors. While some are feeling ground down by the relentlessness of the pressure at work, others are availing themselves of the social facilities now burgeoning in many workplaces – gyms, pool and ping-pong tables, coffee shops, conversation pits – designed to relieve the pressure.

The ubiquitous 'casual Friday' concept, where employees are encouraged to come to work in casual clothes one day a week, has been another attempt to ease the pressure of the modern workplace and humanise the working environment. It's unclear whether it has been successful in achieving that goal: some workplaces have abolished casual Friday on the grounds that people were becoming too relaxed and unproductive; others have long since adopted 'casual' as the norm. In many contemporary offices, a male employee wearing a collar and tie would seem odd, perhaps pretentious, and certainly inappropriate. (As Chapter 2 suggested, this is part of a larger cultural trend toward casualisation of dress, speech and manners that makes 'dressing up' an unusual thing to do.)

Particularly among younger people, there's a steadily increasing demand for more flexibility in the workplace. They want jobs where they can have greater control over the management of their work and their pattern of working – when to be in the office, when to work from home, when to take a day off, when to work at full-stretch without a break. Older workers are also beginning to join the hunt for greater flexibility and control, as it becomes clear that much of the stress at work is related to a lack of control over the working environment and the flow of work. Compressed weeks, rostered days off, the possibility of working from home when you need solitude or silence, the ability to juggle domestic and working responsibilities through more imaginative use of IT connections to the workplace . . . all these options are now being considered. People who are experiencing the workplace as a generally tougher environment than it used to be are looking to greater flexibility as a way of compensating themselves for increased pressure and insecurity.

Working mothers, particularly, speak of the need for greater flexibility in their approach to work – both in the ways they are able to work and in the ways employers accommodate their changing circumstances at different points in the life cycle. When single or as part of a couple, their requirements are generally indistinguishable from those of most men at the same stage. The birth of the first child, though, is the great life-changer for both mother and father, and inevitably changes the attitudes of both of them to work as to almost every aspect of their lives, from insurance to home ownership to the kind of car they drive. For first-time mothers – now likely to be over 30 and well established in the workforce – the new responsibilities of motherhood generally lead to a reappraisal of the place of work in their lives, at least for a while. Maternity leave (still unpaid in most cases, unlike all other OECD countries except the US) provides welcome breathing space, but doubts often begin to form about when, if ever, will be the right time to return to the previous level of work.

The availability of childcare – especially the unpaid, grandmotherly kind – will be a huge factor in the decision. The working hours of many mothers are limited not only by the availability of childcare, but also by their capacity to pay for it. The Human Rights and Equal Opportunity Commission's 2007 report, *It's About Time – Women, Work, Men and Family,* has called for a more flexible approach to working hours, especially for the parents of young children but also for those with responsibilities to care for aged parents and for ill or disabled family members and friends. It has also described paid maternity leave as a top priority for Australia, proposing a scheme of 14 weeks of paid leave, and suggests that governments should look at ways of limiting working hours, because of the damaging effects of overwork on family life (see 'Overworked and underemployed; overpaid and underpaid' later in this chapter).

In The Ipsos Mackay Report, *Australians At Work* (2006), employees consistently remarked that they feel a sense of liberation when they are trusted to manage their own time in more flexible ways than were possible or practical in the past.

> *These days, you can work more flexibly – and potentially even from home. I do when I need to. I've got a full office set-up at home. Last Monday being the first day of the school holidays, I was at home and when people ring and hear the kids in the background, they're attuned to it these days.*

Information technology creates new possibilities for increasing workplace flexibility. Some of the boffins of the telecommunications industry are working on the assumption that within the next five years or so, half of us will be 'teleworking' – working from home via electronic linkages, at least for part of the working week. According to a 2006 survey conducted by Sensis, the figure is already 30 percent.

In a speech delivered in California in May 2006, Telstra's CEO, Sol Trujillo, referred to the revolution in the way we work, courtesy of email: 'Ten years ago there was no email. Five years ago people complained there was too much email and it was interfering with their work. Now email is the way we work.' For all its shortcomings and hazards, email has transformed the workplace by making it possible to be physically absent from it but still closely in touch, at least at the level of data exchange if not human interaction. It has also quickened the pace of work to the point where many people feel under increased pressure from being permanently online: 'email stress' has become an observable phenomenon in many workplaces. Some people are trying to resist the assumption that if you've received an email you should respond immediately, but the pressure is often relentless: instant email response is the norm and such well-intentioned advice as 'try to reduce email stress by only checking your emails every 30 minutes' is ignored in the face of a management expectation of continuous attention to the flow of messages.

Paradoxically, all this stimulation via IT can be a source of workplace boredom. Human beings thrive on social interaction and the sense of being connected to each other. They need to chat; they need to wander around the office; they need to 'waste time' together, over coffee, a lunchtime stroll, an exchange of jokes or a bit of tearoom gossip. When their working environment is characterised by non-personal activities – being locked onto a screen, for instance – the need for personal relief becomes correspondingly more acute.

Writing in *The Psychologist* (Vol. 20, No. 2, February 2007) Sandi Mann reviewed the available research from the US and the UK and concluded that workplace boredom is closely associated with the inability to control your working environment, especially among people who feel as if they are on the job 24/7 via electronic links. She also partly attributes the rise of white-collar boredom to the sharp rise in the number of people with tertiary qualifications which make them overqualified for much of the work they do, and to the Western world's increased need for 'self-actualisation' or self-fulfilment, leading to a more critical appraisal of job satisfaction (though, as the British philosopher Alain de Botton is fond of reminding us, the idea that we should *enjoy* this thing called work is very modern, and possibly unhelpful).

The combination of new workplace technology and more flexible working arrangements has led to the emergence of the 'hotdesk' (now, inevitably, a verb as well as a noun) in offices where individuals no longer have their own exclusive work station but simply occupy whatever desk is available when they happen to call in. If you want to create some of the traditional signs of territorial space, including photos of the family, you set them up as screensavers on your computer so your 'cyber-territory' goes with you, wherever you happen to be working. Phone directories, address lists, documents, scribbles, reminder notes, files – all the paraphernalia of the traditional office desk – are similarly stored on the computer, mobile phone and/or the BlackBerry.

New, more flexible ways of working are still regarded by many employers as experimental and exceptional, though employees typically claim that greater freedom to manage their own workload often results in a greater commitment to the job.

Not all workplaces are capable of being responsive to these possibilities, of course. Many jobs are tied to particular times and places and greater flexibility is a mere fantasy. Children still sit at their desks, for instance, awaiting instruction from a teacher who has very little flexibility in deciding when to work from home (though marking pupils' work is still like overtime done at home for most teachers). And many jobs rely on a collegial sense of connection through free-flowing discussion and interaction that's hard to simulate electronically.

Even people who do most of their work by phone or email generally feel the need to call into the communal office from time to time, simply to warm up their personal connections and engage in chit-chat that might appear to be unrelated to the work, but is crucial to the maintenance of mutual understanding and trust between colleagues. Still, the growing demand for more flexible working arrangements and more control over one's own work processes points to an increasingly fluid interpretation of the very word 'workplace', even for people in permanent full-time jobs.

Should I work for myself?

Needless to say, the dream of self-employment becomes more appealing when the workplace begins to feel more pressured and less secure, and when a desire for more flexibility and control isn't being satisfied. Some employees who feel that 'the boss is always calling the tune' imagine that if only they could get into their own business, they could take greater control of their lives. In particular, they assume self-employed people have more latitude in their working arrangements and are able to strike a better balance between their working and private lives.

In response to these motivations and others (including the steady stream of executives who find themselves retrenched at their prime and decide to fight back by becoming self-employed consultants beyond the reach of a cost-cutting corporation), there has been a marked increase in the number of people going into business for themselves. By the beginning of 2007, John Howard was able to describe the turn of the century as a 'tipping point for a more aspirational Australia as the number of owner-managers in the economy exceeded the number of trade union members' (*The Australian*, 28 February 2007).

Among those who do decide to go it alone, the stories are very mixed. *Australians At Work* quoted cases of self-employed people who were glowing with pleasure and pride in their achievement and whose attitudes to work had been transformed by the experience of being their own boss. It also reported cases of dismal, abject failure and disappointment, especially among people who found the stress of financial uncertainty too much to bear, or who were overwhelmed by an unexpected burden of administration – 'death by paperwork'. Many self-employed people, whether happy or unhappy with their lot, claim they work far longer hours than they did as employees and that it becomes very hard to 'switch off'.

> *Working for yourself has its rewards, but it's a 24-hour, seven days a week job. You get home, but instead of relaxing you're doing quotes, doing bookwork. When I worked for myself I always said I'd take six weeks off but I never did. I never took a break. I couldn't. It's better to be working for someone else.*

But when it's good, being your own boss can be very, very good:

> *My husband might come in at ten o'clock at night, having left at five in the morning, and he'll whinge about the day but he'll happily jump in the truck the next morning, because that's what he loves to do.*

While becoming an employer does bring a greater sense of control, it inevitably involves an increased sense of responsibility and a distinct move out of 'the comfort zone' to a new sense of financial vulnerability and a new set of management challenges. The decision to hire the first employee, for instance, represents a major leap of faith for many beginners, but can be an exciting symbol of the fact that 'I'm on my way'.

I'm never going to be Kerry Packer, but it's a great feeling having my own little empire.

Overworked and underemployed; overpaid and underpaid

Although official unemployment figures are hovering around five percent, some economists argue that they seriously misrepresent the true situation. *The Sydney Morning Herald* economics editor, Ross Gittins, suggests the true figure is probably about twice the official figure at any given time, since the official figure excludes anyone who has even one hour of paid work per week (regardless of how many hours they might want to work), and also excludes those who would like to work but have not registered themselves as job-seekers.

The ABS's 2007 *Year Book* reports that 1.8 million Australians are either unemployed or underemployed: that is, they want a job or, if they have one, they want more hours. That means about 17 percent of the workforce are either unemployed or underemployed. Yet an ABS survey published in May 2007 revealed that 37 percent of employees work overtime, and about half of them receive no extra pay.

The official figures for hours worked show strong growth in part-time and casual work, partly reflecting a stronger demand for more flexible working arrangements, but partly also reflecting a shift towards a more inequitable distribution of work. As a result, the 'standard working week' has become a meaningless term in Kaleidoscope Nation: there's a still-widening gulf between the overworked and the underemployed. Although the average number of hours worked by Australians is coming down (currently standing at 37 hours per week), this is largely the product of the rise in part-time work. Full-time workers are employed, on average, for 44 hours per week; part-time workers are employed for an average of 18 hours per week.

What these figures fail to reveal is the actual number of hours worked at the high end of the scale: the category '45 hours or more' includes people who are working for 60, 80 or even more hours per week, many of them absorbing the equivalent of at least half another full-time job in their overtime. According to the 2007 report, *An Unexpected Tragedy*, published by Relationships Forum Australia, 22 percent of employees work 50 or more hours per week, and 30 percent regularly work on weekends. The report claims that two million Australians now lose at least six hours of family time to work on Sunday and that those hours are not always fully compensated for by time off at other times of the week.

Internationally, this puts Australia close to the top of the heap (or the bottom, depending on your point of view) of high-income nations when it comes to long working hours, weekend work and casual employment. We're second only to Japan when it comes to the number of people working more than 50 hours per week (28 percent of Japanese, compared with our 22 percent); second only to Italy for weekend work (33 percent of Italians, compared with our 30 percent) and second only to Spain for casual or 'temporary' employment (31 percent of Spaniards, compared with our 27 percent). For the dangerous combination of all three factors, we're way out in front.

Some people trapped in a cycle of long working hours claim they are doing so against their will: many overstretched employees, particularly those juggling work and family responsibilities, fear losing their jobs should they try to confine their working hours to a reasonable 40 or so per week. In many organisations, long hours are treated as a symbol of commitment, even if they sometimes achieve little more than being seen to be in attendance for more than the requisite number of hours.

There are many kinds of overworkers. Some are ambitious young lawyers struggling to cope with the relentless demands of the 'billable hours' treadmill; some are senior executives with a crushing burden of responsibility; some are in industries such as retail and hospitality where evening and weekend work is mandatory but sometimes comes on top of a solid week's work as well. Many are self-employed, small business owners and operators – shopkeepers, tradespeople, contractors, consultants – who would rather work long hours than complicate their lives by taking on more employees.

To balance the picture, it must be acknowledged that some overworkers are keen to spend as much time as possible at work as a means of escape from the pressures of a demanding home life or the strains of an unhappy personal situation. In moments of candour, some admit they are never happier than when they are at work, or that work takes their minds off other problems they'd rather not face. And there's a potential vicious circle here: spending too much time at work can take its toll on personal relationships, and when those damaged relationships become difficult to manage, work can become a welcome refuge.

This unusual combination of overwork and weekend work imposes inevitable strain on personal relationships – especially in marriages with children. It doesn't take much imagination to realise that if relationships require attention, and that kind of attention requires time, then a shortage of sufficient time to devote to a relationship will have adverse consequences for the relationship. ('Quality time'? Forget it. Relationships with partners or children can't be hothoused.)

Drawing on a significant body of international research, the Relationships Forum report suggests that established patterns of long and unusual working hours have a direct effect on health, family relationships and the wellbeing of children. These conclusions are partially supported by Australian research. In the *Australian Journal of Social Research* (1998), David Fryer and Anthony Winefield quoted a number of studies that linked the stress of overwork to such health problems as anxiety, depression, cognitive failure, headaches, sleep loss, skin disorders, hypertension, chronic fatigue, substance (especially alcohol) abuse, aggression, coronary heart disease and many others. Incidentally, the researchers noted a remarkably similar pattern of health problems among the unemployed and underemployed: the stress of not having a job, or not having enough hours, appears to be as potentially hazardous to health as the stress of overdoing it.

The 2001 HILDA (Household, Income and Labour Dynamics in Australia) survey jointly conducted by the Melbourne Institute of Applied and Social Research, the Australian Council for Educational Research and the Australian Institute of Family Studies, revealed that 37 percent of full-time workers would prefer to work fewer hours, though by the time a follow-up survey was conducted in 2004, almost two-thirds of them had been unable to make any adjustment to their hours. The same pair of surveys showed that part-time workers were more successful in matching their desired hours to their actual working hours, perhaps because most of them were wanting to increase their hours rather than ease back, and it's the easing back that most of us find so hard to do – either for financial reasons or because we become addicted to the rituals of overwork.

Not surprisingly, the redistribution of work has resulted in a steady redistribution of wealth. Although it's true to say that, from the top to the bottom of the economic ladder, we are all significantly better off than we were ten years ago, we are living with a longer ladder than we've been used to: the distance from top to bottom is now among the greatest in the OECD. We are also witnessing the gradual shrinkage of the economic middle class, as more people drift towards the top or bottom. In *The Weekend Australian* of 4–5 June 2005, George Megalogenis pointed out that, 20 years ago, nearly 50 percent of working men and women were clustered around the middle-income band. That proportion has dropped to 37 percent for men and 44 percent for women.

The average annual personal income for all workers in Australia in 2007 stood at $827 per week – or $43 000 per annum, rising to an average of $52 000 for full-time workers. The highest incomes were in the mining industry (averaging $1729 per week for men and $1318 for women) and the lowest were in the so-called service industries: the retail trade ($834 per week for men, $731 for women) and accommodation, cafes and restaurants ($770 for men, $725 for women).

Those averages can be misleading, because they are distorted by some very large earnings at the top of the heap. In fact, the top of the heap doesn't even sound like the same heap: while 80 percent of all employees earn less than $75 000 per annum, the average annual remuneration for the 50 highest-paid executives in Australia exceeds $6 million. Multi-million dollar payouts to departing – especially unsuccessful – CEOs make the top seem even more remote from most wage- and salary-earners, including those at quite senior levels.

A 2006 study published by the National Centre for Social and Economic Modelling makes it clear that the past ten years has been a period of rapidly increasing prosperity: almost all of us are

25 percent better off than we were ten years ago, though, in real money terms, this obviously produces very different outcomes for high- and low-income-earners. For the poorest ten percent, the increase amounted to $29 per week, after allowing for inflation; for the richest ten percent, it has yielded $256 more per week.

Perhaps a better way of understanding the distribution of income and wealth is to look at households rather than individuals. According to economic analysts IBIS*World*, the average annual household income in Australia in 2006 was $102 470. For the top 20 percent of households, the average is $225 350. Those households receive 45 percent of all household income and own 60 percent of the wealth.

The bottom 20 percent of households have an average annual household income of just $22 500. They receive 4.5 percent of all household income and own just one percent of the wealth.

With a shrinking middle and growth in the top and bottom income bands, contrasts in experience and attitudes towards money are becoming predictably sharper:

The kids are due back at school next week, and they all need new shoes. We can't afford a new pair for one of them, let alone all of them. Sometimes you feel like giving up – there just seems to be no end to it.

The school got very sniffy about the fact that we were going to get the kids back a bit late for the start of term. We were skiing in France, and we only get away as a family once or twice a year, so there was no way we were going to cut it short. Anyway, the connecting flights didn't quite work to get back before school started. They only missed a day or two, and they never do anything serious on the first couple of days. It's not as if it was their HSC year.

Among the rich, the making of money has nothing to do with 'making ends meet'; it can sometimes come to seem like an end in itself, since wealth is so easily equated with happiness, or even with 'worth' in a more general sense. From there, it's a short step to the growing sense of *entitlement* among those in the wealthiest 20 percent of households: 'We're doing well; we're entitled to what we've got; we've worked hard for it; our kids will be fine.' Such attitudes suggest a waning of the egalitarian dream, especially when wealthy people contemplate (as they rarely do) the plight of the less well-off:

> *There's poverty? Not really – not in Australia. Sure, some people aren't doing so well, but that's inevitable in any society. You always get winners and losers – there's always a certain proportion of drop-outs and drop-kicks.*

Lower down the economic heap, where 'rich' is an impossible dream, other consolations are sought – believing that 'too much money only brings unhappiness', for instance, or that 'rich families fight over money' or even that 'rich people have forgotten about the simple pleasures of life'.

The prosperity of the early years of the 21st century has come at a high price: our epidemic of anxiety and depression appears intractable and many Australians are now questioning whether the ruthless focus on material prosperity has blinded us to some non-material values – such as loyalty, a sense of duty, pride in a job well done, honesty, prudence, restraint – highly esteemed by previous generations. That niggling thought is starting to affect attitudes to work: the 2006 Ipsos Mackay Report on *Australians At Work* quoted a number of people who admitted they were working too hard ('feeding the habit') because they had fallen for the idea that wealth equals worth.

You establish this lifestyle based on your earning power, and then you can't afford to pull back. So what if we don't go skiing this year? The sky won't fall in. But we keep running harder – it's not to keep up with the Joneses so much as to keep up with ourselves. Crazy stuff.

The range of Australians' responses to the current period of economic growth is starkly revealed in two contradictory attitudes to work. One is that we are enjoying such unprecedented prosperity, we need to make the most of it. The other is that, precisely because we are enjoying such prosperity, we have the luxury of being able to rethink our values and our priorities: 'How much money do you really need to have a good life?' The first attitude is an expression of max-out materialism – wealth for its own sake – which drives a relentless money-making ethic. The second expresses the desire for more *balance* and questions where all this growth is taking us, both personally and societally: *We're becoming more competitive, more commercial, more ruthless bastards. It's true. Is that necessarily good for us or for our way of life?*

Many people in two-income households find themselves wondering whether they are paying too high a price for their own prosperity. Especially among working mothers, the thought that 'life shouldn't have to be so busy and stressful' is often followed by this one: 'Weren't our parents happier and more relaxed, even though they didn't have as much stuff as we do?' and then this one: 'Do we really want to raise our kids to be little materialists? Are we setting the right example?'

Such reflections sometimes trigger a decision to downshift or simplify. Sometimes, it leads to the development of a more gradual strategy for easing back to a less frenetic pace and a less 'stuff-driven' life. But the magnetic appeal of material prosperity, the sheer exhilaration of 'retail therapy', the glamour of travel, the glitz of fashion and the social pressure to conform often overwhelm such decisions, and so the treadmill grinds on.

Even when people resort to the old line that 'money can't buy happiness', they are inclined to wonder whether just a little more money might buy just a little more happiness, especially when their smart friends say, 'You think money can't buy happiness? You don't know where to shop.' The ABS's 2001 National Health Survey shows a startlingly direct correlation between income and life satisfaction, and the idea that more money might bring more happiness is constantly and powerfully reinforced by the buzz, the pace and the seductions of a consumerist society. Still, there's a growing body of research (see Richard Eckersley's *Well & Good* and Clive Hamilton's *Affluenza*) suggesting that, beyond a certain level of material comfort, extra wealth does not produce a corresponding increase in wellbeing, so rumination about such matters seems timely.

Work till you drop?

When the then federal treasurer, Peter Costello, foreshadowed in 2005 the possibility that we might have to make a radical reassessment of the concept of retirement (caricatured by the Opposition at the time as the 'work till you drop' policy) he was responding to two important trends in contemporary Australian society – one demographic, one cultural.

We might be tired of hearing about the ageing society, but it's a core fact about us that must be faced. In Chapter 8, we will be pondering the implications of the fact that Australia's birthrate is now so low – far lower than the replacement rate – that we are in the process of producing our smallest-ever generation of children as a proportion of the total population. At the same time, proportionally the largest-ever generation of children – the Baby Boomers – are charging towards the point where previous generations were expected to settle into retirement: the oldest Boomers turned 60 in 2006 and are enjoying the prospect of greater longevity than any previous generation in our history.

Taken together, a low birthrate and the increasing longevity of the Baby Boomers mean that by the time this generation of children reach their middle years (assuming the birthrate stays this low or goes even lower, and assuming levels of immigration remain fairly constant), 25 percent of the Australian population will be over the age of 65 – double the proportion we have now. If we were to go into that future with the same attitudes to retirement we have now, the economic consequences would be catastrophic. We would be facing the prospect of a veritable army of retirees, many demanding pensions, health care and other social security provisions, and expecting to be supported by a shrinking base of taxpayers. (The Boomers did it for today's retirees, but it seems unlikely we are going to be able to do it for them.) So the economic imperatives demand that we rethink the whole idea of retirement and adopt a more flexible, more gradual approach to our eventual withdrawal from the paid workforce.

That sounds like a good idea for society as a whole, not only because it will help to spread the taxation burden more widely, but also because it will avoid – or at least mitigate – the social and economic impact of a huge increase in the number of retirees.

It's already starting to happen. Listening to today's pre-retirement generation talking – those now well into their fifties and even some already into their sixties – the traditional idea of retirement is being seriously reappraised. 'Sixty is the new 50', they want to assure us, because it reinforces their conviction that they are much 'younger' than their parents were at the same age: they eat younger, dress younger, act younger, think younger, feel younger. They are sure they are healthier and fitter than any previous generation, and many of them regard their continuing participation in the workforce as a sign that they're not finished yet.

Quite apart from the pleasing symbolism of remaining in the workforce, many of them can't afford to retire: they've been too busy borrowing and spending their way through middle age. They may have been notoriously poor savers, but they do have the highest rate of home ownership of any generation of Australians – 80 percent – and according to Professor Ann Harding of the National Centre for Social and Economic Modelling at the University of Canberra, they seem to have their debt under control. If they do get into financial trouble when the time comes to leave the workforce, the prospect of a reverse mortgage on their fully owned and highly appreciated homes beckons as a welcome safety net (as we will see in Chapter 8).

The traditional concept of retirement represents an unwelcome challenge to the Boomers' view of themselves as perpetually young. In fact, 'retirement' is a word they'd rather not use, because it carries connotations for them of elderly folk sitting on the verandah with pipe and slippers, watching the sun sink symbolically into the west. Far from being over the hill at 60 or 65, they prefer to think of themselves as approaching an airy upland where they will have more control over their lives, more choice, more opportunities to achieve the balance they've long craved. They will be looking for creative ways to de-stress, without appearing to have dropped out or given up.

And they've found the word to go with it. In Boomerspeak, the downbeat *retiring* has been replaced by the upbeat *refocusing*.

For the men and women of this and following generations, paid work – even if at a lower level of seniority and intensity – will continue to be an important symbol of vitality and effectiveness. This is why Peter Costello's ruminations had considerable emotional appeal to people still in the workforce who had already been thinking of ways to remain useful and engaged. Their motivation is partly selfish – they want to continue to feel valued, especially as they are looking forward to ten, 20 or 30 more years of active life – but it is also partly altruistic: many Boomers approaching their sixties feel as if they have plenty left to offer the community, either in their present roles, or in some voluntary capacity.

Many of them know, or suspect, that they will run into the problem of 'ageism' – the prejudice that says if you're past a certain age, you're either invisible or useless – and the more stories they hear about friends or colleagues who have retired, voluntarily or involuntarily, and then felt their experience was no longer valued by anyone, the more they are determined to find ways of hanging on. People with a wealth of valuable experience and a great deal of accumulated wisdom have often been frustrated to find that, after resignation or retrenchment from a job, it was almost impossible to find new employment in organisations that, apparently obsessed with the culture of youth, regarded older people as being too inflexible to adapt to new ways of doing things, or perhaps even too expensive to employ.

The good news is that this situation is about to change. As they've moved through the various stages of the life cycle, the iconoclastic Baby Boomers have changed our attitudes to almost everything; ageism and retirement are bound to be their next targets.

This doesn't imply an automatic dream run for the over-fifties from now on. The mere size of the generation now approaching the traditional age of retirement will not, of itself, be enough to guarantee a change in our attitudes to them as effective employees. If they are to be attractive to employers, older employees will have to demonstrate they are flexible enough in their attitudes and performance to adapt to the swiftly changing world of work.

If 60 is indeed the new 50, employers will be delighted.

Is there a cure for Retired Husband Syndrome?

No matter how long it may be postponed, retirement will eventually come to most of us. In the future, though, given that 45 percent of the workforce is now female, the dynamics of retirement will change. The old story, where a man retired to stay at home with a wife who was herself already at home, will gradually give way to a new story, where partners who both work will need to negotiate ways of co-ordinating their retirement (or 'refocusing') plans.

Even then, given the fact that women are still bearing most of the domestic workload, the probability is that an age-old problem will recur: the problem of Retired Husband Syndrome (RHS).

When he first retired, it was just awful. He seemed to think it was his job to take over the organisation of the household, so he started suggesting

ways I could become more efficient with the housework. He even came
shopping with me and tried to change the way I wrote my list. I thought
I was going mad.

That was a research respondent describing the impact of her husband's retirement on their marriage. Like many women in her situation, nothing had prepared her for the possibility that her husband, a senior executive with a major corporation, might start using their home as a new focus for his management skills. Typical of many men who retire, he had failed to anticipate the seriousness of the change or to make much effort to imagine how his permanent presence at home might affect his wife.

Wives are often more successful than husbands at sorting out their own sense of identity. Women who have been housewives, mothers, grandmothers and have full- or part-time jobs as well, typically create structures and routines that express the many facets of their identity – often including time for leisure and recreational activity that balances the other more demanding aspects of their lives and gives them crucial 'time out'. Though it seems like a dangerous generalisation, the evidence of several of my own research projects suggests that women also tend to be more conscientious than men at the business of maintaining friendship circles outside their working environment – including family circles.

Men, especially those holding senior positions in management and the professions, are often less careful about creating a balanced and well-rounded sense of personal identity. If they have defined themselves too narrowly in terms of their work, there's often a period of disorientation, or even panic, following the loss of that all-consuming identity.

In their search for a new sense of identity, some men put pressure on their wives to compensate them by becoming a newly enthusiastic couple. If they've previously neglected this aspect of their lives, or taken it for granted, it is easy to imagine their wives' initial resentment at finding that 'suddenly he's all over me, wanting to be part of a couple again and needing constant reassurance that I love him' (especially if declining sexual potency is simultaneously becoming a problem).

That new-found sense of dependency may be expressed as a constant desire to be with his wife, to go everywhere with her, or, if she's going out without him, to know exactly where she's going, with whom, how long she'll be gone, whether she will be back in time to make his lunch. (And if not, what should he do?) To a wife suffering from RHS, a simple question like 'Who was that on the phone?' can feel like an interrogation or even an invasion.

A retired husband's dependency might also be expressed in the expectation that his wife's established routines will be abandoned in favour of spending time exclusively with him: elaborate travel plans are sometimes hatched as a ruse to make this happen. This is not to deny, of course, that many couples actually welcome retirement as a phase of their life when they can spend more time together than has been possible since they were newlyweds. RHS is by no means a universal affliction.

Wives' accounts of tension arising from an unexpected sense of dependency among newly retired men suggest that if the situation is not well understood and sensitively managed by both spouses, it can create a gulf between them that will be hard to bridge. So perhaps it's not surprising to learn that many of the wives of newly retired men find themselves echoing the famous line attributed to the Duchess of Windsor: 'I married him for better or worse, but not for lunch.' Others complain of the flagging energy of their retired husbands, at a stage of life when they themselves are feeling more liberated: 'I feel as if I'm on the up escalator and he's on the down.'

But there's another problem for the wives of even the most well-meaning men who retire from positions of influence and authority: such men tend to assume that someone should be around to do their bidding, and that things should be done their way at home, just as they were at work.

> *I found he was ordering me around as if I was on his staff. He got a real shock when I suggested that if he knew a better way, he should do it himself. Actually, in the end, he did start being more helpful and that made things a lot easier. But some of my girlfriends are still battling with husbands who refuse to help around the house – except painting the outside, of course. They all do that as soon as they retire: I think it's a rite of passage.*

These are not new problems; nor are they exclusive to Western societies. In Japan, RHS has been formally recognised as a medical condition since 1991, and several psychiatrists specialise in its treatment. Reporting for the *Washington Post*, Anthony Faiola describes a Japanese wife who had developed stomach ulcers, slurred speech and rashes around her eyes within a few months of her husband's retirement. She characterised her relationship with her husband as a gradual transition from wife to mother to servant and, in despair, sought the help of a therapist whose advice was to spend as much time as possible away from her husband.

There are other solutions. One of them is to be found in the 3000 self-help groups that have sprung up in Japan, designed to teach retired men not only how to cook, clean, shop and be generally more independent, but also how to be more communicative with their wives.

RHS is an awkward reality for many Australian couples, which is perhaps one reason why the divorce rate remains high among the over-sixties. Perhaps it will become easier as we move into an era when both partners typically will have been in paid employment, or perhaps it will be harder. The experience of many couples, especially those who have raised a family, is that this can be make-or-break time for the relationship: having more time to spend together than at any previous stage of their marriage, they may 'rediscover' each other and perhaps find a new and deeper sense of mutual affection and respect. Their relationship may blossom in new ways. On the other hand, they may find that they have grown so far apart, probably without noticing it, that retirement is a time for the embarrassing discovery that they have little in common, little joy in each other's company, and are better off leading separate lives – much as they did when one or both of them were at work.

Many men need more active psychological preparation for retirement than is generally acknowledged, especially if they find themselves pitch-forked into it through retrenchment. Buying a new set of power tools or golf clubs is rarely the complete answer: the challenge is not simply to fill in your time or 'take up a hobby' but to establish a clear sense of personal identity that will avert your partner's risk of succumbing to RHS.

Gradual retirement seems to help, and a willingness to share in the housework and other domestic tasks – including care of grandchildren – appears to be crucial to the avoidance of RHS. To quote one enlightened (and richly rewarded) retiree from Faiola's research: 'I will never forget the look of happiness in her eyes the first time I cleaned the house while she was taking a bath.'

Are the under-thirties 'different'?

At the other end of the age spectrum, there's a new generation of young employees now crossing the threshold into the world of work. They're more savvy, more materialistic, more media-saturated and more impatient than any generation that's preceded them. They're also better educated, having stayed at school longer and engaged in tertiary education to a greater extent than any previous generation. Thirty years ago, only 12 percent of people in their twenties were attending a tertiary education institution; today, it's 25 percent. The change is even more dramatic for women – up from nine to 24 percent – and there are now more female than male tertiary students.

The generational mind-set of the under-thirties was described most recently in Rebecca Huntley's *The World According to Y* (2006). This is a generation that's easy to misunderstand, especially in the context of work. Older people who share workplaces with them often regard them with bewilderment, accusing them of having unrealistic expectations about what they should be doing at this early stage of their working lives, and how much they should be paid for doing it. In The Ipsos Mackay Report, *Australians at Work* (2006), some went so far as to suggest that the members of this new generation of workers have failed to grasp the essential concept of reciprocity inherent in the implied contract between employer and employee.

I find with the younger ones, if they don't want to do something, they don't do it, whereas we'd be anxious to please and would do anything we were asked.

This is a generation whose attitudes to work have been shaped by two very different influences. On the one hand, they find themselves in a society enjoying almost unprecedented economic prosperity and so, like the Baby Boomers of the 1950s and '60s, they are being conditioned to think of economic prosperity as their birthright. On the other hand, they watched their parents learn some painful lessons during the economic correction of the early 1990s – the recession the former governor of the Reserve Bank, Ian Macfarlane, described in his 2006 Boyer Lectures as both inevitable and economically beneficial, though actually less deep than the recession of 1982.

To quote from *Australians at Work*:

Observing parents whose loyalty to an organisation was devalued by the economic imperatives of cost-cutting or downsizing, young people have naturally developed more wary and self-protective attitudes to their own employers. Seeing the negative impact of long working hours on their parents' personal and family lives, young people are understandably inclined to think twice before jumping onto the very same treadmill.

To older people, a fresh generation of young Australians who seem determined to live life on their own terms, to assert their own values and to keep their options open can easily look as if it lacks loyalty, commitment or a proper sense of seriousness in its attitudes to work. But the attitudes of this generation to work are consistent with its attitudes to many things. This is a generation marrying later (if at all), having children later (if at all), buying a house later (if at all) and settling into the idea of a 'career path' later (if at all).

But generalisations are always dangerous, especially when they are based on a cohort of young Australians who have grown up in the midst of such kaleidoscopic change. So there is no single trend in their attitudes to work: this, after all, is the generation that has already increased the demand for apprenticeships, created a spate of high-flying entrepreneurs, and insisted on a more flexible approach to work than any previous generation. For their parents, 'job insecurity' has been a shock and a challenge but it's simply part of the reality for the members of this generation, and they are incorporating it into their approach to work.

At the same time, they've been conditioned to borrow for what they want, on the assumption that even if they keep changing jobs, the economic escalator will carry them in a generally upwards direction. To them, debt is no scarier than job insecurity: in this respect, at least, their parents – the Boomers – have set an enthusiastic example for them to follow.

5

Paradox:
The IT revolution

Back in 1994, the chairman of Microsoft, Bill Gates, told *The New Yorker* that he always combs his hair before sending an email, 'hoping to appear attractive'. Perhaps he was joking. Or perhaps he was making a serious point, knowing, even then, that email had the potential to confuse the idea of data transfer with the idea of communication. By combing his hair – literally or metaphorically – Gates may have been reminding himself that the message he was about to send was a *substitute* for the person-to-person, face-to-face contact that has always been fundamental to the process of communication between human beings. Combing his hair could not, of course, make him seem more attractive (though it might if he were meeting someone), but it could be a useful little ritual – a reality check – that would encourage him to pause for a moment and focus on the difference between an exchange of emails and a personal conversation. Combing his hair could have been like a 'note to self: remember what this email is *not*'. On the other hand, if Gates's email traffic has burgeoned in the past ten years as it has for most of us, his scalp might by now be irreparably damaged by excessive combing.

Here's another quote from that *New Yorker* interview: 'Email is a unique communication vehicle for a lot of reasons. However, email is not a substitute for direct interaction ... Email helps out with other types of communication. It allows you to exchange a lot of information in advance of a meeting and make the meeting far more valuable.'

Good to know, isn't it, that the high priest of the information technology revolution understood something we are now in danger of forgetting. The cleverness, accessibility, convenience and speed of the new IT products seduce us with the promise that we can be in closer-than-ever touch with each other – and, if we wish, with the whole wide world – and that we will be smarter, info-richer, more savvy and, above all, more *connected,* more 'wired', more 'switched on' than ever.

And so we will. And that's obviously wonderful, in so many ways. Who would want to turn back the clock? Who would dare? And yet, with every passing week, the hazards of our immersion in new media technology become more apparent, especially that constant temptation to confuse data transfer with human communication; to confuse one meaning of 'connected' with another, when the core message of the IT revolution is that the word now has two meanings, both valuable. It's easy, but wrong, to assume that because I've sent you some data and you've sent some back, that is simply an alternative to what Gates calls 'direct interaction'. It's not an alternative: it's a different process altogether. Email (or text, or whatever's next) can never do the whole job of communication because the human stuff – the emotions, the nuances, the things you'd normally convey through tone of voice, rate of speech, posture, gestures, eye movements – is all lost. On the other hand, when we are communicating face to face, our words are often contradicted by the messages in our tone of voice, our eye movements or our posture and when this happens, almost without exception, we pay more attention to those non-verbal messages than to the verbal ones.

The words on the screen might be the words you want to say but, from the receiver's point of view, most of the really interesting, really revealing stuff is missing. And let's not forget that the words we say or write often get in the way of human communication because they conceal our thoughts. (Voltaire thought that was actually the purpose of the words.) But even when we are valiantly trying to express our thoughts, the words are only ever a small part of the total message. Body language carries valuable freight.

So the great irony of the IT revolution is that, when it comes to the quality and the subtlety of our exchanges with each other, we are being conditioned to settle for much less than pre-revolutionary generations had to work with. More and more data; less and less communication.

The printing press, the Industrial Revolution, and now ...

Quite apart from the empirical evidence, it's clear from the tone and intensity of Australians' conversation about IT that this is a revolution likely to have been as powerful and transformative as the Industrial Revolution of 200 years ago. Its social and cultural effects – quite apart from its economic effects – are on the scale of the invention of the printing press, the generation and transmission of electricity, the invention of the steam engine, the development of factories, cars and aeroplanes. The IT revolution (now being called ICT, to slip 'communication' in there) is in that heady, heavy league. It is changing the way we live, the way we work, the way we contact each other, the way we inform and amuse ourselves. It's affecting the pace, the content and the focus of our lives.

All revolutions that transform us have the capacity to bring out the best and worst in us. The internal combustion engine gave us the automobile which gave us, in turn, unimagined freedom and flexibility, but has also polluted our air, clogged our cities, and killed us off in numbers to rival warfare. The printing press gave us mass literacy, but encouraged a hazardous separation of the author from the message which seemed to give messages – words – a life and meaning of their own. Print also taught us the straight-line disciplines of reading and writing which led to a tendency to admire the rational at the expense of the emotional, and to think in formal, logical, straight lines that serve us well in many contexts, but not all (which is why Edward de Bono had to reintroduce us to lateral thinking). The era of mass production brought us cheap and plentiful goods, but condemned millions of people to work in William Blake's 'dark Satanic mills'.

So the IT revolution was always going to be a blessing and a curse, and we all saw that coming a quarter of a century ago. The Mackay Report, *Computers, Technology & the Future* (1981) revealed a high level of anxiety about the looming revolution: people who had not yet come into contact with computers at that time were almost incapable of clear or calm thought about them and dreams of a 'golden age of leisure' made possible by computers were balanced by nightmares of a dehumanised, brutal, technocratic society. Few jobs were seen as safe from the potential effects of the revolution, and there was speculation about whether, if 'knowledge is power', the controllers of the computers would be the new power elite.

A blessing and a curse? Twenty-five years later, we're still trying to work out how much of each we're getting.

Families scattered around the world can now be in constant touch: every passing thought can be converted into an email and sent to the entire family, all at once, all in an instant. Businesses can move mountains of information in the twinkling of an eye. Scholars can exchange ideas, references, scraps of insight with colleagues in universities on the other side of the city, the country or the planet. People who are isolated and lonely, or socially inept, divorced, bereaved or depressed, can tap into a network of 'friends' in cyberspace – faceless but curiously real and, over time, reassuringly familiar – who will be there at any hour of the day or night, to listen, comfort, advise, amuse, flirt, or simply distract us from the dark places in our minds. For some people struggling with the ache of aloneness, the internet has proved to be as therapeutic as any medication. Online sites such as *Reach Out* provide instant, anonymous counselling for troubled young people, including those contemplating suicide.

And . . .

The internet has stimulated demand for pornography to previously undreamed-of levels. For all the talk about the internet giving us access to vast tracts of rich and diverse information that could open a window onto new and wonderful worlds of human possibilities, the reality is grubbier than that: an estimated one-third of internet users in Australia are accessing porn sites. Though some couples use shared exposure to online porn to stimulate their physical relationship, others have been driven apart by one partner's resentment of the other's habitual, solitary use of porn, sometimes amounting to an addiction. Even the loathsome trade in child pornography has prospered in the wake of the IT revolution.

The internet has added a new meaning to 'infidelity' in matters of the heart. Even without physical contact, some people have virtual affairs that are every bit as distracting, and distressing to their partners, as the real thing. The net can facilitate clandestine contact between old flames who rekindle their romance under the cloak of the spurious intimacy generated in the virtual world where, rather like the telephone, the absence of physical cues can stimulate the imagination and appear to increase the intensity of the encounter.

Some people feel liberated by their online anonymity, and that doesn't always bring out the best in them. The internet phenomenon of 'flaming' – hurling through cyberspace the kind of abuse you'd never say to someone's face – is a revealing feature of the new media: people often overplay their hand when they are released from the constraints and courtesies of face-to-face contact. Cyber-bullies are even less restrained than the other kind.

The anonymity of the internet also allows us to free-associate, to fantasise, and to project false and misleading images about ourselves; to obfuscate and deceive in ways difficult to achieve in contacts via other media. That statuesque, 28-year-old Swede you've fallen helplessly in love with might actually be a pimply-faced 14-year-old in New Jersey who delights in sending you (and thousands of others) photos of 'himself' in various stages of undress and has perfected the halting style of a non-native writer of English. That wise philosopher who keeps tossing *bon mots* into the online conversation might be a sad neurotic with a well-thumbed book of quotes at her elbow. That mole in the CIA might actually be a frustrated, fantasy shock-jock who dreams up conspiracy theories while driving his truck across

France. Wikipedia, billed as the largest encyclopedia-of-everything in the history of the universe, includes rubbish, falsehoods and fiction (whether deliberately misleading or not) as well as authentic, accurate and illuminating entries.

Since we half-know all that, does our exposure to the internet condition us to be less strict about the accuracy of the information we encounter there? Does that, in turn, lead us to be less strict about the integrity of information in general? The evidence suggests it does, and that the traditional mass media are playing a part in the process as well: The Ipsos Mackay Report has been noting a steady decline in respect for TV news and current affairs, as viewers have felt increasingly unable to distinguish the 'truth' from the carefully contrived tales of political spin doctors, or the opinions of journalists or commentators. The embedding of journalists in combat units in Iraq was a particularly disturbing development for many TV viewers: 'are we just seeing what the US military wants us to see?' In that case, the internet gave millions of viewers the chance to see alternative versions of the war story from other sources but this only reinforced the view that 'the news' is a more slippery thing than we used to imagine.

Perhaps the upside of this is that we have become more sceptical. The downside, though, is that we may no longer care so much when we are deceived – deliberately or not – by politicians, journalists, advertisers, or each other. When women discuss the possibility that much of the material they read in gossip magazines is 'made up', it's hard to tell whether they are complaining or entering into a jokey conspiracy with the publishers.

While the internet gives students access to a world of information to draw on for essays and assignments, it has also led to the phenomenon of mass plagiarism, sometimes detected by teachers, sometimes not. Students can help each other online; they can do each other's assignments across the world, and who would know? (And, if we are in the process of devaluing information because of the plethora now available to us, who would care?)

The very accessibility of the net, and its seductive pull, creates another danger for us. Radio and TV have proved themselves effective as surrogate companions – even offering, in the case of radio, the pleasing illusion of one-to-one intimacy – but the internet has a magic all its own. Because we interact with it, we seem to be in control of it, and yet it 'leads us on' in ways the mass media can never do, with its immediacy and its mesmeric power of access to an apparently infinite flow of people, places and information. Like all media for the transmission of information – from books to television – the internet can be a source of fascinating or even vital information and stimulating entertainment, it can be a pleasant pastime (literally, a way of passing the time), and it can also be an insidious time-waster and a merciless muncher of whole evenings:

> *I sat down to do a couple of things, one thing led to another, and before I knew what had happened, it was midnight. And when I thought about what I'd been doing, none of it mattered. I was just wasting time. But it was fun while it lasted. No worse than TV, I suppose, but it sort of gets to you in a different way. You're more in control of it, and there's such variety, you think, 'I might just have a look at this . . .'*

It's not only other people that might be neglected in favour of the screen: sleep is often a casualty, as well. Thanks to the internet, a new breed of nocturnal creatures is emerging: they work at night, they play at night, they socialise at night, even if they're not going out. They inhabit a virtual world where the lights are always on and something is always happening. It can be hard to drag yourself away and, when you eventually fall into bed, it can be hard to switch off the effects of all that stimulation.

A school counsellor, used to seeing sleep-deprived high school pupils struggling to keep pace with the demands of a busy school life, sums it up like this: 'Night is the new day. If they are up half the night, how can they expect to function normally during the day? Simple lack of sleep seems to contribute to many of the problems I see.'

According to the ABS's 1997 national survey of mental health and wellbeing, 27 percent of young people in the 18–24 years age group had experienced mental health problems – the highest proportion of any age group. Those problems are caused by many factors but, knowing what we know about the debilitating effects of lack of sleep, internet-related sleep deprivation may well be a contributing or exacerbating factor in some cases. (Is the old-fashioned concept of bedtime due for a comeback? Perhaps 'how to sleep' workshops will soon appear on the extracurricular agenda at high school.)

In The Mackay Report, *Living with Technology* (1993), Australians were already identifying five moral issues arising from the onrush of technology. With minor variations, those same questions are still being raised today when people – especially parents – discuss the impact of the IT revolution on our lives.

Is this just another example of mindless consumerism? Consistent with the widespread belief that the sophistication of modern marketing makes us buy things we don't really need, the ever-expanding array of products spawned by the IT revolution sometimes prompts the question: are we just buying all this stuff because it's there, or because we really need it? Have these products and services – and even information itself – become a new focus for our materialism?

Is electronically stored information ever really secure? This continues to be a concern for older people who are new to the technology. Younger people, by contrast, are more accepting, more relaxed, often to the point of indifference about the issue.

Has 'the system' taught us to become too dependent on electronic data – for example, in our increasing reliance on intangible money via credit cards and online transactions? And an associated concern: is new electronic technology so sophisticated, and so mysterious to most of us, that we have no alternative but to 'trust' it?

Does technology increase unemployment? Most people find it impossible to answer 'no' to that question. In spite of relatively low levels of unemployment in 2007, this question is still being raised, as people recognise that IT breakthroughs can occur unexpectedly and jobs can suddenly become redundant as a result.

Is technology depersonalising our society? This was a hot topic in 1993, but it is more likely to be discussed in a spirit of resignation in 2007: we know the process is well advanced, and we sense that we have lost something along the way. We appreciate the efficiency, but we know the human content has been removed from many transactions (including emails), even though we talk to each other more than ever via the mobile phone. As we adapt, we are starting to accept that there's a new meaning for words like 'communication' and 'connected'.

Such questions highlight the fears that continue to lurk beneath our enthusiasm for new technology. Parents constantly wonder, even as they indulge their children with the latest electronic gadget, whether IT is doing undesirable – and unpredictable – things to their children. Are they losing their social skills? Will their health be affected by the amount of time they spend in front of a screen? Is it too late: have we already lost control of our children's access to mediated information?

IT is evolving so rapidly you can hardly keep up. Don't get too attached to your iPod: your next mobile phone probably will have made it obsolete. Don't imagine your new phone, or your BlackBerry, is the last gasp in technofab. Don't forget, when you're shopping for your plasma TV, that TV is on its way to your mobile phone, and you'll be spending less time sitting in one place to watch it. As in so many aspects of Kaleidoscope Nation, the IT revolution is partly about convergence and the blurring of traditional distinctions to create new patterns: while the newsagent has also become a betting shop, spouses have become partners and the Right and Left of politics have become almost meaningless labels, the mobile phone is rapidly becoming a nimble, pocket-sized computer.

In a 1999 article reprinted in *The Age*, 'Keep tabs on technology', the US academic and author of the 1985 classic, *Amusing Ourselves to Death*, Neil Postman, suggested that as each new piece of clever technology arrives on the scene, we should ask ourselves the question: 'What is the problem to which this is a solution?' The answer to the question might be 'I need access to more information' or 'I'd love to have brighter colours on my screen' or even 'I need more fun in my life'. Whatever the answer, it's probably worth asking the question before we decide to spend our money, especially as the price of new IT tends to fall quickly, once the market has adopted it on a large scale. If we can't identify a problem to which the latest IT miracle is a solution, perhaps we should remain sceptical.

Reinventing Australia described an enthusiastic section of the community whose fascination with ever-new technology was part of their general impatience to get to the future: 'The compulsive futurists are almost exclusively interested in the short term, are attracted to quick and easy solutions and want instant gratification. Debt is fine, because credit is the magic mechanism for bringing tomorrow into today.' In 1993, they were a somewhat eccentric group of uncritical apologists for new technology. Today, they are close to the mainstream of Australian thought. Back then, I wrote: 'As we move through the Nineties, we may well decide that the only constant is change and that the most appropriate response to that is simply to react and adapt to every new event with no underlying sense of vision or purpose beyond a constant willingness to experience the new.' By 2007, that had become characteristic of us: like media-saturated societies around the world, we keep looking for the next thing, and the next. The thrill of the new tends to obscure the lessons of the past, and the capacity to distract us is one of the greatest of all the appeals of the IT revolution.

Consumers suspect that IT is increasing our work rate, putting us under more pressure, reducing our privacy and robbing us of time for reflection and relaxation, but they also know the IT tide is running strongly, and they are keen to catch the next wave.

A bleak footnote: in our enthusiasm for the IT revolution, it's easy to overlook the fact that IT is yet another divisive influence on our society. We speak glibly of 'information-rich' and 'information-poor' without always realising that there's a strong correlation between that and the other kind of wealth. If you simply can't afford to participate in the revolution because you can't pay the price of entry – a computer linked to the internet and a mobile phone, at the very least – you're being gradually pushed to the margin of a society that is bedazzled by its love affair with electronic data.

Connecting us and keeping us apart

When people reflect on their use of IT, and especially when parents reflect on their children's use of mobile phones and computers ('the generation that beeps and hums' one father calls his kids), a recurring question is this: are we in danger of losing something more precious than we're gaining? In particular, are we being seduced into thinking we don't need to spend so much time together?

It's not as if we spend over-much time together, as it is. In 2001, Sweeney Research's *Eye on Australia* reported that Australian couples spend an average of only 12 minutes a day talking to each other (and that's an average figure: some couples would regard 12 minutes as an eternity, especially if they happened to be 12 consecutive minutes).

We sometimes call these IT gadgets 'communication technology' as though they bring us together. But the paradox is that they also keep us apart. Our communing, such as it is, takes place at a distance. The very fact that we are using a phone, or email, means we are not together, and the more we use those media as alternatives to personal, face-to-face conversation, the more we run the risk of settling for contacts at that level. This doesn't mean we should eschew the opportunities IT gives us to maintain contact when, for reasons of time or distance, we simply can't get together. Phones and email are wonderful ways of augmenting and supplementing our relationships – keeping the pot simmering until we can re-stoke the fire with some full-on personal contact. The danger is that we might acquire a mind-set that says 'I'll send her an email' when picking up the phone would be better for the relationship, or 'I'll pick up the phone' when a chat over coffee might be a better setting for what you want to say. Personal, face-to-face interaction represents a quantum leap in the quality of any contact, even for the routine purpose of keeping in touch. The IT alternatives are superior for speed, precision and convenience, but efficiency is not the same thing as efficacy.

The phone is better than nothing, but it's not better than meeting. And neither is an SMS text or an email. An online chat-room offers us neither a chat (as traditionally understood) nor a room. All wonderfully clever as ways of transferring data; but not quite what we have traditionally meant by communication. None of which is to deny Bill Gates's point: data transfer, in any form, is useful as preparation for a meeting, for recording the outcome of a meeting, or for keeping in touch between meetings; it's just not a meeting.

People who work almost exclusively from home usually feel the need for occasional visits to the office to maintain personal contact. People who have only ever met by email, or even by phone, usually find that their perceptions of each other are modified in significant ways by the experience of a face-to-face meeting. Who's surprised? Humans are, after all, herd animals. We enjoy being in groups. We get our sense of identity and emotional security from the experience of belonging to the herd. We even enjoy grazing with the herd. So if we're going to be spending more time cut off from the herd – keeping in touch via electronic mooing – we'd better pay serious attention to the need to compensate for what we're giving up.

There's truth in the claim by Telstra's CEO, Sol Trujillo, that email has become 'the way we work'. But the fact that we've integrated email into our ways of working doesn't mean email is the only way we work nor that it is necessarily the way we work best. The faster the data exchanges, the less time we have for interpreting them, and that may be one of the greatest hazards of all. If we are constantly distracted by the flow of information into our heads, and addicted to the pleasing sense of stimulation it provides, will we become less committed to the idea of keeping in touch with each other? Will we even start to find each other less attractive, less stimulating and less biddable than the machines that seem to hum inside our heads?

If our data diet becomes too rich, we may starve ourselves of the emotional nutrition we get from actually being together in the same place, at the same time. If we let that happen, there'll soon be a new form of RSI – Reduced Social Interaction syndrome – with loneliness, paranoia and depression its symptoms, and doctors prescribing more frequent contacts with the herd.

No need for panic . . . yet. When you observe the rising generation of IT-saturated young Australians, some have become internet hermits but, more generally, there's no sign that they are less personally in touch with each other because of their electronic linkages. The reverse might even be true: they use IT to maintain almost continuous contact when they are apart, but not at the expense of time spent together. For the children of this revolution, 'connectedness' has acquired two meanings instead of one. In fact, many enthusiasts believe the internet connects them in a unique way to the vastness of global human experience. The World Wide Web is a perfect name for it.

Being connected to data, no matter how personally intimate the content, is not the same as being connected to other people, though the illusion of personal connection is very powerful. And if it is an illusion, it's an engaging one. In *The Gutenberg Elegies* (1994), Sven Birkets refers to 'sense-extending technologies' that distort the traditional time-space axis and lead us to think of communication – even quite intimate communication – taking place without real human presence. Birkets foresaw the development of a kind of electronic human hive (he called it an 'amniotic environment of impulses') creating a condition of apparent connectedness that was nevertheless spurious. Reflecting on the vast web of connectedness created by precisely the kind of IT networks now operating, Birkets fantasised about how strange and exhilarating it will be, in the future, to stand momentarily free of all this connectedness – just as it now feels for a city-dweller to be out in the country at night and see a sky full of stars.

Not all analysts of the IT revolution have as grim a view as Birkets. In an article published in the 1997 *Annual Review of Sociology*, Karen Cerulo argues that 'new communication technologies have freed interaction from the requirements of physical co-presence. These technologies have expanded the array of generalised others contributing to the construction of the self.' In other words, Cerulo – like many enthusiastic users of the new technologies – believes a sense of connection with others no longer depends upon the central requirement of traditional interpersonal communication: *being there.*

Birkets was not simply anticipating a society in which we might risk sacrificing too much personal contact in favour of the electronic kind. He was also anticipating Cerulo's point that the new forms of connectedness would create a new *kind* of intimacy, which helps to explain the emerging challenge to our traditional view of privacy (see 'Redefining privacy', later in this chapter).

A glimpse into the new way of thinking about connectedness comes from a young woman who has fallen in love on the internet, but has yet to meet the object of her affections:

I feel as if this is better than falling in love in person. On the net, it's more like a kind of pure thing – you're not distracted by things like personal appearance, or how someone sounds. It's more like the true essence of things. You can be completely open and you're just being judged on what you say. Nothing else comes into it.

Others might argue that those 'distractions'– how we look, how we sound, how we smell, how we dress, how we walk, sit or stand, how we eat – are integral to human relationships in general and to falling in love in particular. But for that woman, and for thousands like her, there's a different kind of love, a different kind of relationship, that feels utterly real, profoundly 'connected' and possessing a 'purity' not available in settings less ethereal than cyberspace.

The internet game Second Life, described by its devotees not as a game but a 'virtual world', is a logical extension of the idea that the cyber-world is not only authentic but can be experienced as real. Participants in Second Life can establish an idealised identity (their 'avatar'), complete with physical features tailored to suit their taste or their mood – or perhaps their whimsical fantasy. They can buy virtual land, build virtual houses, take on virtual jobs, meet virtual partners, have virtual sex, establish virtual households and neighbourhoods, all while sitting at their keyboards. Some of them talk of Second Life as if it really is a second life, possibly lived with more flair and imagination, or more recklessness, than their three-dimensional life. 'I've made a lot of money in Second Life' is a statement that sounds odd to non-participants who might think this has about as much significance as saying 'I made a lot of money playing Monopoly' but those making such statements may regard Second Life as being rather like a second chance – in particular, a chance to 'show what I can really do'. The crossover point between the two worlds is, predictably, money: via a conventional credit card, participants can acquire currency to spend in Second Life.

Online activities like Second Life can be everything from a pleasant distraction to a mesmerising or even delusional experience that saps the motivation to participate in the here-and-now. If such games consume too much of the time and energy required for our flesh-and-blood relationships with partners, friends and neighbours, then their potential as an emotional hazard is obvious. But if they are a way of trying out life strategies – whether commercial or emotional – in a harmless environment, they may have some educational as well as therapeutic value. What is clear, though, is that Second Life is a signpost to a future in which, for many people, the distinction between electronic data transfer and human communication is further blurred.

Behold the undisputed champion of the revolution!

Australians have always shown the keenest enthusiasm for new technology that makes it easier for them to do things they already want to do. The home computer received a lukewarm reception at first, because we were somewhat at a loss to see what it could do for us, beyond its obvious appeal as a sophisticated new form of typewriter. Keeping a record of the contents of your pantry so you could generate a shopping list was a cute idea, but a notepad and pencil still seemed pretty efficient. But when the internet arrived, the computer was transformed: it became what we had dreamed it might become – a means of access to a world of unlimited information, a gold mine of data, a source of constant stimulation with the potential for serious mind expansion. We started to see it as a mega-magical version of the mass media.

And, of course, it gave us email, thereby changing the way we work, the way we keep in touch with each other and the way we exchange contact details ('give me your email address' replacing 'give me your phone number'). And yet, for all its marvellous convenience, email can't claim the title of IT champion: it has created too much stress, put us under too much pressure, brought us too much spam and consumed too much of our time to be a champion. We want it to be our servant, but it keeps acting like our master and we're not sure how to put it in its place. 'I deleted 200 emails and cancelled my address' sounds reckless: we keep thinking there must be a more constructive, more reasonable way of dealing with the problem.

No, the undisputed champion of the IT revolution is not email, nor even the computer, but the mobile phone. With each new refinement, its users become more admiring, more astonished, and more addicted. It started as the perfect example of technology at its best – letting us do what we already wanted to do, namely, call people from wherever we happened to be – and then carried us to unimagined new realms. The mobile concept itself was magical enough, but the subsequent additions of ever more amazing and useful facilities to the mobile phone – SMS, email, video calls, TV reception, internet connection – have transformed it into the must-have technology: the must-have accessory for the young; the must-have lifeline for lovers; the must-have access to their children for worried parents;

the must-have convenience for busy people everywhere; the must-have symbol of personal importance: 'people *need* to reach me'.

In the process, it has transformed us. For a start, it has changed the way we greet each other on the phone. It's no longer 'how are you?' but 'where are you?' It has transformed our phone bills, too, plunging many people into unexpected debt: we had always resisted the concept of timed local calls when we only had phones attached to landlines, but our resistance crumbled before the magic of the mobile. It has also created a marketplace crowded with complex deals and 'plans' that have so confused consumers, they are inclined to shrug helplessly and hope for the best. (This is an unusual example of a marketing strategy that irritates customers, sometimes to the point of fury, without dimming their enthusiasm for the product itself. The losers are the reputations of the mobile phone companies.)

The mobile phone has transformed our behaviour in social settings. Not having yet fully evolved a set of generally accepted manners for mobile usage, we are still feeling our way. It's apparently okay to talk on your mobile when you are sitting in a restaurant with someone else; indeed, it's okay for everyone at the table to be talking on their mobiles to other people. (It's a pleasing fantasy to imagine that the couple over there in the corner, both talking on mobiles, are actually talking to each other, and it's not entirely inconceivable: conditioning is a wondrous thing.) It seems to be okay to speak more loudly on your mobile than you would in a face-to-face conversation, since we all understand the vagaries of mobile reception. Public transport is widely thought by mobile users to be a suitable place to conduct private conversations, though there's often less enthusiasm among their fellow travellers. (Can the 'silent carriages' of some UK, Japanese and US trains be far away?)

Mobiles are completely out of place in church, at conferences, concerts, theatres or lectures. Drivers using hand-held mobiles are at risk not only of prosecution, but abuse from other drivers. You can answer a mobile in a retail store, but if you're already at the checkout, you must sacrifice your place in the queue. Provided you're discreet about it, you can check your SMS messages or use your BlackBerry almost anywhere.

The main transformation wrought by the mobile phone is that it makes continuous contact possible. No owner of a mobile need ever feel isolated. If no one has actually rung you and you can't think who to ring, you can always recall your old voicemail messages and create the impression that you're in touch; you're in demand; you're loved, wanted, needed. Indispensable, even. (What's the use of a lifeless mobile? What would its silence say about me?)

Children spend all day together at school, then get on the bus or train to go home and whip out their mobile phones to maintain contact with each other. (It's serious stuff, too: 'Where are you now? Who are you with?') Lovers can breathe their every thought into each other's ears when they are apart. Spouses can make detailed arrangements about the shopping, the children or the movie tickets. And young people can modify their arrangements from moment to moment, as fresh possibilities emerge. The mobile phone has reinforced their natural tendency to hang loose – keep your options open – so this is dream technology for them. It lets them make plan A as a kind of marker, so plans B, C, D and E can evolve, apparently seamlessly. It's no wonder parents are bewildered: they haven't grasped that the mobile is like a magic wand that controls the universe, an instrument for maintaining the dynamic tension of constant change. It's not for making plans; it's for exploring alternatives, considering options, letting life's possibilities unfold, right up to the last minute: 'Where are you? Oh, there. I see you!'

Occasionally, there's a note of wistfulness in young people's enthusiasm for their mobiles: 'Sometimes there's nothing left to say when we meet, because we've said it all on the phone.' But, for most mobile users, that's a risk worth taking.

Our dream is always that technology will both enrich and simplify our lives; that it will do more *for* us than *to* us. The mobile phone and, to a lesser extent, the internet-linked computer have come closer than any other of the fruits of the IT revolution to convincing us that such a dream can come true. But there are many other marvels on offer.

We were slow to adopt the ATM because it didn't seem to be letting us do what we wanted to do (i.e., conduct a transaction with a teller in a branch). It was only when it gradually dawned on us that the banks didn't want us inside their branches – since they were intending to close many of them – that we took to the ATM and discovered its extraordinary convenience, though we still prefer withdrawals to deposits. EFTPOS, by contrast, was an instant success because it was convenient for us to use the retail store's cash register as a bank withdrawal facility. (And guess who gets the credit for EFTPOS? The retailer, not the bank.)

The credit revolution has been facilitated by the IT revolution and, according to The Ipsos Mackay Report, *Living with Debt* (2007), it's over. It's happened. We are converts. The speed and convenience of online banking has made financial services seem as accessible, as easy and as painless as booking an airline ticket or sending an email. The distinction between money and credit has been blurred by electronics ('you can't see it; you can't feel it'), and many of us no longer even think of credit as debt.

Since the 1974 launch of Bankcard – forerunner of Visa and Mastercard – credit cards have become so integral with our way of life, they are perhaps the closest rival to mobile phones for the title of IT champion. *Reinventing Australia* reported that 'instant credit, combined with invisible money, created the new hazard of accidental debt'. It's no longer new, but our record levels of personal and household debt suggest it is still a hazard. Australians began 2007 with a record \$40 billion credit-card bill, representing a tripling of credit-card debt in six years.

Consumers love their credit cards for their convenience, their symbolism ('I'm *approved*') and their power ('I've got thousands of dollars to spend') and any guilt they might feel at overspending can be postponed, at least until the bill arrives and, even then, by the slow and gradual repayment of the debt at interest rates that are as invisible as the money.

In direct response to the easy credit mentality created by the impact of the IT revolution on our financial system, debt has become 'normal': 'If you're not in debt, you're not in the race,' said a participant in the *Living with Debt* study – a far cry from the days when debt was feared, when saving was a virtue (rather than a waste of time) and when banks were expected to err on the side of caution when they assessed a credit risk.

Revving up our lives

We are being swept along by the pace of the IT products, services and processes we have so enthusiastically embraced. Their speed has generated demand for more speed. Speed has become a virtue. And if speed is good, faster must be better. 'I sent you an email' means 'Why haven't you replied?' But we no longer simply expect instant replies to emails; we expect instant reactions to everything.

Our insatiable appetite for speed – for 'saving time' – can be seen not only in the swiftness of our email exchanges, but also in the short cuts we take in composing them. SMS (short message service) text has led the way, with its arcane language of abbreviations and symbols that seem to people raised on a more leisured approach to literacy to be shredding the written language – or, perhaps, to be inventing a new kind of language. Emails are increasingly adopting the same abbreviated style, but we no longer simply use 4 for 'for' or tx for 'thanks' or gr8 for 'great' or btw for 'by the way' or pos for 'parent over shoulder' (useful as a warning to expect a change of tone when a parent mooches into a child's room to check what's happening on the screen). Now we've started dropping capital letters entirely, since we can't afford to waste the time or effort it takes to hit the shift key. Full stops are on the way out, too: another waste of time. And as an email already includes the addressee's name, repeating it in a salutation would be both redundant and a waste of time. Emails are increasingly taking on the appearance of stream-of-consciousness output. (What might James Joyce have made of this endless, unpunctuated, free-associative, quirky use of language? His style might have been partly a revolt against the conventions of the print medium: this lot is driven by the opposite – a capitulation to the very nature of the medium.)

The fast food revolution is a cultural offshoot of the IT revolution and so, too, is the 'slow food' counter-revolution – a resistance movement led by people who don't merely want to enjoy eating more;

they want to enjoy life more and feel it is becoming blurred by pace. For them, the kaleidoscope is not merely turning; it's spinning.

The short break – a couple of days snatched in the middle of a week, or tacked on to a weekend – has become a fashionable alternative to the full-blown holiday. It's quicker, it's cheaper, and you can justify every kind of pampering on the grounds that you're trying to cram the benefits of a 'proper' holiday into a few days. For people in the grip of job insecurity, the short break also has the advantage that you won't be away from the office long enough for people to have noticed you've gone, and you're less likely to come back to find you've been made redundant.

You need a book of household cleaning hints? *Speed Cleaning*, the hugely successful sequel to *Spotless*, promises 'a spotless house in just 15 minutes a day'. And if you're trying to squeeze in a quick bedtime story for your children, Shari Lewis's *One-minute Bedtime Stories* should do the trick.

Speed dating is another child of the revolution. Put 20 people in a room – ten men and ten women – and let each spend ten minutes with each of the ten people of the opposite sex. At the end of the session, let's say Josie is interested in 'taking it further' with Brad and perhaps with Rick. She lets the organiser know that if either of those men asks for her contact details, that's fine; no worries. If not, no sweat. And if anyone other than Brad or Rick asks for her details? No way. End of story. (btw, in our newly abbreviated world, either *no worries* or *no way* can convey your response to most situations.)

It's neat. It's as safe as any other way of arranging a first date, with the possible exception of having your parents arrange it for you. And, above all, it's quick: a ten-minute sampler with each of ten men or women, and you haven't wasted an entire evening. You've also saved endless hours mingling in coffee breaks at tedious conferences, drinking in bars, going to dance parties, attending popular church services, or doing any of the other traditional things that might put you in the way of romantic prospects. Kaleidoscope Nation comes to dating: ten minutes with this one, then twist, then twist again, and let's see if a pretty pattern appears.

Speed has become a factor in other aspects of courting behaviour, too. In a February 2007 program on ABC radio's 702 in Sydney, the attitudes of older and younger Australians were being compared on everything from food to dating. Barry Oakley, novelist and former literary editor of *The Australian*, was recounting his adolescence, when the height of a young man's romantic ambition was to kiss a girl on the lips. A twentysomething guest on the program, Samantha Brett, who writes a blog (a term derived from 'web-log') for *The Sydney Morning Herald*, was clearly astonished by the contrast between Oakley's revelation and what she described as today's 'three date rule' – that is, not having sex until the third date – though she conceded that some couples might actually wait as long as three months. She also remarked rather wistfully that it might be nice if things were still the way they had been in Oakley's youth.

Further down the age scale, teenagers are becoming wary of declaring their love for one another via SMS because of the risk that an answer may be slow in coming, and then what? Does that mean he doesn't love me, or doesn't love me enough to reply this instant? Or is he too busy texting his mates, or . . . 'Of course I love you – it's just that my mobile battery was flat.' Oh.

Television started the process of shortening our attention span. It didn't take TV directors long to realise that the small screen demanded a faster pace than the big screen: perhaps because the flickering tube had a soporific effect on so many people, quicker cuts were needed to keep them awake. Editing has become progressively more frenetic as scenes in soaps and other material produced for the small screen are cut into smaller and smaller pieces. Even in news and current affairs, the ten-second grab became the five-second grab and now it's sometimes the two- or three-word grab.

If the director hasn't allowed for the shrinking attention span of viewers, they can do it for themselves. Right up there with the mobile phone and the credit card as heroes of the IT revolution is the TV remote-control wand, universally and affectionately known as 'the remote'. The contest to hold the remote is a familiar power struggle in many households. Its greatest value is not that it saves us having to drag ourselves off the couch to change channels, but that it gives us the power to flick, flick, flick constantly between channels. A commercial break? Quick, flick! Then, if you become briefly engrossed in what you find, you'll need to flick back to see what you're missing on the channel you so recently left. On the way, you might check what else is going on. TV, like life, has become a kaleidoscope.

The journalist David Dale, one of the most perceptive commentators on Australian popular culture and the author, most recently, of *Who We Are* (2006), has unearthed some remarkable facts about our TV viewing practices. In *The Sydney Morning Herald* of 28–29 April 2001, he quoted research conducted by David Keig, showing that, on average, only 36 percent of those who dip into a program end up watching the whole show. Typically, 51 percent of the total audience for any one program watch less than one-third of it. Of course, some programs attract more loyal viewers than others, but The Ipsos Mackay Report, *What We Do with Television* (2003), suggests that even viewers who are theoretically watching an entire program may well be doing a bit of flicking as well.

Shortening our attention span also means lowering our boredom threshold. People who have opted for a diet of fast data need ever-faster data, and they need it to be coming at them constantly. It's no accident that 'I'm bored' has become the agonised cry of a generation of highly stimulated young people. Constant stimulation creates a need for constant stimulation. TV taught us that when nothing seems to be happening, you can turn on the set and – hey presto! – *something is always happening*. From those simple days of not so long ago, it's been a short and logical step to the present situation where, for a growing number of IT-savvy Australians, stimulation doesn't mean having television on; it means instant messaging a couple of friends while browsing MySpace, keeping an eye on eBay (the online auction service), checking emails and maybe dipping into a channel or two of television as well. With the mobile to hand, of course.

The need for constant buzz is like an addiction, and it has some interesting effects on us. Not only do we crave instant reactions, instant responses and instant gratification, but we expect everything to be stimulating – to amuse us, distract us and entertain us. Television might have led the way, but the whole IT revolution – and the very culture of Kaleidoscope Nation – reinforces the idea. Whether it's education, politics, religion or current affairs, we need pace, colour and movement; we are in constant need of *something else*. 'What's new?' is no longer a laconic greeting; it's a pointed question. Even in the arcane world of celebrity, speed and variety are the watchwords. We need a new name; a new scandal; a new face; a new revelation; a new illness; a new diet; a new bit of cosmetic surgery gone wrong on a famous face or body. And we need it all *now*.

Well back from the cutting edge of technology, the women's magazine market has been transformed by the spirit of the IT revolution. It now caters brilliantly to the need for pace, variety and visual stimulation. Fifteen years ago, the market was dominated by a handful of big-selling titles: *The Australian Women's Weekly, Woman's Day* and *New Idea* were firmly established, selling close to one million copies each, with *Cleo* and *Cosmopolitan* rising fast and pointing to what was to come. *Who Weekly* was carving out a new niche for celebrity gossip, also a harbinger. Today, the women's magazine market – increasingly drifting towards gossip and increasingly appealing to men as well – has fragmented and segmented to the point where more than 15 titles like *Famous, OK!, NW, Hello!, That's Life, New Woman* and *Take 5* jostle for the reader's attention. (Did I say 'reader'? Mostly, these are picture-books.) And if some of the stories seem like fabrications or exaggerations, so what? We're here for the soft focus, not the hard facts.

If we keep speeding up the rate at which we receive and digest information, the process itself will change. Interpretation, normally involving some considered reflection and contemplation, will become increasingly superfluous. When the next thing, and the next, are already here, when will we stop and consider what we've just seen?

In *The Triumph of the Airheads and the Retreat from Commonsense* (2006), Shelley Gare bemoans the triumph of style over substance everywhere from the boardroom to the classroom, partly under the influence of the mass media. One factor driving the trend towards 'dumbing down' is, surely, the sheer pace of data transfer. If we don't have time to weigh, assess, reflect and interpret the information cascading over us, how can we become wise? Might we lose our sense of which bits are relevant? Might we lose our perspective under the weight of so much data? When will we have time off to think?

Redefining privacy

The generation raised in the thick of the IT revolution appears to be less interested in traditional notions of privacy than older Australians are. When information about almost everything is so freely and readily available, and when electronic exchanges, both financial and personal, are transacted with dizzying speed and in a context of kaleidoscopic transience – *what's next?* – it's probably not surprising that privacy is becoming something of a non-issue.

New privacy laws, enthusiastically enacted by governments in response to older people's concerns about the security of information about them (especially when it is stored electronically), have generally failed to capture the attention of young people. To them, the IT revolution is all about the *sharing* of information, rather than the withholding of it, and they appear more trusting of online transactions and less concerned about what will happen to the information about them held by banks, ticketing companies, online retailers or government agencies. Whereas some older people might ponder the privacy implications of releasing their credit card details for an online purchase, younger people simply accept that this is how it's done.

A more telling symptom of the culture shift in attitudes to privacy comes from the growing number of people who are using the internet to display their wares – their life stories, their diaries, their innermost thoughts and even pictures of their daily lives – to all and sundry.

The blog is the most straightforward example – more like a personal publication, perhaps, than a revelation of anything that might once have been thought of as private. But the blog can easily transmogrify into something more edgy, more intimate and more lurid: some of the web diaries now appearing in the new so-called 'social networks' like MySpace or Facebook look like exhibitionism gone wild. In a *Guardian* article reprinted in *The Sydney Morning Herald* on 13 March 2007 ('A brave new teen world in blog land'), British columnist Anna Karpf expressed the view of a generation of bemused parents who compare the openness of their offspring's blogging with the intense privacy of their own diaries: 'What's shocking to us is the extent of self-exposure they embrace. These kids live their lives online, but to their parents it feels like public nudity ... Those of us from the generation of the book inevitably sneer at and fear MySpace, where teenagers think nothing of recording their late period alongside their favourite band.'

Why do people do it? One answer: because the internet lets them. But a better answer is this: the IT revolution is ripping the veil of secrecy from our culture. Thanks to the internet, we know more and more about more and more: in the context of such unrestrained disclosure, tiny bits of information about ourselves can seem like a legitimate part of the vast web of data that vibrates with a kind of universal life.

In *The Sydney Morning Herald* of 3–4 March 2007, Jenna Hand wrote about the increasingly frank, personal details now being posted in various forms on the internet as part of the social networking phenomenon.

A friend of mine recently enjoyed a night of athletic lovemaking that resulted in a broken bed frame. On the same day, my primary school nemesis split up with her boyfriend and a work acquaintance had a messy run-in with a chicken dealer in Vietnam.

None of these individuals told me of these exploits. So how do I know about them? Facebook.

Facebook, MySpace, Friendster and similar networks enable their users to reveal whatever details of their lives they choose, on web pages with attachments offering extensions into video footage, friends' exploits, and the opportunity for people on the registered 'friends list' to make comments about each others' pages. Says Hand: 'In real life, this would be called stickybeaking. Online, it's expected.' It means that when you meet someone you've been tracking on a social network you might realise you know more about them than is normally the case with casual social encounters. One of the young people quoted in Hand's article concedes this can sometimes make for uncomfortable conversations: 'Someone will be speaking about an event and think I don't know about it, and I'll say, "Oh, I saw your photos". It makes things a little awkward sometimes.'

Hand points out that although people using these new networks treat them as if they are cosy communities, this is a misguided view. Like almost everything posted on the internet, contributions to social networks are publicly available and can be accessed for years. The prospect of a potential employer or an inquisitive teenage daughter, yet unborn, using Google to find out something about you and coming across some of this material in future decades doesn't appear to dim the enthusiasm of those involved.

Perhaps the mentality that drives people to offer the world moving images of themselves cleaning their teeth or undressing for bed also insulates them from the embarrassment others might feel. But the phenomenon of 'web display', whether verbal or visual, is a sign that the boundary between public and private – and perhaps also the boundary between the individual and the tribe – is blurring. If this is a signpost to our cultural future, it suggests a return to a more primitive cultural framework rather than a great leap forward. Anthropologists, rather than social forecasters, might be the ones to draw us a map of where we're going.

Changing the way we woo and wed

The advent of mass literacy gave us the love letter and, like all new media, the love letter changed the courtship rituals of literate people. It allowed them to say things that needed reflection, careful expression and, perhaps, more tenderness than could easily be put into words when confronted by the beloved, especially in social settings not conducive to the expression of private thoughts and feelings. Paradoxically, the letter permitted more bravado, more courage and hints of greater intimacy than might have been possible in the hesitant, face-to-face encounters of a more genteel age. The love letter sped things up.

The phone has long been an instrument of seduction and romance, partly because it creates an illusion of physical intimacy that encourages recklessness: a voice close to the ear; the sound of quickened breathing; no observers to worry about; the delectable disorientation of being both connected and unconnected.

As the IT revolution gathers momentum, its products are becoming fully integrated into modern courtship rituals. People routinely fall in love on the internet, though they are often disappointed when they meet (proving there's more to romance than the words). But the net has become a popular meeting place and *The McKinsey Quarterly* reported in 2006 that 12 percent of US newlyweds that year had met online. The early stigma associated with online dating has gone, and people of all ages and from all walks of life are now able to make exploratory overtures in a safe environment. While it's true that exploitation and deception still take place, it takes only one live meeting to establish whether you have been the victim of misleading advertising.

Text messages, redolent with private codes, have become the contemporary equivalent of the love letter, though it's doubtful whether they'll appear in anthologies of the future. And ditching someone by text is about the most heartless of all modern applications of IT.

Telstra's CEO, Sol Trujillo, mentioned in a 2006 speech that young people in Dubai have devised new courtship rituals using mobile phones. Nothing as simple as just asking a girl for her number, though. One trick is for boys to buy a pre-paid mobile, install a picture of themselves, drop it into the handbag or through the car window of a girl they like, then call the number.

But there's a catch. According to Trujillo, it has become such a common practice, girls are refusing to take the call if the handset is not top of the range. (Adds a whole new meaning to 'chick magnet'.)

A new form of democracy?

In *Media Mania* (2002), I wrote that 'it has become fashionable to speculate about the possibility of the internet being harnessed in the service of democracy, uniting us all in a mega-forum in cyberspace where we can participate, with equal access, in the democratic process and express our views on any issue . . . Could cyberspace,' I asked, 'offer a new kind of village green where we could all assemble at an electronic version of the public meeting, and where our leaders could take their cue from us at every turn?'

It's true that market and social researchers are making increasing use of the internet as a medium for contacting large numbers of people very quickly. The internet 'panel' is becoming a popular and inexpensive way to obtain information about everything from product usage to political opinions. Over time, such panels have the capacity to provide useful trend data, provided rigorous sampling methods can be applied to the selection of respondents, and provided people can be trusted to tell the truth when they are so disconnected from the source of the questions: even a telephone interview is more demanding of our attention and honesty. (Early research into internet survey techniques has shown, ironically, that a reminder to complete a survey task stimulates a higher rate of response if it is sent via 'snail mail' rather than email.)

No doubt the speed and efficiency of the internet will also be harnessed by politicians – partly to gauge public opinion on particular issues, partly to evaluate the effectiveness of particular strategies and partly as an irresistible new medium of propaganda and persuasion. (In the federal electorate of Wentworth, Malcolm Turnbull's newsletter is a model of the genre.) Speed and efficiency are the essence and strength of the internet, but they hardly sound like the crucial ingredients in the process of decision-making, whether personal, commercial or political.

Democracy depends on the quality of consultation, the free interplay of debate and, above all, the provision of time for reflection, consideration and careful discourse. Democracy, at its best, is not about the speed with which decisions are made, or even about the quantity of available data. Brilliant leadership is unlikely to be enhanced by a web-based version of the town hall meeting; it may even be eroded by an excess of uninformed opinion. (Aren't we already in danger of our political system being weakened by too much reliance on public opinion research?) And the proposition, occasionally advocated, that the internet could take us into some idealised, cyberspace version of the old Roman Forum, where everyone can vote on everything, is both a distortion of that very elitist historical concept and a rejection of the whole process of parliamentary democracy. We could certainly dream up ways to improve our democracy, but full-scale citizen participation in online decision-making doesn't sound like one of them.

Leadership has its problems but mob rule, whether electronically or otherwise, hardly seems like a sensible alternative. Isn't leadership about creative thinking and a willingness to take bold and even unpopular initiatives, to propose visions of what we might become, and to display moral courage? Smart, sensitive and responsible leaders are assiduous students of public opinion, but they use it as an input to the decision-making process, not a substitute for it. The internet, and other IT miracles yet to be performed, can illuminate the political process and create new opportunities for engagement with it. But the prophets of a brave new democracy where we all participate continuously, online, are offering us a recipe for chaos.

A word to the wise

In a 1999 article, 'A Waste of Time', published in *The New York Times*, the Pulitzer Prize-winning US novelist Richard Ford described a dilemma that is echoed in the concerns of many contemporary Australians. Ford is sceptical about the claim that the new information technology is morally neutral and has no impact on human nature. On the contrary, he regards the IT revolution as morally dangerous because of its impact on the pace of our lives, and the way it distracts us from being able 'to experience [our] lived days as valuable days'. Ford admits he has neither email nor a mobile phone – not even 'call waiting' or a beeper, and confesses the fear that 'if someone can't find me using any or all of these means, they will conclude that, for technical reasons, I don't exist any more'.

Many people feel vaguely uneasy about the impact of the IT revolution on their working lives, on their children and on society at large. Some are as resistant to the technology as Ford is: I spoke at an IT conference in Brisbane in 2007 and was asked by one woman what she should say when people ask her for her (non-existent) email address. She felt embarrassed about not having one, but was determined to resist the pressure. I suggested she should say 'I don't have one' and leave it at that. Any minute, she'll find herself at the cutting edge of a counter-revolution, if the growing number of complaints about email is anything to go by.

But most people are no longer resistant to the use of some, at least, of the technological marvels now on offer. Even if they regard MySpace as a kids-only zone, or YouTube as offering more choice of video material than they could possibly handle, they can see value in the speed of email or the convenience of the mobile phone for both voice and text. Yet Ford's anxiety is theirs, too: are we being affected by this revolution in ways we don't fully understand? Are we being changed – not just in the way we spend our time, but in our priorities as well? Are we judging things to be important that we once thought unimportant? Were we to keep a diary of how we actually spend our time, would it reflect the things we claim are important to us, like spending time with each other, face to face? 'Privacy' and 'identity' and 'connected' and even 'communication' might be acquiring new meanings, but the old meanings are still valid, too.

As even the most passionate advocates of the new technologies would agree, information is not, of itself, the pathway to happiness or enlightenment. We can easily be distracted from the quest for the meaning of our lives by our dalliances with data; indeed, some of us have discovered the guilty pleasure of insulating ourselves from a three-dimensional reality that's too daunting or demanding by immersing ourselves in more and more information.

At the same time, there are those who, before the IT revolution, would have suffered agonies of isolation and loneliness because of geographical remoteness, crippling shyness or mental illness. For them, the revolution has been an emotional boon, at least, and possibly even a life-saver. Sometimes, connectedness via that vast worldwide web is the only kind available.

6

Diversity: The identity revolution

It is hard to know whether this is the greatest or the least of the revolutions transforming us. 'National identity' waxes and wanes as an issue: it's rarely mentioned when Australians meet and talk informally about whatever is on their minds, but it bubbles to the surface when something happens that reminds them that, these days, we are virtually defined by our diversity. Given that we are creating a society from the blending of people who have come here from nearly 200 different birthplaces around the world and that, right now, 50 percent of us were either born overseas or have at least one parent born overseas, the question of national identity is bound to be somewhat elusive. We seem less sure of who we are, and where we belong in the world, than we were 15 years ago, but we know there are revolutionary changes taking place on both scores.

In *Where to Now?: Australia's Identity in the Nineties* (1993), the Hungarian-born writer and literary critic, Andrew Riemer, wrote: 'A society is something fluid, constantly changing, being redefined perhaps almost as soon as it has defined itself.' True of every modern society, no doubt; especially true of Australia, given the ever-increasing diversity not only of our ethnic composition, but of our cultural life as well. Who is the typical Australian? What is the typical Australian way of life? In Kaleidoscope Nation, the answers to such questions are no longer simple, if they ever were.

We used to think we could define ourselves by our Britishness – partly because so many of our institutions were derived from British models, partly because our non-Indigenous founding population was mainly British and partly, of course, because the British monarch was – and, astonishingly, still is – our head of state. In *Claiming a Continent* (1996), historian David Day reports there was uproar in our federal parliament in 1936 – just 70-odd years ago – when it was revealed that the proportion of immigrants coming from the UK had dropped from 98 percent to 97 percent.

Yet Britain itself has always been, in effect, a multicultural society, with regional dialects so broad they were virtually incomprehensible to outsiders: a fisherman from Cornwall, a farmer from Yorkshire, a cutler from Sheffield and a banker from London might as well have come from different planets. There was a unifying sense of Britishness, of course, deriving from a shared national history and from institutions, myths and legends, some of which, like the class system, actually preserved divisions. Today, British society is increasingly pluralistic and increasingly black-skinned. Oxbridge graduates now affect Dockland accents and the very concept of Britishness is itself in decline, yielding to the resurgence of separate English, Scottish and Welsh identities. In *The London Review of Books*, 5 April 2007, Neal Ascherson quotes the most recent *British Attitudes Survey* showing that in the ten years to 2005, the number of English people who felt they had a British identity had declined by eight percent to less than half the population. The Scots' sense of Britishness has been in sharp decline for years, and is now down to 14 percent. There's a growing preference for the use of English, Scottish and Welsh flags over the Union Jack.

Though Australians who came here – or whose forebears came here – from the UK still respect our British heritage and admire many aspects of it, that heritage has no particular significance to those of Irish, Greek, Italian, Lebanese, Chinese or Vietnamese descent. The proportion of UK-born residents has been declining steadily: over the past 25 years it has dropped from about 33 percent to about 20 percent of the population. The biggest proportional rises in that period have come from people born in China, Vietnam, India, the Philippines, New Zealand and South Africa, though the UK is still the single largest group. Residents born in China and Southeast Asia together still account for only about three percent of the total population.

In terms of recent arrivals, the largest proportion still come from the UK, but they are no longer a dominant group: 15 percent of the 123 000 permanent settlers who arrived in 2004–5 were from the UK, 14 percent from New Zealand, followed by nine percent from China, eight percent from India and five percent from the Sudan.

Regardless of where people or their parents might have been born, there appears to be an increasing willingness to identify themselves as Australians. Newcomers have no doubt that 'Australian' is what they want to be, and perhaps the very fluidity – the very dynamism – of our evolving identity is what makes it easy for them to identify with us. In the same way, second- or third-generation Australians who, 30 years ago, might still have identified themselves as being of English or Scottish origin, no longer seem keen to do so.

To the extent that our increasingly independent (and increasingly diffused) sense of identity is tied to any other country, it would be the US rather than the UK. That is partly a result of our increasingly close military and foreign policy links, and partly cultural: when it comes to cinema and television, we're hands-down American in our tastes. The twang and idiom of the US sitcom is never far below the surface of young Australians' conversation.

And yet, from a tourist's point of view, Australians are equally alien in both countries and the US and UK seem equally unlikely to treat us well as a trading partner. China and Japan loom larger, from that point of view, and our sense of identity is therefore also being gradually influenced by our economic engagement with Asia.

There's a gradual awakening to the idea that we belong to a region – the Asia Pacific – in which we are a middle-order nation, dependent on larger countries for economic sustenance and increasingly involved in the affairs of smaller countries (East Timor, the Solomon Islands, Fiji) via humanitarian aid, military, police, medical, legal and other support. But we don't yet *relate* to the region in our attitudes, except with some nervousness about the long-term prospect of China's economic domination of us and Indonesia's potential hostility to us either as a highly unlikely aggressor, or through diplomatic tensions arising from Australian drug offenders and/or our determination to prevent asylum-seekers using Indonesia as a staging post en route to Australia. The push to learn regional languages – especially Indonesian and Japanese – appears to have lost momentum since the federal government stopped funding earmarked for Asian studies in schools.

We know we invaded and occupied Iraq as allies of the US, and the presence or absence of UK troops was irrelevant to that commitment. Our military ties to the US – in equipment and administration as well as allegiance – are about as close as can be imagined and although many Australians express uneasiness about the strength of the link and Australia's subservient role in the relationship, the trade-off is obvious: whether justified by the terms of the ANZUS treaty or not, there is a widespread assumption that the US would come to our aid if we were ever threatened militarily. (Such a threat is almost unimaginable to most Australians, by the way: they assume we are more at risk from terrorism, due, ironically, to our close identification with US foreign policy, especially in Iraq.)

Though Australians may deride many aspects of the American way of life – especially its health and welfare systems and an employment market that has spawned 'working poor' on a large scale – the US is still unambiguously regarded as the world's only superpower and the fountainhead of capitalism. Americans are praised for their 'niceness' (nicer at home than abroad) and, at its best, the US is thought capable of leading the world – intellectually, commercially, industrially and even culturally. Hostility to the administration of President George W. Bush has been widespread, but it has rarely been the product of a generalised anti-Americanism.

The ugliest word in the language

There's something else we've recently borrowed from America that is far less attractive than its scholarship, enterprise or entertainment. A new word has entered the language, apparently with the purpose of trying to stifle open debate about our culture, our values and our politics. The word is *unAustralian* and it has begun cropping up in the media, in the rhetoric of politicians and, unhappily, in backyard conversations around the nation. It's tempting to make light of it, but it may be a symptom of something dark.

Here we are, in these early years of a new century, offering an example to the world of a tolerant, fair, prosperous society. Yet we have begun to use a word which carries the quite alien connotations of an infamous era in America's history when anyone suspected of 'unAmerican' (i.e., pro-Communist) activities was branded a 'fellow traveller' and pilloried. Our circumstances are different, of course, yet the growing use of 'unAustralian' suggests a new form of pressure to conform to a particular view of Australia. The implication is clear: those who use the word believe they have such a firm grasp of what it means to be Australian, they are in a position to judge whether others are falling short of that standard. They don't even have to tell us what the standard is: it's as though they alone know the password, the code, that gives them access to this mythical 'Australianness'.

It's the kind of word that goes perfectly with the political rhetoric that says, 'If you're not with us, you're against us'. We no longer have an enemy as specific and identifiable as communism: our enemies are said to be 'terrorists' which is about as slippery a definition as you can imagine. But in the same way as the US (and, to some extent, Australia) became obsessed in the 1950s with 'Reds under the bed' and gripped by fear of communist infiltration of academia and the labour movement, so we are in danger of falling for the idea that anyone who challenges the current political orthodoxy – about the invasion of Iraq, the treatment of asylum-seekers, the injustices of Guantanamo Bay or the erosion of civil liberties – must be 'against us' or, even more bizarrely, 'on the side of the terrorists'.

This is arrant nonsense. You could be a patriotic and committed Australian, yet continue to believe it was wrong for our defence forces to participate in a pre-emptive military strike. You could love this country passionately, yet be deeply ashamed of what we have done to people locked up in our detention centres. You could be fiercely loyal to the principles that underpin our society, yet feel free to speak up when you think they are being violated.

You could even accept the philosophy of 'practical reconciliation' between non-Indigenous and Indigenous Australians, yet still feel there is room for deep contrition, admission of fault, and heartfelt apology before we could expect the forgiveness of those who have been sorely mistreated and marginalised.

Does any of that imply you are unAustralian? Of course not. But perhaps 'unAustralian' is simply the new term of abuse to hurl at those who happen to have a different view of the world from yours.

There's a commercial sting in the tail of this story: some Australians hold firmly to the view that it is unAustralian to buy imported products that compete with Australian-made goods. From time to time, there have been attempts by commercial advertisers and industry groups to promote this idea, though patriotism appears to be becoming less of a driver of purchase decisions as we adapt to the idea of a truly globalised marketplace.

Nevertheless, the 'buy Australian' concept remains something of a conundrum for consumers: what is 'Australian', anyway? Does it only mean products made here, by Australian labour? What about products made here for foreign firms? Products assembled here from overseas parts/ingredients? Products made elsewhere from Australian materials, then imported and sold by local firms?

From the consumer's point of view, it's all too hard. So we take refuge in post-purchase gratification: we buy what we want, what we can afford, what the kids will eat . . . and then, if it turns out that the product is Australian in any sense of the word, that's seen as a nice bonus, but hardly a reason for buying it in the first place.

For some people with a broad, global outlook, the 'buy Australian' philosophy is not only difficult in practice; it also raises a moral issue: If I'm going to think about the importance of the country of origin, should I perhaps be supporting products that have been made in poorer countries than ours?

Is multiculturalism dead?

The word that provokes most debate when Australians think about their sense of identity is not 'unAustralian' but 'multiculturalism'. Though it drifted out of official favour in 2006–7 – being replaced in the language of both sides of federal politics by 'integration' – it has nevertheless come to be accepted as the shorthand way of capturing all that is good *and* all that is threatening about the complexity and diversity of contemporary Australian society.

The good? We see ourselves as a culturally richer, more interesting place; we have more fun; we are noisier and less inhibited than we were, kissing and hugging with less restraint, for instance; we are learning more communal, less insular, more European ways of living; we are discovering (with pleasure) the street as a venue for eating out and, more broadly, for our social lives. And, of course, we have become more adventurous with our food, 'fusion food' being a distinctive response to our cultural diversity, and the modern deli a far cry from the ham-and-beef shops of old.

If we never used the word 'multiculturalism' and spoke, instead, of our cosmopolitan or pluralistic society, who would argue with that? After all, true multiculturalism is not only – or even mainly – about ethnicity or religion: it is about a heterogeneous culture in which people are free to live in many different ways, based on respect for each other's rights and a concern for each other's needs and wellbeing. A multicultural society has the Big Day Out *and* Opera in the Park; churches *and* mosques; Aussie Rules *and* soccer; RSL clubs *and* concert halls; backyard barbecues *and* A-list charity balls; conservatives *and* liberals; public libraries *and* multiplex cinemas; cathedrals *and* casinos.

Multiculturalism, as a word, carries some negative baggage. It suggests to some people that subcultures will be preserved in a way that slows the process of establishing social harmony. Others believe it poses a threat to the whole idea of 'shared values'. It also sounds like an official policy imposed on us, rather than something we created all by ourselves.

And it can't easily be unhooked from our attitudes to migration. As ever, we tend to be resistant to the latest wave of immigrants – whether Lebanese, Sudanese or Burmese or whoever the next group might be – just as we were to Greeks, Italians and other 'wogs' and 'reffos' after World War II. Back then, we were nervous about the influx of Roman Catholics from southern Europe, the '40s and '50s having been a time of great sectarian tension between Protestants and Catholics, especially in Melbourne, with strong anti-Catholic prejudice especially evident in corporate life, conservative politics and the 'establishment'. Today, it's Muslims who make us nervous. Though we regard Muslims more warily than we used to regard Catholics, the claim that this is because they are non-Christian has an oddly familiar ring: among postwar Protestants, there was a widespread view that Catholics weren't quite Christian either ('the Antichrist', some thought). As late as 1961, a popular worry was that John F. Kennedy, the first Catholic president in US history, might 'take his orders from Rome'.

Writing in the *Journal of Democracy* ('Identity, Immigration & Democracy', April 2006), the renowned US scholar Francis Fukuyama reminds us that 'at many periods in history Muslim societies have been more tolerant than their Christian counterparts' and that 'it makes no more sense to see today's radical Islamism as an inevitable outgrowth of Islam than to see fascism as the culmination of centuries of European Christianity'. But, in Australia, the facile attachment of 'extremist' or 'radical' to 'Muslim' has had considerable political currency which, in turn, has reinforced our nervousness. We are not quite at the stage of assuming that 'all Muslims are potential terrorists' but there's a dangerous drift in that direction, helped along by reports of anti-Western propaganda being preached in some mosques.

A popular source of antagonism towards Muslims was the assertion often heard around the turn of the century that primary schools were being prevented from holding celebrations of Christmas – carol singing, Nativity plays, decorated Christmas trees – because such events might give offence to Muslims in the school community. Pauline Hanson made much of this during her brief period of political prominence as the leader of the One Nation party, though the assertion had no more status than an urban myth. No school could ever be found where this had actually occurred, though dark murmurings persisted.

The rumour may well have sprung from cases where Muslim children were not permitted to take part in Christian ceremonies.

In fact, many enlightened primary school teachers have seized the opportunity to mark all the festivals celebrated in the cultures represented by the children in their schools, from different religious and ethnic backgrounds, so the children's understanding of each other's cultural context is enriched. Naturally, Christian children are encouraged but not forced to take part in Muslim ceremonies, and vice versa. Thus are rumours born, and thus do rumours foment prejudice.

In fact, our xenophobia has little religious content, since Australia is itself such an avowedly secular society and only about 15 percent of us regularly attend Christian church services. So anxiety about Muslims is more about 'otherness' than religion; more about identity than spirituality (as, indeed, was the earlier prejudice against Catholics). The true source of current uneasiness is the worry that Muslims might be more inclined than other ethnic or cultural minorities to hang back from fully embracing Australian culture and identity. Nothing irritates or offends long-term Australian residents like the thought that any group of immigrants might choose to be anything less than wholehearted Australians.

In 1999, John Howard had launched his National Multicultural Advisory Board with these words: 'We respect and understand the fact that you were born in another country, you retain a special place in your heart for that country, and there is nothing, in my view, that diminishes the wholeness of the Australian nation in that being fully recognised.' That captured the general view of multiculturalism at that time and would still resonate today, with this proviso: we are uncomfortable about any sign that suggests another source of identity – whether ethnic or religious – is being rated more highly than the Australian identity.

Attitudes towards multiculturalism have gone through several stages, from initial resistance to wary acceptance, qualified approval and now back to a more questioning, ambivalent attitude. While we take great pleasure in our more liberal, more cosmopolitan way of life, we have been shaken by occasional media reports of race-based hostility, especially when it involves violence: the riots at Sydney's Cronulla beach in 2006, sparked by an attack on lifesavers by Lebanese-Australian youths mainly from Bankstown in Sydney's southwest and exacerbated by massive revenge attacks by local youths from the Cronulla region; press reports of crimes associated with particular ethnic groups; continuing enmity between supporters of soccer clubs with strong ethnic heritage. Such events, rare as they are, revive long-standing worries about whether we are taking too big a risk with multiculturalism; whether we have been too relaxed about the standards we expect from new settlers.

Some of our attitudes to multiculturalism are tied directly to a lingering concern about the size and composition of our immigration program and our traditional fear of being culturally 'swamped'. In many ways, those attitudes have scarcely changed over the past 20 years: we still believe that immigrants should feel more grateful to us than we do to them; that anyone who comes here should make the learning of English a top priority; that immigrants should leave their own ethnic tensions and conflicts behind; that immigrants should not take 'our' jobs or lower our standard of living.

The Mackay Report, *Mind & Mood* (2003), noted some turning of the tide on multiculturalism:

During the past 20 years or more, Australians have prided themselves on their reputation for being a tolerant and hospitable society. But, over the past three years . . . we have been taking refuge in prejudices of various kinds and, as part of that process, we have become a more intolerant society. Some Australians blame the concept of multiculturalism: they believe . . . that by promoting the strong identity of various ethnic sub-cultures, we have written a prescription for social dislocation and disharmony.

Other participants in that study welcomed the enrichment of our society through multiculturalism but wondered whether 'we might be letting the wrong people in'. In 2003, there were distinct signs emerging of a backlash against multiculturalism and a greater assertiveness in the voicing of prejudices against Muslims, Lebanese, 'Asians', Aborigines and anyone outside the Anglo-Saxon–Celtic circle. These prejudices ranged from a belief that certain ethnic groups were disproportionately associated with crime to the view that, in the case of Muslims, they were actively trying to undermine the Australian way of life, perhaps even with the long-term hope that Australia would become an Islamic nation.

But personal experience is usually a great softener of attitudes, and that's reflected in the accounts of people who have lived or worked closely with migrants towards whom they had felt some initial prejudice. Our remarkably high rates of intermarriage between the offspring of immigrants from different birthplace groups, and between immigrants and members of the host community, also tell an encouraging story of a society that is learning how to become truly multicultural.

One impediment to progress towards greater acceptance of our ethnic and cultural diversity has been the community's continuing irritation and impatience with asylum-seekers, egged on by what some saw as explicit permission from the federal government to dehumanise 'illegals':

> *The Tampa incident really legitimised racism in this country. From that time, it's been okay to speak out against other races. Before that, people might have had an opinion, but you kept it in your back pocket. Now it's almost okay to be racist: it's like the government's given you permission. It's all been pretty laid back – until now. Now we have comments from people like Peter Costello targeting Muslims. You get the impression the government would prefer to have a monoculture.*

> *You know what I reckon? Push the boats back out to sea. The navy's doing a good job – why doesn't the air force bomb them?*

At the height of hysteria about asylum-seekers arriving in small and scarcely seaworthy fishing boats, John Howard made one of his most memorable – and characteristic – remarks: 'We will decide who comes to this country and the circumstances in which they come.' It sounded unexceptionable; it sounded tough; it sounded strong. It also sounded like the kind of thing any nation could say if it felt its borders were being penetrated. In this case, the numbers involved were tiny and incarceration of asylum-seekers in harsh detention centres, sometimes for years, struck many Australians as brutal and unreasonable. (Others simply didn't want to know: see Part Four.)

But for how much longer will we – or any developed nation – be able to assert that we will decide who comes here? Part of the national character we like to project is that we are hospitable, tolerant and compassionate, and these qualities are likely to be put to a much tougher test in the future than they ever have been in the past. There are about 25 million refugees adrift in the world: 25 million human beings who, tonight, have nowhere to call home. When will we be called on to take a larger share of them? And what will we say when the call comes? Will we dare say, 'We will decide who comes...'?

When the disastrous occupation of Iraq by US-led forces, including ours, finally comes to an end, our moral obligations will become clear: we will be obliged to offer whatever help we can – medical, engineering, peace-keeping, educational, diplomatic – but won't we also be obliged to share in the inevitable resettlement program for thousands of Iraqi refugees?

And if the dire predictions about the effects of global warming are even partly realised, what will be our response to the greatly increased number of refugees whose coastal areas are no longer inhabitable or whose food supply has run out?

Of course, there's another issue that transcends the question of who will come, or how many will come, or how they will come: what will we expect of them when they get here?

Amidst all the talk of citizenship tests and other ways of ensuring that new settlers understand what we stand for, we should perhaps be placing more emphasis on the things that bind us to the ideals of a liberal democracy and less on specific bits of Australian history and custom. Who cares if new citizens have never heard of Phar Lap, or are confused about which was Burke and which was Wills or what Australia Day commemorates? Isn't it better that they understand, from the start, our commitment to tolerance, gender equality, the rule of law or parliamentary democracy? The rest may come when they start trying to help their kids with their homework or when they watch game shows on TV. Some of them – like some of us – will be interested in Australian history, and some won't.

•

Multiculturalism is not dead, but it is being re-evaluated in the light of the experience of the last quarter-century. Some say it has run its course, by which they mean that we have become so well established as a pluralistic society, we no longer need to wear a badge that declares it. Others passionately want to keep displaying the badge, fearing that recent revisionist talk might actually undermine the principles of tolerance and fairness that inform the concept of multiculturalism. But others want to discard the badge altogether, seeing it as a relic of a misguided idea: for them, recent talk of 'integration' sounds like a welcome return to the old days of assimilation when we were all either Australians or 'New Australians' – a term designed to make newcomers feel welcome but which, in practice, often had a distancing effect. (Inevitably, New Australians became 'Naussies' before the term lapsed with the advent of multicultural social policy.)

Two striking conclusions emerge from an analysis of Australians' current attitudes to multiculturalism. The first is that, even if we want to scrap the word itself, we still see ourselves as a shining example to the world of a society that can blend people from almost everywhere into a tolerant, harmonious society, and make it work – perhaps better in Melbourne than elsewhere, but we're generally doing pretty well. Here's part of a news item that appeared in *The Sydney Morning Herald* on 26 December 2006, written by Deborah Snow and Dylan Welch:

> In the kitchen a row of six women wearing hijabs dice vegetables and slice fruit. Nearby another group of young Muslim women are tearing open packets of pasta by the dozen and throwing them into

a huge pot of boiling water. Across the room, two young men wearing skullcaps are stirring a sizeable pan of beef curry.

Aiming to give their Christian counterparts from the charity Just Enough Faith the day off, the dedicated Muslim volunteers spent most of Christmas Day preparing and distributing homecooked meals to more than 500 homeless men and women at [Sydney's] Cook and Phillip Park.

The volunteers come from Al-Ghazzali Centre for Islamic Sciences and Human Development, in Roselands, and see their role as building bridges between the faiths. The founder of the centre, Imam Afroz Ali, said . . . 'This service is directly for our Australian brothers and sisters. What has made this successful is that the younger generation, particularly Muslims who were born here, have been dying to do something like this.

'Their parents, the older generation, still have connections back to their places of birth overseas, so a lot of charity goes back there, and there is no hiding from that. But Islam requires us to provide charitable services in our own neighbourhood first. So we have to do this as Muslims, right here in Australia, regardless of gender, race or religion.'

The second conclusion is this: among the things with the potential to divide us, multiculturalism rates way below socio-economic inequality. We are more concerned about the emergence of winners and losers, about the growing stratification of our society, about the cultural and economic chasm between city and country, and about the impact of a harsher commercialism and more ruthless competitiveness than we are about our cultural diversity.

Is the quest for those distinctive 'Australian values' misguided?

The debate about Australian values, like the debate about national identity, comes and goes. While we might be ready to accept that our national identity is an evolving concept that can't yet be articulated very precisely, some of us still cling to the idea that there must be some distinctive values that spring from a unique Australian ethos and help to define the kind of people we are, or aspire to be.

Yet most of the values we claim as cornerstones of our way of life are simply the touchstones of any modern liberal democracy: respect for persons as individuals, regardless of age or sex; respect for democracy and its institutions, including the rule of law and the principle of parliamentary representation; the right to freedom of speech, belief and assembly. We discourage the exploitation of the weak by the strong; we abhor prejudice that judges people by the category they represent – ethnic, religious, or otherwise. We condemn the oppression and abuse of minorities.

It goes without saying that we don't all live by all those values all the time, but we could scarcely claim them as uniquely ours, without offending every other liberal democracy on the planet.

There have been similar attempts, from time to time, to identify a unique Australian spirituality, and to discern some distinctive, spiritual essence of Australianness in our art, music or literature. While some people have been tempted to look to Indigenous art, culture or spirituality as a source of distinctive Australianness – perhaps hoping for a unique fusion of Indigenous and Western or other traditions – Professor Gary Bouma reminds us in *Australian Soul* (2006) that there has been a sharp decline in the number of people identifying with Aboriginal traditional religions. Although Indigenous Australians have been practicing religion and spirituality for over 40 000 years, this has been a highly diverse heritage (reflecting the many 'nations' that lived here before European settlement). In any case, as Bouma points out, most contemporary Australians who identify themselves as Aboriginal also indicate that they are Christians. Quoting 2001 Census figures, Bouma notes that only 1.2 percent of Aboriginal people said they held to their traditional religions whereas 69 percent identified with a Christian denomination in proportions that roughly follow those of the Australian population as a whole.

The reality is that in our religious faith and practice, as in our broader cultural life, we are highly diverse and we share that diversity with – and indeed derive much of it from – many different cultures from around the world, both past and present. The Australian physical and cultural context naturally exerts its influence on our creative artists, yet there is no reason to suppose that the most profound and universal human impulses and yearnings should find a unique expression in Australia, disconnected from the flow of creative evolution around the world – whether in religion, art, music, literature, values, or any other aspect of our culture. The Australian landscape painter Ross Lawrie, for example, sees his highly distinctive work as being set squarely in a tradition that runs from Rembrandt and Tintoretto via Willem de Kooning to Lawrie's studio on a sheep farm in Walcha. Similarly, there's no reason why cultural expressions of deep human impulses from other parts of the world should seem alien or unacceptable to us.

While there has been a surge of interest in the subject of values, it has little to do with *national* values. When politicians try to hijack the values debate, they miss the point: our keenest interest in values is almost entirely confined to the private realm: How should we live? How can we manage our lives better than we're doing at present? How can we restore balance to our lives?

In the 1993 paper referred to earlier in this chapter, Andrew Riemer noted that 'in the case of national identities and national prototypes, perhaps even national fictions, there are profound myths, legends and beliefs that become part and parcel of the cultural fabric of a society. It is those things we ought to try to explore.'

In Australia, there are plenty of myths, legends and beliefs that sustain our sense of ourselves: the Anzac tradition, Eureka Stockade, Burke and Wills – though those are all tales of heroic failure. More broadly, we respect our military history and revere the exploits of explorers and the privations of pioneers who opened up 'the outback' (itself a sustaining myth that has sold an awful lot of four-wheel-drive vehicles, elastic-sided boots and 'country' furniture to city slickers). Our painters, poets, writers and composers have framed a national story for us and inspired us with a deep sense of Australianness that sometimes springs from our distinctive environment – the land, the sea, the sky – and sometimes from the very tensions inherent in the process of creating a cultural amalgam out of a highly eclectic collection of immigrants.

But it's early days. We've only been a federated nation for a little over 100 years. Think of Greece and Italy. Think of England, Scotland, Ireland, Wales. Think of France, Spain, Mexico, Brazil, Peru, Cambodia. Think of Egypt, Iraq, Iran. Think of India, China and Japan. Think of Hungary, Poland, Austria and Germany. We need another century or two, at least. The process of identity formation has scarcely begun.

Three of our favourite 'national values' sound suspiciously as if they were borrowed from the French Republic's *liberté, egalité, fraternité*, though they are generally presented in the reverse order as Australia's own: mateship, egalitarianism and the 'fair go'.

So how do they stack up? Though it may be an unpopular view to take, I suspect this particular trinity offers more comfort than illumination. Myths are fine when they inspire, but what if they actually weaken us by blinding us to the truth about ourselves?

Take mateship – a perennial favourite among back-slapping blokes, though not so immediately appealing to women. Derived largely from the legends of survival in the harsh outback, comradeship in war, the solidarity of trade unionists, and the bonding rituals of sport, mateship is actually a rather clubby, tribal concept. Our version seems less inclusive than the French: rather than implying that we are one 'brotherhood', it suggests we look after our mates; we care for our own. Well, who doesn't? Throwing a sympathetic arm around a friend in trouble is natural, but hardly noble – and hardly unique to Australia. When two miners were trapped underground for a week in Tasmania's Beaconsfield gold mine, politicians and the media praised the rescue efforts – which were indeed heroic – as a tangible expression of classic Aussie mateship. But wouldn't Russian, German or South African miners have tried just as hard to rescue their colleagues?

What about egalitarianism? Given our increasingly stark socio-economic stratification, it's even doubtful whether this is still our dream, and the more we recite it like a mantra, the less clearly we'll perceive the contradictory reality of unequal access to education, health care, housing and information. Were we ever a truly egalitarian society, compared with, say, Denmark or Italy, both of which have far flatter distribution of wealth than we do? The dream thrived in the 1950s when it looked as if the suburban middle class would become our paradigm, but the gap between wealth and poverty now seems unlikely to narrow. We've always had our own jumped-up version of an aristocracy, mainly based on money and as deluded as any other, and we weren't even egalitarian in our attitudes to women until the last 25 years or so. There's still a common view that immigrants should first 'learn their place' before they can expect to be accepted as equals here, and we're highly elitist in our treatment of sports stars and celebrities.

The 'fair go'? That certainly sounds like us. Dinky-di. Unless you're an asylum-seeker, of course, or the kind of refugee we don't want, an Aborigine, poor, homeless, or have a mental illness or some other disability. (Come to think of it, we're quite adept at marginalising people.) We're not even particularly good at ensuring a fair go for those in rural and regional Australia who watch the prosperity gap between them and the city widen (the income of non-metropolitan Australians is an average 16 percent lower than for those living in metropolitan areas) and who are being disadvantaged by the steady withdrawal of commercial, health, education and other services.

That 'holy trinity' of Aussie values, however appealing, doesn't quite capture the real us. If you had to be brutally honest about the values that drive us at present, materialism would have to top the list, perhaps followed by pragmatism. But these hardly sound noble enough to be enshrined as the values that define us.

Is there something unique to celebrate?

Why don't we abandon the clichés and focus on what really is distinctive about this vibrant, exciting, infuriating place we call

Australia? We're highly urbanised, highly mobile, highly innovative – and so are plenty of the countries we like to compare ourselves with. We consistently produce world leaders in science, technology and the arts: we're over-represented in the list of Nobel prize winners. We excel at sport. We're richly endowed with mineral deposits that underpin our prosperity (though we can hardly take credit for that).

Beyond all that, surely there is a distinctively Australian achievement: we are world champions at creating a harmonious society from a blend of people who, over the years, have come here from every imaginable birthplace.

That suggests tolerance should be a cardinal virtue in the Australian character, but that's a pretty feeble contender for a defining value: who wants to be merely tolerated? Aren't we overdue for a bit more healthy curiosity about each other? Isn't it time to develop a heightened respect for difference, alongside our natural affinity with people who are like-minded? Nothing breeds prejudice, suspicion and mistrust like ignorance, and we won't shake that off until we take a more active interest in those whose cultural backgrounds are different from our own.

Then we'll start to realise that diversity – in a society as in an ecosystem – breeds strength, and homogeneity is bad for us. We're more mongrel than purebred, and what's wrong with that?

Kaleidoscope Nation is a work in progress – a brilliantly creative work of art to which each of us is making our own unique contribution. Our national character is still evolving. Yes, we need to cling to the values that distinguish liberal democracies from other societies, and distinctive Australian bits (like compulsory voting) will ultimately emerge. But who can imagine what the term 'Australian identity' will mean, 50 or 100 years from now?

PART THREE

Snapshots from the family album

'Ooh, look how we've changed! I'd hardly recognise us.'

7

The 'relationships' era: Reinventing marriage and divorce

The figures speak for themselves. In Kaleidoscope Nation, more than 40 percent of contemporary marriages are likely to end in divorce. About 66 percent of marriages are first marriages, compared with 90 percent just 30 years ago. The marriage rate is the lowest in 100 years, and falling. Thirty years ago, almost 90 percent of Australians were married by the age of 30; today, fewer than 50 percent have taken the plunge by that age. In the past 30 years, the proportion of women marrying by age 20 has fallen from 25 percent to just three percent, and there are now more unmarried than married women in Australia (though many technically 'unmarried' women are in live-in relationships that qualify as de facto marriages). Most couples live together before they marry (up from 16 percent to 76 percent in the past 30 years), and about one-third of all babies are born to unmarried parents.

If present trends in marriage and divorce continue, it seems safe to predict that, before long, the marriage market (like many consumer markets) will be almost equally divided between light users, heavy users and non-users: those who marry once, those who marry two or more times, and those who never marry at all – at least not in the legal sense.

None of this need be interpreted as either good or bad news, but it certainly suggests we are prepared, as a society, to accommodate a more flexible, more transient attitude to marriage, and to view de facto marriage as a perfectly acceptable alternative to the legally sanctioned variety. 'Partner' has become part of the language, even being adopted by some married couples wishing to sound as cool as any less conventional liaison. In 1992, when I was writing *Reinventing Australia* and casting around for the word most likely to emerge as a label for a de facto spouse, 'partner' was scarcely on the radar: 'de facto' itself seemed a serious prospect – as in 'Hi, this is Jodie, my de facto.' But 'partner' came from nowhere to win the popular vote and has even wormed its way onto official forms where some married people might actually prefer to see 'spouse'.

Changed attitudes to marriage are inseparable from changed attitudes to divorce. A sustained high rate of divorce is interpreted by some (mainly older) people as a symptom of moral decline; a sign that we have lost our 'fibre' when it comes to upholding the institution of marriage and have surrendered to a more self-centred, self-indulgent view of the world. Others interpret our divorce rate as welcome evidence that we are a society that takes a 'modern', healthy, critical attitude to marriage; a society that acknowledges the pain of divorce will sometimes be preferable to the pain of an unhappy marriage. In between, there are those whose ambivalence allows them to see the value of divorce as an opportunity for a couple to abandon a hopeless marriage and seek happiness with someone else, but who still wonder whether divorce has become so easy as to discourage people from making sufficient effort to work things out when the going gets tough.

Divorce is never a pretty sight. Pain and anguish are etched on our divorce statistics – pain for the couples themselves, for any children involved, and for the circles of family and friends affected by the split. A high rate of divorce means that such pain is continually being experienced in our society on a very large scale.

On the brighter side, it also means people are less willing to settle for relationships they find unsatisfactory, unfulfilling and perhaps even damaging. Most people don't divorce lightly, so the transformation of Australia from a low-divorce society 30 years ago to its status as one of the world's high-divorce nations signals a profound cultural shift. The stigma attached to divorced people has almost vanished. The legal requirement to establish 'fault' in divorce proceedings disappeared with the Family Law Act of 1975. The idea that divorce is a symptom of a character flaw has all but evaporated: which family, after all, has not by now experienced the trauma of separation or divorce somewhere in its extended ranks?

Many human consequences flow from the high rate of relationship breakdown in Australia, whether of legal or de facto unions. Separating and divorcing couples themselves obviously pay a high emotional price in bitterness, loss of trust, protracted recriminations and the fracture of family and social connections. In-laws become 'outlaws'. Grandparents often find access to their grandchildren limited by the parents' custody arrangements, and may also find themselves grieving over the loss of a much loved son- or daughter-in-law from their extended family. Such difficulties can be greatly magnified when separating couples feel such bitterness towards each other that they can't bear the thought of a continuing relationship between their ex-spouses and their own families. Sometimes it's a case of 'If he doesn't want me, he can't have you either'; sometimes it's 'I don't ever want to see him again and I don't want you to, either.' Either way, grandparents often find such adjustments painful, especially when they are expected to behave as if one of their grandchildren's parents doesn't exist.

We always loved our son-in-law and we were terribly sad when they split up. He is still the father of our grandchildren, after all, and we want to stay in touch with him. But our daughter can't see it like that. Not yet, anyway – she may come around in time.

Friends of the separating couple may be similarly conflicted. While some will declare their determination not to take sides, and to remain equally friendly with both partners, it may turn out to be more difficult to maintain that balance than they assumed it would, especially if either or both of the people separating are resentful of any contact between their friends and their former partner.

It isn't always painful, of course: some couples – usually without children – describe their split as amicable and claim to remain the best of friends. Some couples with children make serious attempts to ensure the children are not caught up in the conflicts or tensions surrounding the split, but 'putting the children first' is a goal recognised as worthy by more people than seem able to achieve it. Even when a split is managed tidily, things can change dramatically when an ex-partner unexpectedly 'moves on', forming a new relationship with someone else. Such a development often creates strain, resentment and estrangement, even when the original couple had agreed to part, perhaps with sadness but with no particular acrimony. Curiously enough, the bitterness associated with re-partnering can be most intense among those who had initiated the original split, but had assumed the 'ex' would remain emotionally accessible to them. 'I don't want him, but I don't want anyone else to have him either' may seem an irrational position, but isn't irrationality the currency of most transactions of the heart?

Adults are expected to cope with the vicissitudes of life, or at least to know where to go for help. But the consequences of divorce can be especially painful for children not yet emotionally robust or mature enough to understand the issues at stake or to make much sense of their altered living arrangements. About 50 percent of divorces involve children under the age of 18 and, as a result of our sustained divorce rate, more than one million children – 22 percent of all children aged 0–17 – now live with only one of their natural parents and have another parent living elsewhere. Only about 50 percent of those children have face-to-face contact with their non-resident parent at least once per fortnight. For 26 percent of them, the contact is less than once a year or never (though even that is a slight improvement on the situation of ten years ago).

Living apart from a parent can be tough for children, and for the absent parent. But the regular contacts between children and absent parents (usually fathers) can also be tough for all concerned. More than 500 000 children are making the weekly or fortnightly trek from the home of the custodial parent to visit the home of the non-custodial parent. That many kids regularly to-ing and fro-ing amounts to mass migration at best, and large-scale social dislocation at worst. It's a round trip fraught with emotional hazard in both directions.

Understandably, many children in this situation use television, iPods, computer games and mobile phones as security blankets. Such media will sometimes seem to offer fixed points in a confusing world of shifting moods and situations. And the mobile phone can supply a precious link to people who might represent much-needed stability at a time of transience or upheaval.

Not only are the children regularly unplugging themselves from one domestic situation – one parent, one bedroom, one home, one set of friends and neighbours – and plugging themselves into another, but they are also repeatedly switching from one parental world view to another. Stark differences in styles of parenting, not always evident while the marriage was intact, may surface within weeks of a separation as parents try to assert their independence from each other (or, less nobly, to score points off each other). For the children, conflicting values and divided loyalties lurk in their path like landmines.

A welcome initiative by the federal government has been the proposal to establish a network of 65 family relationship centres. Since 1 July 2007, it has been compulsory for separating couples to attend a dispute resolution session at one of these centres, or another accredited agency, to formulate a parenting plan before they will be permitted to file a dispute with the Family Court. Writing in *The Sydney Morning Herald*, 3–4 February 2007, Adele Horin describes this as 'vital work' and notes that 'the weight of worldwide evidence, as complied by the Australian National University researcher Bryan Rodgers, shows it is less divorce that damages children than the conflict, violence and bitterness that precedes and follows a marital break-up.'

'The Government should be congratulated,' Horin says, 'for providing three hours of free counselling to help separating couples sort out their differences [and to] civilise marital breakdown for the sake of the children.'

Early in a separation, the actual moment of changeover for parental access visits can produce some of the most stressful of all the experiences of divorce, especially for children. The idea of 'handover centres' has sometimes been proposed as a way of reducing the stress for children inherent in the moment of switching from one parent to another, and defusing the risk of emotional or even physical violence between the parents, with the children as miserable witnesses. It is easy to imagine a network of *'tween centres*, set up by preschools and kindergartens, schools, churches, service clubs or other community organisations in places familiar to the children, where properly staffed and supervised spaces and facilities could allow a brief transitional period between being dropped off by one parent and collected by the other.

However it is managed, this is heartache territory for all concerned. Some children adjust with amazing flexibility and a remarkable tolerance of their parents' occasional flashes of anger or outbreaks of irrationality. Others reflect, as they look back on a childhood dominated and regulated by administrative arrangements designed for their parents' convenience (or perhaps merely to look good on their parents' mental scorecards), that their childhood seemed to have been stolen from them. They were too often on the move, and too often feeling as if it was their job to make their parents' lives easier or happier. Thrust into such a demanding role, too little time seemed to have been left for playing with friends on the weekend, mucking about or just 'being myself'.

'Keep your options open'

Perhaps we shouldn't be surprised that as the children of the most-divorced generation of parents in our history reach marriageable age, they are inclined to hang back. When they say, 'I'd like to get married but I'd hate to get divorced', they know whereof they speak. Marriage beckons for all the traditional biological, romantic, social and cultural reasons, but in the light of their direct or indirect experience of divorce, many young Australians have a more hard-edged, sceptical view of marriage than was typical of their parents' generation. At the same time, having endured the pain and mess associated with the wreckage of their parents' marriages, many young people are determined to make their own marriages work.

Even without the chastening influence of growing up in a more divorce-aware society, the rising generation of young Australian adults view marriage, as they view everything else, through the prism of their generational ethos. Having grown up in the thick of the multiple revolutions described in the opening chapters of this book, they have learnt something: be prepared for constant change; don't get too committed to anything too soon; keep your options open; hang loose; wait and see – you never know what's coming next.

For those now into their early thirties, this ethos can be particularly testing for parents who assumed that, by now, everything would be settled – partner, job, mortgage and children. But their children's keep-your-options-open approach means the parents are having to adjust to the idea of a prolonged emotional adolescence, perhaps stretching into the late thirties.

This is the generation who, at the younger end of the age spectrum, change their plans from moment to moment, partly because they are generationally programmed to keep things flexible and partly because they hold in their hands a magic wand – the mobile phone – that allows them to hold off until the last moment before making a firm arrangement and, having made it, to change it. And change it again.

Such behaviour, characteristic of the under-thirties, is most pronounced in the mid-teens and younger. 'But I thought you said you were going to Karen's,' say their parents, minds clagged by their own linear habits, assumptions and expectations. 'She's doing something else. We're going to a movie.' Encouraged by this spontaneous offer of information and unable to help themselves, the parents may stumble on in the same fruitless direction: 'So, what are you going to see?' There's only one answer: 'Don't know yet.'

In *Generations* (1997), I dubbed them the Options Generation. Growing up in a world of ever-expanding choices, they have made a virtue out of keeping their options open, and they have adopted *What else is there?* as their generational catchcry. It's a question that comes up whether the topic is a course of study, a job, a sexual partner, a musical genre, an outing, a set of religious or political beliefs, a fashion label, a food fad or a make of car. 'This is fine – nothing wrong with it – but what else is there? How do I know if this is the best I can do if I haven't tried the alternatives?'

A generation with that mind-set is hardly likely to rush into marriage: when they do fall in love and decide to cohabit, or even to reproduce, they may still baulk at the ultimate commitment implied by the tying of the legal knot. If their caution leads them to make safer, more thoughtful choices, it may yet result in a declining rate of divorce; it will certainly keep the marriage rate down. Although their parents' generation has offered them a more transient example of marriage than was typical of Australia for the first three-quarters of the 20th century, they are not necessarily impressed by their parents' approach.

To quote from *Generations*:

The Options Generation look at their parents' marriages and frequently decide that, when it's their turn, they will try to handle things rather differently. They are inclined to see their parents as having been in too much of a hurry, as having accepted 'the strain' of children too early in their married lives and, as a result, as having closed off too many options too soon. The [Baby] Boomers themselves believe they exercised far more freedom of choice than their own parents had been able to do, but their children see them as having been highly conformist in their approach to marriage and parenthood, even though the fabric of family life has been shredded in a growing number of cases. Indeed, the rising generation are inclined to think that 'too much, too soon' is actually a prescription for failure in marriage and family life: they prefer to approach it steadily, cautiously and tentatively. When the time comes, they want to feel that they have both the emotional and financial security to be able to make a go of it.

All this might seem to contradict their relaxed and accepting attitude towards divorce. For the members of the Options Generation, though, there is no contradiction: they expect to be committed to a partner when the time comes to have children, but they acknowledge – with less dreamy sentimentality than they might discern in their parents – that some marriages are not 'forever'; that ten years might be 'a good innings'; that children's needs should be taken into account but not allowed to 'destroy your life'.

If the experience of parents' divorce creates a certain wariness in young people's attitudes to marriage, their generational inclination to *keep your options open* would only reinforce it. All this inhibits an early commitment to marriage and, for a growing number of young

Australians, inhibits *any* commitment to marriage. Paradoxically, some young people see parenthood as being both a more serious and less daunting commitment, in the sense that it involves no continuing choice: once a parent, always a parent, whereas a spouse can become an ex-spouse. A marriage can be unscrambled; parenthood can't.

The institutional versus the instrumental view of marriage

There's another factor driving the marriage rate down, and the divorce rate up: attitudes to marriage itself have changed, and the language of matrimony has changed to reflect that. Marriage used to be spoken of as an institution: once you were in it, you stayed in it, as if the institutional door clanged shut behind you as you entered. (Groucho Marx: 'Marriage is a wonderful institution, but who wants to live in an institution?') In that era, stable and secure marriage, like stable and secure work, was seen as a cornerstone of a stable and secure society.

Today, marriage – whether legal or de facto – is spoken of as a *relationship*. 'If our relationship works, we might get married. Once we're married, if the relationship breaks down, the marriage will be over.' This is new language designed for a new set of cultural norms. The institutional, cultural view of marriage has given way to a more instrumental, personal view: is it working *for us*? And sometimes the question is even more ruthlessly individual: is it working *for me*?

When the grandparents of today's young people hear this kind of talk they are typically either appalled or mystified: 'What's all this talk about relationships? They're married, aren't they? Why don't they just get on with it?' In the days of a more institutional view of marriage, the quality of the relationship between the spouses was not central to anyone's thinking: people fell in love, got married, had children . . . and got on with it. If the result, in some cases, was prolonged misery, then 'you made your bed so you must lie in it'. The retreat into alcohol, analgesic or sedative abuse – or perhaps even into extra-marital affairs – was quite widely regarded as preferable to divorce. The institutional view of marriage meant the institution was to be respected above the difficulties faced by individual couples. Divorce, in that climate, was a Very Big Deal.

No longer. Such talk would strike today's young Australians as misguided, heartless and rather silly (as would the view that divorce should be based on one party's proven 'fault'). Marriage, for them, is essentially about the quality of the relationship. Even when children are involved, a popular view is that it is bad for children to live in an atmosphere of tension and unhappiness where they will learn poor lessons about relationship management by seeing their parents trying to flog the proverbial dead horse of a doomed marriage.

At the same time, young people generally regard themselves as being better educated about the conduct of relationships than their parents were, and therefore better equipped to handle the difficulties and tensions that inevitably arise in the course of any long relationship. Many of the current crop of young men, in particular – especially the New Blokes described in Chapter 3 – see themselves as better prepared and more willing to discuss relationship issues than their own fathers or grandfathers were.

Some parents of today's young adults concede that this is a change for the better. When they look at the marriages and de facto marriages of their offspring, they see the advantages of the new approach to marriage already emerging: a kind of 'bonded independence' (together *and* separate); genuine liberation; an insistence on friendship as the best basis for commitment (since mere sexual attraction is nowhere near the big deal it once was); both parties expected to work at the relationship. In the brightest, most successful cases, 'love's work' is no longer thought of as woman's work – and that may be the biggest generational shift of all.

The board of the Marriage Guidance Council of Australia, the country's pre-eminent marriage counselling service, anticipated this change of emphasis when, in 1994, it changed the name of the organisation to Relationships Australia. That was a prescient acknowledgment of the looming reality: marriage was soon to become just one of the many forms of relationship, sexual and otherwise, for which people would be seeking professional help. Relationships Australia (NSW) now reports that only about 46 percent of its clients are 'married' in the legal sense of the term.

One important implication of the shift in emphasis from 'marriage' to 'relationship' is that the distinction between legalised marriage and de facto marriage blurs, and we come to recognise them as two roughly equivalent versions of the same idea – as, indeed, the legal system increasingly does and no doubt will, eventually, for committed, enduring homosexual as well as heterosexual pairings.

And yet, in spite of the tectonic shifts in our attitudes towards marriage, divorce, parenthood and family life, something thought of as *a relationship* is still likely to be subject to more scrutiny, and perhaps more sceptical evaluation, than something called *a marriage*. Even in the present cultural climate, there is a lingering sense in which 'relationship' strikes us as a less determinedly permanent state than 'marriage'. Couples who have never seriously contemplated a legal marriage and decide to marry only when they have children often seem to be responding to an implicit assumption that being legally married will somehow make the union seem more proper from the child's point of view. Some are more explicit, believing that the arrival of a child is a signal that the time has come for a more formal, binding commitment.

Nevertheless, those who choose to settle for a relationship that doesn't involve 'a piece of paper' insist their commitment to each other is no less than if they were married; they may even declare that a shared mortgage is a more significant piece of paper than a marriage certificate. Others are drawn to the idea that something with the status of 'relationship' will seem easier to terminate than a marriage. That attitude is reflected in the general acceptance, especially among the under-thirties, that the end of a relationship, no matter how painful and disruptive, is less of a drama than a divorce.

The language of matrimony will continue to evolve. But, for the time being, 'I've had several relationships' still sounds to Australian ears like a less momentous declaration than 'I've been married several times'. Similarly, 'repartnered' still seems to carry a bit less freight than 'remarried'.

The dangerous cult of perfectionism

Our attitudes to marriage have been affected by another culture shift. In the past 15 years, we have been increasingly caught up in the idea of *perfection* – in personal appearance (fuelled, as always, by the beauty industry but now boosted by the aggressive promotion of cosmetic surgery), in diet and health, fitness, furnishings, bathroom fittings, kitchen design, vacations, entertainment, cars, food, coffee, and even in the education of our children: 'We want him to have the perfect teacher in the perfect school – why settle for less?'

The star rating system adopted by film reviewers has been enthusiastically taken up by people in all aspects of their lives. 'I'd give it about three-and-a-half stars' might be an assessment of a lecture, a holiday, a school, a date or a meal. Encouraged by the cult of celebrity – always with us, but grotesquely exaggerated over the past 15 years – we have fallen for the idea that everyone can be 'extraordinary', 'excellence' is the new standard, 'winners are grinners' and everyone should be experiencing life to the max. (Would you dare send your child to a school that *wasn't* a centre of excellence in something or other?)

From the perfect latté to the perfect storm, the idea has taken root in our culture that perfection could be within our grasp if only we had enough money, enough persistence, enough beauty, enough talent, enough charm, or enough luck.

This makes it tough for mere mortals, struggling with the private knowledge of their own frailties, flaws and imperfections, particularly where intimate personal relationships are concerned.

The cult of perfectionism, if unchecked, can lead us to expect too much from a partner, and from a relationship. It can make us too cautious in our approach to prospective partners and unrealistic in our demands and expectations. It can infect our experience of love and happiness by introducing the gnawing doubt that this isn't as good as it should be; that perfect bliss is eluding us; that romantic love should never fade; that we should be able to establish perfect (or even excellent) relationships without too much hard work.

The hazard here is obvious: if we're banking on the perfect relationship, we're bound to be disappointed. If we're banking on having perfect children in a perfect sitcom family – everyone happy, obedient, high-achieving yet bathed in the glow of a charming humility – we're in for a nasty shock. (Many parents are disposed to regard their own children as miraculous, of course, but that natural tendency is in danger of getting out of hand since perfection entered the scene as a possibility.)

The human journey is characterised by chaos and contradictions, and the cult of perfectionism can blind us to the fact that 'perfectly reasonable' may be as close to perfection as life gets, for most of us, most of the time.

The cult of perfectionism has already damaged many relationships that might otherwise have survived (and has also put too many children under too much pressure to succeed). It has caused many couples to decide they could do better with someone else – only to find that 'someone else' turned out to be human, too, and that feet of clay are standard issue, after all.

Low marriage and high divorce rates are caused by many obvious and non-obvious factors – cultural, social, economic and even technological (since, as we saw in Chapter 5, the mobile phone and the internet are generating new varieties of coupling and uncoupling). But the cult of perfectionism is making its own quiet contribution by raising the threshold of contentment. It is certainly making a contribution to the wedding industry. Regardless of misgivings about marriage, weddings are bigger business than ever. In fact, it's tempting to conclude that the greater wariness about marriage, and the greater awareness of its potential fragility in the relationship era, have contributed to the idea that if we're going to get married, let's have the perfect wedding, at least.

Wedding planning services typically send out a checklist to prospective brides, reminding them of all the things that need to be done in the lead-up to the Big Day. First item on the list provided by one wedding planner: cosmetic surgery. Implication: if you need a nose or boob job, or to remove some of those facial blemishes, then act now! No time to lose! (It would be churlish, presumably, to mention that those blemishes might have been among the things that attracted your man in the first place. Moles were once called 'beauty spots' for a reason.)

A perfect dress, perfect hair, a perfect limo, a perfect location. A perfect video, of course, since you're going to be a celebrity for a day. And even in the digital age, a perfect set of photographs. Some professionally produced wedding albums now come in a wooden box, complete with a set of white gloves to be worn by anyone granted the privilege of leafing through the album.

This kind of thinking has always been present to some extent: which bride has not dreamed of a perfect wedding on a perfect day? But the cult of perfectionism seems to be exerting increasing pressure, aided by a commercial wedding industry that has managed to boost the cost of an average wedding to more than $30 000. More than ever, the perfect wedding is being treated as a symbol of perfect love. ('What? You're not having a big wedding? Aren't you sure about him?')

As we'll see shortly, the fewer children we produce, the more fuss we are likely to make over them. And the same goes for weddings:

as the marriage rate falls, the significance of the wedding event itself looms larger than ever.

We are marrying less ... and more

Young Australians are postponing or avoiding marriage in record numbers, and only 40 percent of marriages are now conducted by ministers of religion. Young people still fall in love, still want to cohabit and still want to procreate, but they are, paradoxically, both more relaxed and more uptight about these matters than their parents and grandparents were: while they are inclined to regard all relationship permutations as 'cool' and to accept that whatever people want to do is their business, they are also less inclined than previous generations to rush into making commitments that sound too daunting.

In previous generations, the combination of hormonal and economic imperatives often drove people into marriage at an early age: today, independence has become a virtue – as has 'hanging loose' – so marriage requires a more deliberate decision than it used to. Most young people speak as if they expect to get married at some stage or, at least, to have a stable, long-term partnership. But they are more clear-eyed and less romantic about the idea than their parents were, even though they may give in to helpless romanticism as the wedding day approaches with the alluring prospect of starring in your own reality video.

They are more obviously troubled by the idea of commitment than previous generations were, and more open about expressing their doubts and reservations: 'How could you ever know that someone was the right person to spend the rest of your life with?' In *The World*

According to Y, Rebecca Huntley noted that 'the rise in cohabitation before marriage is not a symptom of Ys' disregard for marriage but their intense concern about getting it right'.

This is not a generational shortcoming, but a realistic assessment of the chances of things coming unstuck. For some couples, the idea of living together without any talk of marriage is appealing precisely because it creates an opportunity to see what it would be like, to see whether it is going to evolve into something special or permanent, or perhaps even to see whether it will be comfortable enough to settle for.

> *I've just about given up on the idea of perfection. I know ours is not the greatest love match of all time, but it's okay, and I don't know if I could face putting myself back on the market. We'll see. Strangely enough, my partner occasionally talks about having kids, so he seems to be thinking long-term.*

Some young women, in particular, have a more pragmatic explanation for their reluctance to marry: they are simply too busy, too career-orientated and too independent to contemplate the thought of a long-term, committed relationship, especially if, as many of them claim, they can obtain sexual gratification when they need it.

It would be quite wrong to conclude from the falling marriage rate that marriage has become unfashionable or unimportant in our culture. For those who choose legal marriage, the symbolism may be even more intensely important than it was when marriage was the conventional thing to do. Our increasing tendency towards multiple marriages is also a sign of the continuing importance of legal marriage. People who marry two or more times are not doing so, presumably, because they love getting married so much they want to keep having another crack at it, but because they still believe in the whole idea of marriage – in the ideal of 'happy marriage' – and keep striving to achieve it in spite of setbacks and disappointments. The triumph of hope over experience it may be, but, in our culture, the hope of personal fulfilment through marriage remains a compelling motivation.

Amidst this confusing and sometimes contradictory set of shifting mores and changing attitudes, a stable and satisfying marriage is still widely regarded as the gold standard in sexual relationships. Whether it is postponed, avoided, embraced, respected or mocked, marriage is an ever-present reference point, and it figures somewhere, sometime, in the dreams of most Australians. Parenthood may have more far-reaching effects on the quality and trajectory of our lives, but the public declarations implied by marriage are still typically regarded by those who marry as the most serious they ever make.

The end of the story has to be a reminder that most Australian marriages survive. Almost 60 percent of marriages will never trouble the Family Court. Although this is a smaller proportion than it used to be, it's a relatively stable majority: the official divorce rate does not appear to be rising, and may yet fall as a consequence of the falling marriage rate. Many of those marriages don't merely survive; they thrive. Some couples find that if it wasn't quite 'happily ever after' for them, their marriage has brought benefits, joys and gratifications that come very close to that. When it works brilliantly, marriage can be experienced as blissful human harmony. When it works even tolerably well, it can be a source of deep physical and emotional comfort, reliable friendship and shared experience that creates the powerful bond of a common history and the prospect of companionship into old age. A couple committed to their marriage running its full course (and that's the expectation of most married people) draw strength from the security of knowing they can rely on each other, trust each other and be open and relaxed with each other.

Only a dreamer would ask for a stress-free marriage (or, indeed, a stress-free life). Only a fool would expect perfection in human affairs, including marriage. But those in long-term committed marriages typically report that when the romance fades and the relationship settles down to the long haul of conjugal love characterised by mutual support, encouragement, respect and affection, the rewards are incalculable. Minor irritations? Yes, often. Occasional strong words? Yes. Disagreements? Of course. Even murderous fury, sometimes. But a stable, fulfilling marriage remains, for most Australians, a dream that either has, or might, come true.

8

Formula One prams: Wheeling out our smallest-ever generation

A mother is standing in a cafe, pram by her side, waiting for her takeaway latté. Another customer peers into the pram, admires the baby and asks, 'Is this your first?'

'Yes – and my last,' replies the mother without hesitation.

Advocates of zero population growth would approve of her, given the parlous state of the planet. Growing numbers of her generation are saying the same thing: one only, or if not one, then none.

If members of the Options Generation – *hang loose; wait and see; what else is there?* – aren't rushing into marriage, you can be sure they won't be rushing into parenthood either. The birthrate in Australia plummeted to an all-time low of 1.7 babies per woman in 2004, and seems likely to follow countries like Britain, Canada, Italy and Japan even lower. But we can't see around corners, which is why the ABS wisely offers three quite divergent projections of population trends up to 2051. The lowest is based on a long-term fertility rate of just 1.5 babies per woman; the highest on a rate of 1.9.

There has been a slight increase in the birthrate since 2005 but there's no way of knowing whether this is a temporary pause in a downward trend or the beginning of a significant upswing. Anecdotally, many people claim to have seen the evidence of a mini baby boom (though 'mini' and 'boom' seem oddly incompatible notions). The baby bonus of $5000 per child was widely thought to have encouraged many couples to take the plunge, either by making their first foray into parenthood or by following the advice of the former federal treasurer, Peter Costello, to have 'one for Mum, one for Dad, and one for the country'. (Shades of the old 'populate or perish' slogan of the 1950s, when the more sedately named Child Endowment Payment offered a similar financial incentive to produce more children, though it's doubtful if that was a key factor in the postwar baby boom – an unstoppable trend, here and elsewhere, that ran for 15 years from 1946.)

Perhaps the baby bonus has helped power the short-term lift in the birthrate, but there's always more than one explanation when trend lines unexpectedly turn up or down. Sifting through the available evidence, another factor also seemed to be contributing to this particular rise: the forehead-slapping syndrome. This describes the behaviour of a significant number of women, well into their thirties, who – metaphorically, if not literally – are suddenly slapping their foreheads and crying, 'A kid! Quick! I almost forgot!'

As well they might. At the age of 37, the fertility of most women drops dramatically. By 40, most would have only a five percent chance of conceiving naturally. So 30 is a milestone in more ways than one. Thirty-year-olds typically describe this as the most significant birthday they've ever had; the end of being really 'young'; the beginning of serious adulthood or, as one of my respondents in The Mackay

Report, *Turning 30* (2001), grimly expressed it, 'the beginning of the end'. When they say '30 is the new 20', today's 30-year-olds mean it. At 30, they feel as if they are at about the same stage in the life cycle their mothers had reached at age 20. Thirty years ago, most first births were to women in the 22–24 years age range; today, for the first time in our history, most first-time mothers are over 30 and the majority of all babies are born to women over 30.

So a certain amount of haste is in order for women who, having kept their options open while they sailed into their thirties, now find that nature is not quite as accommodating as they had assumed or hoped it would be. There's a significant attitude shift bound up with all this. Women who have grown up feeling powerful and in control – *I can have it all! I'm free to choose!* – in a world where everything can be 'fixed' (including too-large noses or too-small breasts) are naturally inclined to think that even if they've left it a bit late for nature to take its course in the matter of conception, this, too, can be 'fixed'.

Such reliance on last-minute intervention via biotechnology has increased the incidence of multiple (especially twin) births, so some women conceiving late, via IVF, may be unintentionally boosting the birthrate. 'We badly wanted a baby and ended up with two' reflects the fact that assisted reproduction has a 15–20 percent chance of producing multiple births, compared with 2–3 percent for natural conceptions.

Yet even the increasingly sophisticated techniques of biotechnology aren't miraculous and can't guarantee conception for an older woman: IVF, for instance, can increase the chances of conception for a woman over 40, but only from the five percent probability of a natural conception to a ten percent chance of conception *in vitro*. Some high-pressure, high-wire women are making the most of their fertility by freezing their embryos while they are still young enough to conceive with ease, and then waiting for a convenient time to implant them. (Yes, it's happening.)

But let's not get too carried away with the idea of a mini-boom – or, at least, let's put heavy emphasis on the 'mini' until harder evidence is in. After all, in the real baby boom, the birthrate hit 3.5 babies per woman and the current upswing is still modest: having hit its 2004 low, the birthrate has only struggled back up to 1.8 babies per woman and may well fall again.

Why?

As with most attempts to explain changes in human behaviour, the key word is *multifactorial*. There's unlikely to be a single explanation for a change as marked as this one, especially in Kaleidoscope Nation. Obviously, easy access to contraception makes it possible for women who choose not to have children – or not yet – to avoid becoming pregnant, but the real question is why so many women are making that choice. We've already noted a generational attitude shift that casts some light on that question: if you want to keep your options open, parenthood would be about the last thing on your mind.

The fact that young Australians are partnering later than in previous generations is also relevant: if you're not settling on a partner until you're around 30, there's less time available to have children.

The rising education level of women is another contributing factor that can be observed all around the Western world. Generally speaking, women who are more highly educated tend to have fewer babies than less-educated women. It's not an immutable law of nature, of course: there are many exceptions in both directions, which is why this couldn't be anything more than one factor among several. But it's probably no accident that Canberra has the most highly educated female population in Australia and the nation's lowest birthrate.

You can see where this leads us in the short term: the population will tend to grow more rapidly in lower socio-economic areas typically associated with lower levels of educational attainment and greater economic disadvantage. This is hardly a new phenomenon: poorer and less well-educated families have traditionally tended to be somewhat larger than better-educated families. But the rapid expansion of educational opportunities for women may well increase that imbalance, especially as the decision to have no children at all will, from now on, be quite commonly made among the most highly educated women, and the offer of a cash incentive to breed will inevitably be most attractive to the least well-off.

So it's clear what politicians must do if they are determined to get the birthrate up: simply ban women from universities, keep them undereducated and generally disadvantaged – a bit like they were in the 1950s – and watch the birthrate rise. You'd have a riot on your hands, but you'd soon fill the maternity wards of the nation. Or perhaps not: if ever we returned to the days of a paternalistic culture that treated women as second-class citizens, it would take women a matter of moments to organise a moratorium on sex as a form of strike action – with far more adverse emotional consequences for men than for women. From a male perspective, one of the most dispiriting revelations of the gender revolution was that women are not always as impressed by male sexual performance as men assume they are. (To rub salt into that wound, recent Australian research has shown that, in the over-forties, women without partners have more reliable orgasms, via masturbation, than those with partners.)

The link between more education and fewer babies is neither direct nor inevitable. No one is suggesting that if you educate women more highly, they will become smart enough to realise that having babies is a silly idea. Nor is there any evidence to suggest that education magically eradicates the maternal instinct experienced by many women. But better-educated women tend to get better jobs and, as a result, may become more attached to the very idea of employment as a symbol of their station in life, just as job-related labels have so often served men. They may also be more career-focused than less well-educated women in lower-status or less satisfying jobs. And their generally higher salaries may exert the predictable materialist pressures on them: 'How could I sacrifice this lifestyle for a child – I'd lose income *and* have more expenses.'

There are also lingering traces of the once-core message of the women's movement, conveyed explicitly or implicitly from mother to daughter, that being at home with babies can dull your mind, cut you off from your friends and colleagues and reduce the amount of stimulation and fun in your life. The counter-argument – that motherhood can also be one of the most fulfilling and rewarding experiences imaginable – has sometimes been lost in the din of feminist sloganeering. Though this issue is frequently brushed aside in the rush to embrace childcare – 'I'll have a child *and* a career' – the continuing impact of the women's movement is felt by many young women who see motherhood as an assault on their independence. The growing popularity of the one-child option is at least partly attributable to this factor: 'Surely I can manage *one* without compromising my lifestyle too much.'

And if not even one, then perhaps a cat or dog? It's not uncommon to find young couples, not yet committed either to marriage or parenthood, deciding to 'try ourselves out on a dog'. The proliferation of pet shops – Moggie and Mutt, Pet Heaven – pandering to the role of pets as child substitutes only reinforces the idea that a pet might be commitment enough: fewer sleepless nights, no childcare worries, school fees or orthodontists' bills, though who can say when canine and feline orthodontistry will catch on?

Many other explanations for the falling birthrate have been proposed: the self-centredness of the rising generation of potential parents (now where have we heard that before?); the cost of housing; the cost and competitiveness of education; the reluctance of many potential parents to bring children into a world that seems more hazardous, more ecologically fragile and more generally demanding – for both children and parents – than ever before.

What will it be like to be a member of the smallest generation of children Australia has ever produced?

Because our population continues to grow, the children being born at this time of a record low birthrate do not comprise our smallest-ever generation numerically, though the actual number of children in the 0–14 years age group is projected to decline over the next 20 years. But, relative to total population, this is our smallest-ever generation: they will have the smallest footprint and the quietest voice of any generation in our history. (Even the Great Depression only drove the birthrate down to 2.1 babies per woman, and it climbed steadily from 1934 right through World War II, and then more steeply to its peak of 3.5 in 1961.)

Once they reach the workforce, they'll have a dream run. Unemployment simply won't be an issue for them: they'll be able to pick and choose among job offers and employers will be furiously competing for their services, though their tax bill may make today's taxation rates look dreamily desirable.

But that's all 20 or 30 years away. In the meantime, they will have to contend with two contradictory pressures on them. First, they will have to learn how to absorb the impact of overzealous attention from a generation of parents who have embraced the idea of 'parenting skills'. Then they will have to learn how to cope with life in a less child-friendly society.

When the birthrate falls this far, parents are understandably keen to extract all the joys of parenthood from their one or two babies, and to take extra special – even obsessive – care of them. We've seen what happened in China as a result of the one-child policy: the Little Emperor syndrome is a well-documented phenomenon there, and Australia is now developing its own version.

A really low birthrate almost guarantees a generation of overindulged children who will grow up with the idea that they are the most precious creatures on earth. From an early age, they will have known they were the apple of the parental eye, perhaps to an unhealthy degree, and an overprotected childhood will lay the foundation for an overindulged adolescence. They won't have the sheer generational muscle of the Baby Boomers; they'll borrow, instead, the muscle of parents who have willingly signed on as members of their private army of supporters, advocates, apologists and protectors.

This won't be *all* children in the rising generation, of course: many parents will be balanced, sane and firm even in the raising of a single child and, in any case, the birthrate will continue to remain higher among less affluent parents who couldn't afford to overindulge their children even if they wanted to. The most unbridled expressions of parental zeal are most likely to be found in the middle- and upper-middle socio-economic strata.

These are the parents who will be frequent visitors to their children's schools, constantly checking that everything is to their liking and that their children are not being overlooked or disadvantaged in any way: 'Why has my son got that clarinet teacher – I understood the other teacher was more experienced. Is my daughter keeping up with her reading group? Why was my son dropped to the B team – don't you think it would be fairer if all the teams were called "A"? How many teachers will be going on the excursion? Are they properly trained? Why isn't there air-conditioning in all the classrooms and nicer soap in the washrooms? Why wasn't my daughter made captain – how can I be sure the system's really fair?'

If you think I'm exaggerating, ask any primary school teacher: this is the most overprotective, intrusive generation of parents teachers can recall having to deal with. To some extent, parents' concerns are understandable. They, too, are members of a community dealing with a generalised sense of anxiety, and anxiety about the wellbeing of children is bound to be one of the most vivid forms of its expression. Perhaps children do need more protection than ever – from pedophiles, child abductors, the mass media, the drug trade, heavy traffic on the road, terrorist attacks . . . or unfair teachers. Or perhaps the consumerist, materialist society has found yet another expression, particularly among the fee-paying parents of private-school children who might regard their child's low mark in a maths test as being a bit like an annoying rattle in their BMW: 'I'm paying a lot of money for this, so if there's a problem, you fix it.' Or again, perhaps education is yet another field where the current emphasis on rights is outweighing the acceptance of responsibilities (by both parent and child).

In one private primary school, the preponderance of children receiving coaching from private coaching colleges reached such exaggerated proportions, the school had to appeal to parents to reconsider their enthusiasm for engaging coaching services. The tipping point was the discovery that one boy, aged no more than ten, was being set homework by his coach, so his parents engaged a second coach to help him with the extra work being set by the first coach.

In other schools, a note has been sent home to parents asking them, in effect, not to do their children's homework for them. A bit of guidance, encouragement or support is one thing; marshalling the parents' resources to produce a smashing school project is quite another.

Individual coaching of children with learning difficulties is necessary and desirable. Coaching of bright and accomplished children in the hope that they might garner an extra mark or two in competitive exams (yes, even at primary school) is surely a sign of parental neurosis, if not a form of child abuse.

No doubt it's a good thing that gifted and talented children are being spotted early and given special encouragement. There is the risk, though, that 'gifted and talented' will become a new status symbol and that schools will have to devise 'special' programs for all those children whose parents feel disadvantaged by the discovery that their offspring are neither as gifted nor as talented as they thought they were.

The leading edge of this generation are already into the early years of secondary school and their attitudes and behaviour – in particular, their towering self-esteem and their unabashed assertiveness – are attracting the attention of their astonished teachers:

> *I've never seen such a self-assured bunch of 14-year-olds. They are so used to being told they're perfect, they can't bring themselves to admit they're wrong. I wrote the word 'separate' on the board the other day, and a little forest of hands went up. 'Miss,' they cried, 'you're wrong. That isn't how it's spelt. It's spelt with an e not an a.' I've learned to be calm and patient with this lot. 'Actually,' I said, 'I'm not wrong. Look it up in your dictionaries.' So they all looked it up on their laptops and had to admit I was right. But they are so used to being right about everything, they told me it still looked wrong. They felt it should be 'seperate' even if it wasn't. That's the mentality you're dealing with. I've never struck anything like it in 30 years of teaching.*

It's not just in the classroom that our particular version of the Little Emperor syndrome is becoming increasingly obvious. On the sporting field, too, youngsters are being decked out like little mini-professionals and coached like champions in the making. Even a new bike, if the parents are willing to let their children run the risk of riding one, has to be accompanied by enough kit to make some children look as if they are pre-Olympians. (Yes, safety is an issue but so, it seems, are brands.)

It starts with prams and other nursery equipment that symbolise the disproportionate fuss being made over newborns. As the birthrate sinks to a point where having children no longer seems like the automatic, 'natural' thing for couples to do, those who elect to become parents are finding themselves the focus of new-found attention. 'You're having a child? How wonderful,' is uttered in a tone that almost seems to imply, 'How odd!' When an ABC Sydney radio producer went on maternity leave, the broadcaster and journalist Richard Glover invited her onto his program to discuss the kind of things that were once so routine, so familiar, so ubiquitous as to be scarcely worthy of mention: sleepless nights, feeding routines, the horror of dirty nappies, the joy of the first smile (or was it just a windy wince?).

To match this heightened degree of fuss over the dwindling supply of newborns – and to help baby-carriage manufacturers compensate for a tougher market – you can now buy your baby a huge pram that appears to have all the sophistication of a Formula One racing car in its construction and suspension plus all the comfort of a luxury limousine. Airbags are not yet an option, but be patient. You can spend anything you like: a top-of-the-range pram, with all the accessories, including changeable coloured fabrics matched to the tones of the changing seasons, will set you back at least $2000 and you can buy it with the right brand name, too: Jeep is there, and so is Maclaren (though, to be fair, it might not be the McLaren that puts Mercedes engines into its racing cars). Are Beema prams a cheeky first step into the market by BMW? Can Ferrari or Porsche be far from developing machines to set new standards in performance prams? Or perhaps Bugaboo will soon move into the tricycle market as a prelude to their entry into motor sport.

As these children learn to walk – perhaps borrowing their parents' personal trainers to supervise and encourage their progress – they will be increasingly treated like mini-adults. Overseas trips are already standard fare for upper-middle-class children, to say nothing of their own mobile phones, iPods, computers, and whatever other bits of information/entertainment technology next pop over the horizon. Even their own parents are starting to wonder what treats and excitements will be left for the children to experience when they're teenagers, let alone young adults. (Sex, presumably. Or drugs?)

But indulgence is only part of the story: overprotectiveness is an equally tough burden for children to bear. How will children learn to take risks if they are never allowed to indulge in risky behaviour appropriate to their age? How will they learn to deal with crises if all potential crises are averted for them by parents who are committed to smoothing the way? And what is the advantage of postponing their discovery that the world is an unfair place by having their parents insist on everything being fair?

'Helicopter parenting' someone has dubbed it, and no one who thinks about it dispassionately for more than a moment is likely to conclude it's actually good for children to be cosseted, controlled, supervised and protected by their hovering parents to the extent that now seems to be happening. Yes, park swings are hazardous, but does that mean we have to do away with them? In Canada recently, I spotted a sign in a children's playground: 'This area is unsupervised.' Gosh, I thought, thanks for the warning. And then I wondered: who would normally be supervising a children's playground if it were not the children's own parents, older siblings, nannies or other child-minders?

A newspaper cartoon a few years ago neatly caricatured the problem. 'We're sorry he's late for work,' the parents were saying as they presented their adult son to his boss, 'we forgot to clean his teeth.' When I've described that cartoon to audiences containing the parents of young children, the titters are nervous and tentative; it's only sceptical grandparents and non-parents who laugh without restraint.

There were never enough suburban creeks to match the number of stories told by older Australians about their childhoods spent down at the creek – or riding their bikes to and from the beach, or going to the Saturday-afternoon pictures unaccompanied by an adult. But there's more than nostalgia in their recollections: there's an edge of concern, too, as they ponder the likely effects on today's children of not being allowed to roam a little more freely than they do.

The children of the low-birthrate era may not realise they are the victims of overzealous parenting, since many of them will spend their formative years in a kind of emotional and cultural bubble. The bubble will burst, however, when they make an uncomfortable discovery: the world beyond the home and school environments so closely monitored by their parents is likely to be a less welcoming and friendly place than they might have been led to expect. Their parents may be enchanted and preoccupied by them, but as members of our relatively smallest-ever generation, they may find themselves struggling for attention in a wider society that has become more interested in its elderly than its young. It will also be a society with a larger proportion of non-parents than we have previously seen in the adult population.

One of the factors driving the birthrate down is the sharp increase in the number of women electing to have no children at all. At the turn of the century, it was estimated that 25 percent of Australian women would remain childless, and given the persistence of factors driving the birthrate down, even that estimate might turn out to be conservative. We may well be becoming a society in which only about two-thirds of couples will choose to have children (or, at least, decide to have children in time to actually have them).

As the number of childless couples rises, a significant culture shift takes place. Not only does the idea of having children come to seem like one choice among many – a possibility, rather than an almost automatic probability – but the cultural status of parenthood changes. As we reach the stage where childlessness seems as normal as parenthood, non-parents are likely to become less sympathetic and accommodating in their attitudes towards those who choose to become parents. 'Your kid, your problem' may sound like a harsh attitude, but it will be a sentiment increasingly expressed, in word and deed.

It's already obvious from qualitative research that a culture gap opens up between parents and non-parents as they move into their thirties. And why not? For most parents, the birth of the first child is the most dramatic life-changing experience of all, and those who don't experience it may never quite grasp its significance to those who do.

'We don't really enjoy visiting friends who haven't had children,' say the thirtysomething parents of young children. 'They seem to lead such self-indulgent lives. They're always tripping off here and there, and they eat out all the time. It's just a different way of life, I suppose. We're beyond that now.'

Their non-parent friends are correspondingly reluctant to socialise with them: 'We don't really enjoy visiting our friends who've had kids,' they say, 'because all they want to talk about is the kids. They want to bring them along to everything, and they keep emailing you baby photos. It's all very sweet at first, but it gets a bit wearing.'

Other people's children can be a profoundly uninteresting topic to non-parents (and not necessarily riveting for other parents, either, by the way). In a low-birthrate era, parents who assume that non-parents will be as interested in their remarkable offspring as they are themselves may be in for a shock, especially if they believe they are helping to compensate non-parents for the lack of children in their lives.

The implications of this culture gap soon become clear. Many non-parents, having written children out of their personal scripts, would like to write them out of the wider societal script as well: they will prefer child-free restaurants, child-free resorts, child-free shopping precincts, child-free apartment blocks and eventually, no doubt, even child-free housing estates. Soon they'll be demanding child-free seating zones in aircraft, but will they pay a premium for designated child-free flights?

> *We went out for dinner the other night and the evening was ruined – the people at the next table had brought their kids with them.*

> *Have you ever got on an international flight and discovered you're going to have a young child beside you all the way? It can ruin your journey. They shouldn't be allowed on certain flights, especially in Business Class.*

You've seen what we've done with smokers: children may be next in line – not heard *and* not seen.

The culture gap between parents and non-parents is also being revealed by the disapproval directed at parents whose children infringe on other people's space or peace, and by the tendency to blame the parents whenever a child-related problem surfaces. Two current examples: excessive TV viewing and excessive fast-food consumption. The emerging problem of childhood obesity demands serious attention, but the knee-jerk reaction of many people (especially non-parents) is simply to blame the parents for their lack of discipline.

Richard Glover offers a poignant glimpse into the experience of being a parent on the receiving end of society's growing hostility to parents (which is, presumably, a displacement of its growing intolerance of children). Writing in *The Sydney Morning Herald* Spectrum, 3–4 March 2007, Glover put it like this:

> The latest festival of finger-pointing is over childhood obesity. Parents, it is said, have let the side down. True, there is a lot of advertising of junk food. True, displays of it loom from every surface. But parents must learn to 'just say no' when their children request such rubbish.
>
> Occasionally, in the tiny voices of the thoroughly whipped, we parents answer back. 'Actually, we are very busy saying "no", and mostly it goes pretty well, but I wonder if you could just back off the high-pressure advertising for a moment, just to let us catch our breath.' . . . Some even say, with a smugness that makes me weary to my bones: 'I never had any trouble with my children, you know. I just think parents have lost the art of parenting.'

Growing up as a member of our smallest-ever generation will have its challenges. Being indulged by your parents is nice, in its way, and even being the target for so much commercial attention may be flattering (though, as Glover asks in that same article, 'Why did we ever think it appropriate for highly paid adults to devote all their sophistication and intelligence to tempting children to eat food that would shorten their lives?'). Eventually entering a labour market that is wooing you to fill its yawning vacancies will be some compensation for having to pay higher-than-ever taxes.

Finding yourself in a society that is more indifferent to children and young people than it has traditionally been will create some understandable resentment. 'Hey, we're here, too!' may well become the catchcry of tomorrow's adolescents and young adults. Will they be even more rebellious than previous generations, as a result? Will they be desperate to shake off their overprotective parents? Perhaps, but many of them will be singletons (the demographers' charming label for the only child in a family) and singletons tend to side with authority. They tend to be responsible at an earlier age than those born second or third in a family, who are shaped by the need to fight their way past older siblings in an attempt to attract their parents' attention.

Is the word 'parenting' becoming a problem?

When non-parents – or, indeed, grandparents – criticise the raising of today's children, the most common theme is that 'kids are being allowed to run wild' and that 'parents seem reluctant to discipline their own children'. At its extreme, this criticism suggests some parents are intimidated by their children; too eager to please them; almost afraid of them. This is sometimes interpreted as a form of overcompensation for parents' guilt about the amount of time they are unable to spend with their children, but time-use analyst Michael Bittman of the University of New England says that although most mothers now have paid work outside the home, parents are actually spending more time than ever with their children.

The guilt might still be there: many parents' focus has shifted from the amount of time they spend with their children to the *quality* of that time and this has made them more alert, more cautious, more careful about how the interaction with their children is managed. Today's parents seem to have been made conscious of the damage they might be doing to their children – which may be one of several reasons why so many are sending their children to private schools in the hope that 'values' will be more effectively inculcated and 'discipline' more firmly handled than the parents feel able to manage.

The trend towards parents expecting schools to accept responsibilities traditionally associated with parents themselves is one of the exquisite paradoxes in the current controversy over this thing called 'parenting'. Parents want to spend more and more time with their children but in ways that avoid their responsibilities as parents. And yet they are more acutely conscious than ever of the idea of parenting. Parenting has become a job or, at least, a job description. It has also become yet another source of anxiety – not just about the physical wellbeing of our children, but about their emotional health, and our part in shaping it.

In Britain – can Australia be far behind? – TV programs such as *Child of Our Time* and *Driving Mum and Dad Mad* are attracting huge audiences not only to the programs themselves but also to their associated websites. Program producers claim dramatic effects on viewers' knowledge and understanding of parenting issues and, in many cases, the acquisition of new skills. There is no doubt that such programs (perhaps even including *Supernanny)* are responding to an increasing demand for help from parents who believe the parenting task is tougher than in previous generations.

Parenting used to be something that happened by accident – or, more correctly, by example. Children learned how to grow up by watching what their parents did, helped along by going to school and learning how to live in a community. They were frequently left to their own devices, and that was regarded as an important aspect of childhood.

Their moral formation happened as part of that process. They learned about the courtesies of everyday life, the need to show respect for parents and other authority figures, and the nature of mutual obligation, by observing how it all happened (or didn't happen) in the various adult worlds they encountered, especially at home. The process was helped along, of course, by specific guidance, instruction and discipline at home and at school.

Although it's still the case that our children learn far more from watching what we do than from listening to what we say, we seem to have decided that parenting is an art, perhaps even a science, but certainly a field of serious study. The low-birthrate generation of children in Middle Australia may turn out to be at more risk from overattentive parents than from neglect.

The drive to help parents do a better job of raising their children springs from praiseworthy motivations. What parents wouldn't like to be able to give their children the best possible start, and to restrain themselves from behaving in ways likely to inflict psychological damage on their children? What parents wouldn't like to feel more confident and more accomplished in their approach to the task of raising children, especially when they reach adolescence?

But our current preoccupation with parenting has its downside. In their concern to be wonderful parents, many people now report that it is getting harder to know where to set the limits for tolerance of children's behaviour that offends them. Understandably, parents find it particularly offensive when, having finally reached adolescence and young adulthood, their offspring show them less respect than they would show to other adults, and take their support – and even their indulgence – for granted.

The 19-year-old son of a friend demands a car so he can get to work. Otherwise, he won't go to work. So the parents buy the car, pay the

*registration and insurance, and don't dare ask where he's going or when
he'll be home because he's told them not to. They're offended and hurt, but
they can't bring themselves to say so.*

Examples abound of parents having trouble saying 'no', keeping
their disapproval hidden, or failing to insist that certain standards
be met. Though the problem is likely to increase with the children
yet to enter adolescence, it is already evident among the parents of
young adults – especially those whose offspring are staying at home
for longer than any previous generation. Confirming popular
perceptions, many parents secretly admit to being intimidated by
their own children, or being scared to do or say anything that might
upset them.

It looks as if yet another culture shift is under way: the move
from children feeling the need to please their parents and win their
approval, to parents feeling the need to please their children and win
their approval.

Writing in the *Good Weekend* ('The Parent Trap', 3 February 2007),
Jane Cadzow drew attention to the many books about parenting now
available, from *ScreamFree Parenting* to *Everyday Opportunities for
Extraordinary Parenting*. Cadzow also quoted Sarah Wise, a child
development researcher at the Australian Institute of Family Studies:
'What has changed from previous generations is the emphasis that
we are placing on children and childhood. It's definitely a culture
shift – valuing children to the extent that they overtake your life.'
That certainly coincides with the impression gained from my own
research where parents consistently claim to be 'closer to the kids'
than their own parents were to them (though even the over-sixties
say that, so perhaps greater closeness between parents and children

has been a long-standing goal). They also report that the business of parenting, combined with their paid work, makes them busier than their own parents ever seemed to be.

I never have a minute to myself. If I'm not rushing around taking them to ballet and football, I'm supervising their homework. And projects! Don't talk to me about projects – that's a form of torture for parents. Why do we do it? I guess it's more important to us to be close to the kids than it was for our own parents. I love knowing my children so well. I love knowing their friends. I love that closeness.

Who's going to argue with the proposition that such closeness is desirable? Who would challenge the goal of achieving greater openness, frankness and trust between parents and their children? But perhaps there is a line we are forgetting to draw. Perhaps we need to remember that, in the end, parents are not obliged to be their children's friends (and, by the way, they're not obliged to be sporting or academic coaches either); they're parents, and discipline is part of their responsibility to their children. Loving our kids doesn't mean giving in to them, pretending to share their taste in music, fashion or even friends, or refusing to express legitimate feelings of irritation, disappointment or outrage.

Being human, parents are frail and flawed, and this will be as obvious in their parenting as in every other aspect of their lives. They will inevitably 'damage' their children by making poor judgments in moments of tension or crisis, losing their cool under provocation, and by acting in ways that embarrass their children. (Some parents have even decided it is their parental duty to embarrass their children, and what parent hasn't been made to appear foolish in the company of their children's friends, simply by acting like an adult?)

Children need to learn that adults can be irrational, unreasonable, cranky and intolerant – just like them. They also need to learn that there are sometimes good reasons for this, and sometimes not. And, from an early age, they need to know when they have pushed their parents too far. If parents are offended, shouldn't they at least say, 'I'm offended'? How else will their children learn what 'offended' means? And if they don't learn such lessons at home, where they are loved and nurtured, they are unlikely to learn them anywhere else – and that's the very thing feared by the critics of a one-sided, excessively child-centred approach to parenting.

In her *Good Weekend* article, Cadzow also quotes the author of *Parents Who Think Too Much*, US journalist Anne Cassidy, who concludes that children who are accustomed to having their parents at their beck and call lose the ability to amuse themselves and become 'whiny, passive, self-centred and cheerless'. A harsh judgment, perhaps, but also a timely warning: power imbalances are always unhealthy and children who are allowed to exert too much power over their parents may suffer as much damage as those whose parents exert too much power over them.

Welcome to Botox City

The rising generation of children will be living in a social landscape lush with grey hair and crackling with grey power. The good news is that there may be many surrogate grandparents in search of substitutes for the grandchildren they never had, so that may help to compensate for the lack of interest shown in them by the swelling ranks of non-parents in their midst.

The most obvious demographic consequence of the falling birthrate is the shift in the age distribution of the Australian population, and that has social and cultural implications as well. At present, only 14 percent of the population is over the age of 65. If the birthrate stays where it is – and, in spite of the current upwards blip, it may well go even lower – and if life expectancy also remains stable, then by the time today's youngsters reach their middle years, about 25 percent of the population will be over 65. That's a very different kind of society from the one we've been used to for the past 60 years, ever since the postwar baby boom rewrote our population statistics.

Think of the implications for aged-care medicine, nursing, housing and welfare. Think of the demand for leisure and recreation activities for the increasingly hale and hearty elderly, and the changing demand for media content to reflect their interests – especially their interest in the past which will fuel an unprecedented nostalgia boom. (The BBC's *New Tricks* is just the beginning.) Think of the impact on retailing, entertainment, transport and community services. Think of all the special provisions likely to be needed for a population that is so strongly skewed to the older end of the spectrum, and then think about who's going to pay for it all.

Of course, many of the over-65s will be powering on in the workforce, happily reminding us and each other that since 60 was the new 50, it follows that 70 is the new 60. And so it will be: in terms of their health, their fitness, their diet, their dress, their style, their propensity to travel, their life expectancy and their outlook on life, this will be the 'youngest' cohort of over-65s we've ever seen. And what diet and exercise don't achieve, Botox, collagen and cosmetic surgery will. They'll be determined to *look* as young as they feel.

The Baby Boomers are already leading the way, establishing a trend that will be eagerly followed by the next generation, and the next. As we have already seen, 'retirement' is being dropped from the vocabulary of ageing in favour of 'refocusing' and those who choose to work on – whether full-time or part-time, paid or unpaid – may well regard structured work as a life-prolonging, dementia-postponing pursuit that gives them structure, stimulation, satisfaction and a human herd to belong to, even if their marriages have dissolved and their families scattered.

And if the present rush to take up the new 'reverse mortgage' product is maintained, perhaps the tax burden on younger people won't be as great as is currently feared. This is the product so brilliantly conceived to cater for the army of Baby Boomers who have failed to make adequate financial provision for their old age via savings or superannuation, but who enjoy a high rate of ownership of homes that have appreciated dramatically over the past 15 years. It allows you to mortgage your home, make no repayments and simply live off the mortgage. When you die, the bank sells your house and recoups the loan, so you're dead, the bank's happy, and your kids are furious.

On the other hand, the Boomers have probably lavished more attention, and money, on their offspring along the way than any previous generation has received from its parents. Consistent with their generational reputation as seekers of instant gratification, Baby Boomers like the idea of dishing out some of their children's inheritance *now*, ostensibly because 'it's so tough for young people today – they need all the help they can get' but also, perhaps, so the children can express their gratitude while the parents are still around to bask in it.

Our ageing society may well turn out to be a very lively place, with such a high proportion of elderly people who are healthier, better educated, more widely travelled and more engaged in society than was typical of older people in the past. From the so-called 'grey nomads' who pack up their homes and take to the road in an extended caravan tour of the country to the enthusiastic participants in the University of the Third Age, this will be a more mobile, more inquisitive, more restless generation of over-65s than we are accustomed to. 'Tribal elders' will be a highly visible, vigorous and participative segment of the population. As a result, there may well be a more caring and respectful attitude towards older people, and in spite of the continuing rapid rate of technological change and innovation, there will still be a huge bank of experience among the over-65s for our society to draw on.

When a child born in 2006 turns 20, the youngest Baby Boomers will be 65. By then, 20 may well be the new 30, given the hothouse development of the rising generation, and 65 will have become the new 50. A chronological gap of 45 years may start to feel more like a socio-cultural gap of only 20 years. Perhaps those infamous generation gaps are actually shrinking.

9

The mystery of the shrinking household

Australian households have been steadily shrinking. In the past 100 years, our population has increased fivefold while the number of households has increased tenfold, so we've been creating households at twice the rate we've been growing the population. The average Australian household now contains just 2.6 persons, and falling.

Let's see where that average figure comes from.

At present, about 25 percent of Australian households contain just one person, making the single-person household the most common household type in the nation, closely followed by the two-person household. Together, they account for half of all Australian households, and the single-person household is the fastest growing household type. By 2026, the ABS predicts that 34 percent of all Australian households will contain just one person and the average household will be down to 2.2 or 2.3 persons.

All this seems radically different from the pattern experienced by Australians born mid-20th century, when the typical household was what the ABS describes as a 'couple family with children' (i.e., mum, dad and the kids). As recently as 1986, 60 percent of Australians were living in that particular version of a family household; by 2001, the figure had fallen to 52 percent, and the ABS predicts a further fall over the next 20 years to about 40 percent. Already, lone-person households (1 962 100) outnumber households where couples live with children (1 798 400).

There's been a steady increase in other types of family households, notably one-parent families (12 percent of households, but more than 20 percent of all families) and couples without children (20 percent of all households). But all types of 'family households', lumped together, are still declining as a proportion of total households. They are projected to tumble from 72 percent in 2001 to 62 percent of all households by 2026.

Obviously, many more *people* still live in three-, four-, five- or six-person households than in one- or two-person households. But in terms of *household* statistics, the trend is moving inexorably towards smaller units. About ten percent of the population live in one-person households, though that figure is projected to rise to between 12 and 15 percent within the next 20 years. By then, over three million Australians will be living alone and, in round figures, a further six million will be living with just one other person.

So if you happen to live in a one- or two-person household, you're positively mainstream and becoming more so, year by year. By contrast, if you happen to live with the only spouse you've ever had *and* you are currently living with three or more of your very own children, then, in household terms, you're living on the eccentric fringe (well, almost).

In *Australian Social Trends 2006*, the ABS noted drily that 'most of the change from 2001 to 2026 is projected to be in the numbers of people living alone and the numbers of family households'. They could have added that, in its social and cultural impact, this is the demographic equivalent of climate change.

Who are these 'lone householders'?

Changes in the size and structure of our households are two of the most revealing indicators of the social evolution of Australia. In tracking household shrinkage, we are also, inescapably, tracking fundamental changes in our patterns of marriage and divorce, the birthrate, the age distribution of the population, longevity, the independence of women and in our willingness to explore more diverse and transient living arrangements. We are a more dynamic, flexible society than we used to be: our mobility and our more critical attitudes to relationships are reflected in the changing character of Australian households.

It would be absurd to interpret the increase in the number of one-person households as a sign that we are destined to become a nation of hermits, isolates or recluses. It would also be wrong to interpret a statistical snapshot as if it says more than a snapshot can say. The fact that, at the present time, ten percent of Australians are living alone doesn't mean that ten percent of the population is made up of people who choose to live alone, or intend always to live alone. The rapid changes taking place in our society mean that, for all kinds of reasons, many more than ten percent of us will move in and out of solo households – voluntarily or involuntarily – at various stages of our lives. Many of us will be surprised to find ourselves in that state, even temporarily. Some will have embraced the idea of solo living as a deliberate strategy to suit a particular stage of their life's trajectory.

A much smaller proportion than ten percent will have chosen to live permanently as solo householders

The term 'one-person household' covers a multitude of personal circumstances and situations. Delayed marriage among the young, lower fertility rates, the increased incidence of separation and divorce, and increased longevity all contribute to the phenomenon. And, of course, there will always be a core group of lone householders who choose that state, feel content with it and never assume that a partner would enhance or 'complete' their lives. Some of them are hermit-like in their attitudes; some are gregarious and sociable beings who also happen to place a high value on privacy, independence and solitude.

But none of these factors is simple, neat or predictable in its content or dynamics. For a start, there's the huge emotional difference between those who live alone voluntarily and those pitched involuntarily into the solo state, and between those who accept their state as permanent and those who bridle against it and can only tolerate it by treating it as a temporary or even transitory situation. Some lone householders feel triumphant, exuberant and free; some merely endure their aloneness; some feel like victims. Generalisations about a category as complex and dynamic as this would be patronising and pointless: like everyone else, lone householders are trying to make their own sense of their lives; like everyone else, they are trying to cope with the experiences – some dreamy, some nightmarish – that sweep them towards an unpredictable future.

There are some bereaved elderly people, for instance, who have long since adapted, however reluctantly, to solo living. Others welcome it as an unexpected liberation from a joyless marriage. Some are quietly grateful for the release from the burden of caring for a frail, infirm, depressed, demented or otherwise dependent partner; some simply never adjust to the grim reality of life without their spouses. Some speak of their homes as warm, safe cocoons to which they return with relief after social encounters; others dread coming home to an empty house.

There are people – mostly men – 'left over' from a divorce, who desperately wish they were still living in the former family home, and try to furnish their new homes in ways they hope will seem attractive to their children when they visit. Others – mostly women – are celebrating their release from a burdensome marriage and have no wish to rush into another relationship: they're not even looking, and they hate the very idea of a 'prospect' crossing their path, let alone their threshold.

There are those who, too-earnestly hoping to find new partners, assume their period of aloneness will be brief and can summon no interest in decorating a flat that feels like nothing more than a staging-post: no pictures on the wall, no plants in the balcony pots, the removalist's cartons still packed and waiting for the next step in the tortured process of putting a broken life back together. Some lose themselves in the private consolation of uninhibited drinking, heavily relying on television and radio for companionship. Others seize the chance to live as they have always wanted to live – perhaps more tidily or more messily, perhaps more spontaneously or more creatively, perhaps more contentedly than seemed possible in a family or group household. Some report that in setting up a solo household, they are expressing themselves more transparently and more honestly than ever before.

There are independent, confident young people living alone as a symbol of their independence, revelling in the freedom to stay in bed all weekend if they wish, to eat takeaway Thai three nights running, and to have absolute control over who invades their space. There are others who live alone, theoretically, but whose apartments and houses are home to a constant stream of friends and friends-of-friends.

Then there are the people who find themselves relocated to a strange city or town, transferred there by an employer or simply in search of new opportunities, for whom home is both a refuge and a constant reminder of their new-found aloneness.

Aloneness is a complex state. At its brightest and best, it means freedom – to be yourself, to please yourself, to eat what you like, to work longer hours than a partner might tolerate, to yak endlessly on the phone and to come and go as you please.

But aloneness can also breed a particular sense of insecurity that is more prevalent among lone householders than those living in couple, family or group households. In The Ipsos Mackay Report, *Home Alone* (2005), people living alone reported feelings of vague edginess and uneasiness, anxiety about getting sick with no help at hand, a sense of ultimate financial responsibility ('It's all up to me') and a concern, sometimes even an obsession, with security.

I lock all the doors and windows at night, then I go into my own bedroom and lock that door, too. I always leave a light on at night, and I turn all the lights on when I go out.

The most unwelcome face of aloneness is, of course, loneliness.

Don't ask me whether there are any good things about being alone. The fact is, I want my wife back.

Bereaved partners alone with their grief are, predictably, the least happy lone householders, but an aching loneliness can also be provoked by children leaving a one-parent home, the fracture of a relationship (especially if it involves enforced separation from children), or by certain times in the day that recall a lost intimacy: the 'chardonnay hour', early morning walks, bedtime with its associations of 'pillow talk' and physical closeness.

Not all solo householders experience loneliness, but even the most contented can find Christmas heavy going.

> *I hate waking up on Christmas morning by myself. And I don't like being invited to share Christmas with another family – you feel like a waif.*

> *Last Christmas, I crept out in the morning to see if someone had put a present for me under the tree. Of course they hadn't, because I'm here on my own so I knew I was being an idiot.*

Lone householders with pets describe the great comfort they receive from the unconditional devotion of a dog, or the emotional warmth of a cat on their laps. Some are quite clear about their belief in the superiority of pets over humans when it comes to reliable affection.

> *My pets are my love. I've always been an animal lover and in my older and grumpier life, I like them better than humans. I'm sick of humans with their lies and their crap and their deceit, so these days I'm passionate about my animals.*

> *I've got a dog, so I don't come home to a totally empty house. I'm sure she understands when I talk to her, by the way she puts her head to one side.*

Some lone householders credit their pets with keeping them active, healthy and sane. Others have no time for pets, believing the freedom they relish would be compromised by the responsibilities of having to look after an animal.

The dominant theme in lone householders' descriptions of their lives is that they resent any suggestion that they are weird, pitiable or even unusual. Indeed, if they have access to a warm circle of family and friends, many people living alone would not wish it any other way – at least for the time being.

As usual, social attitudes appear to be adapting to the realities of social change. The demographic shift in the direction of smaller households may be propelled by many factors, but in a society where more people than ever before will experience living alone at some stage of their lives, we shouldn't be surprised to find 'normal' being constantly redefined.

Are we 'meant' to live alone?

Many lone householders report some surprise at finding themselves in that situation, even if they have brought it about. Older, bereaved people might rationally accept that 'one of us was going to go before the other', but having spent a lifetime as one of a couple, solo living can feel like a huge emotional challenge. Even among younger people who may have deliberately sought the freedom and independence of the lone householder, the surprise element is often present: 'How did I come to be living alone, when I always thought I'd be with someone?'

People who have been through separation and divorce frequently ask the same question, with the same note of surprise: 'How did this happen to me?' At one level, they know exactly how it happened; at another level they feel a constant, vague sense that they are living in an unexpected, unplanned situation.

Out of these various circumstances, and among both those who resent their situation and those who embrace it, lone householders are occasionally driven to ask themselves the cosmic question: 'Are we meant to live alone?'

That question contains several layers of possible meaning. At first glance, it sounds a bit plaintive, as if to say no, we are not meant to live alone; the solo state is somehow unnatural for humans; there *should* be someone else in my life. But times are changing, and so are attitudes to aloneness – in a household and in life. The *Home Alone* study found that the stigma once attached to lone householders – *Is he gay? Is she on the shelf? Is he difficult to get along with? Is she a loner?* – has not only given way to a greater sense of acceptance but, in some cases been replaced by a kind of 'aloneness envy' among those who hanker after more freedom and flexibility in their living arrangements.

Gone are the days of 'old maids', 'confirmed bachelors', 'maiden aunts' and 'spinsters' who attracted pity because they seemed incomplete or perhaps unsuccessful in matters of the heart. It has now become fashionable to assert that 'I don't need another to make me complete', even among people who have, or expect to have, a partner. The new wisdom is that we must be 'whole' as individuals, in order to maintain our integrity and sense of identity in an intimate relationship.

The stigma once attached to living alone has not evaporated entirely: some younger people complain that they still find themselves the object of pity among friends and of despair among family members, especially parents who worry that living alone is a symptom of something being wrong. But the days have gone when lone householders might have felt awkward or conspicuous about buying single-serve prepared food or small packets clearly designed for lone householders. Even the traditional reluctance of women to be seen eating alone in a restaurant or going alone to the cinema is waning.

The question 'are we meant to live alone?' is located at the leading edge of social change. The impact of the gender revolution can be felt in the growing determination of some young women, in particular, to assert their capacity for independence, even if they ultimately expect to find a partner. And the growing acceptance of single status following a relationship breakdown also fuels the idea that there's nothing unnatural about periods of living alone and that it might even be a necessary part of the post-separation healing process.

The falling birthrate has also affected attitudes to singleness as part of a general blurring and softening of attitudes to coupledom. In the past, young people generally believed marriage and parenthood were normal, perhaps even obligatory, steps in the process of becoming an adult. That process is now freighted with complex possibilities: will I partner or not, and if I do, will we have children or not? Will we marry or not? Will we take it as it comes, keep our options open, wait and see? In that climate, the idea of living alone, at least for a while, seems as normal, as natural, as conventional as living in a couple or group household.

Developments on the frontiers of biotechnology add extra layers of possible meaning to the question. The prospect of human cloning, for instance, raises serious questions about the need for a partner, as does the technology of sperm donation. While most potential parents would still expect to conceive a baby through conventional sexual intercourse, and to raise their children in a conventional two-parent setting, this is no longer a universal aspiration. Alternative scenarios are no longer regarded as weird or unnatural.

The growing sophistication of medical interventions designed to prolong life seems likely to increase the number of people living alone in older age as a result of bereavement or divorce. The over-65s will be an increasingly common feature of the social landscape, and many of them – more women than men – will be living alone.

Given the sustained high rate of partnership breakdown, periods of solo living (and solo parenting) are now realistically acknowledged as a possibility, so the distinction between 'always solo' and 'currently solo' is becoming blurred. Many lone householders in their thirties, for example, are happy to describe themselves as 'alone' with no expectation that this will necessarily be a permanent state, nor that anyone should read too much into it. 'I might decide to stay on my own; I might not. Do you have a problem with that?'

The change in attitudes to lone householders – particularly among young people and those who have experienced separation and divorce – has been reinforced by enthusiasm for the idea of self-realisation: *this is me, take it or leave it.* If 'the real me' turns out to be a person who is content to live alone, permanently or temporarily, then so be it. Indeed, there is now some pride among lone householders who feel they have achieved something significant in learning how to live alone – perhaps because their aloneness is associated with overcoming the pain and trauma of divorce or bereavement, perhaps because they have confronted the lurking fear of loneliness, or perhaps because 'independence' seemed like a challenge they needed to meet.

Their payoff is in a clearer sense of identity, a greater degree of self-acceptance and a surer sense of what a relationship would have to offer in order to give up the advantages of solo living.

Sometimes I wonder if I'll ever want to give up my freedom. One day I rolled over and realised that it didn't matter if I didn't do my hair and put my make-up on, or get dressed up. I can just be who I am. And it was a huge relief.

What is this freedom that lone householders prize so highly? For many of them, it's the freedom to choose between intimacy and solitude. Friends are precious; socialising is fun (up to a point); romance is usually welcome. But the ability to switch off, to retreat into quiet solitude, to close the door behind you, often comes to be valued by lone householders more than any other feature of their lives. That's partly because they realise they have a flexibility not so readily available to those living in couples or larger households: they can be with people when they choose, and they can be alone when they choose, whereas those in larger (even two-person) households may have more trouble finding solitude.

Some couples, loath to give up the intimacy/solitude flexibility they enjoyed as singles, maintain two separate houses. This affords each of them the privacy and freedom of the lone householder, with the intimacy of a relationship available to them when they choose to be together – which might be part of every day, or part of every week, or less often than that. Or it might be 'a week at your place, a week apart, a week at my place'. Or it might be *ad hoc*. The essential point is that they use their separate households as a bastion against loss of privacy, loss of identity and loss of independence. All this may strike some married couples as a sign of a half-hearted commitment, though others will envy the safety valve offered by a bit of separateness. In the new world of households, all such arrangements are bound to become more common – not necessarily as permanent ways of living, but sometimes as 'test patterns' or as a temporary response to tensions that inevitably arise in closer, more intimate household settings.

A couple's deliberate choice to maintain two households may seem unusual, but the high rate of marriage breakdown means that many fractured families are doing precisely that – occupying two separate dwellings, typically with the mother and children in one house, and the father in another. Such arrangements are often fraught with tension and anxiety but, at any given moment, hundreds of thousands of Australians are trying to make sense of a two-household arrangement.

Smaller households, bigger houses

The desire for freedom to switch between intimacy – familial, sexual and otherwise – and solitude is one explanation for the curious phenomenon of ever-expanding houses for ever-shrinking households. In a one-person household, solitude is easy to achieve; intimacy involves a deliberate decision to go out or to invite someone in. Conversely, the members of a large household of six, seven or eight people accept that they'll probably need to go out to find solitude – for a walk, perhaps, or to sit by the sea, or to visit a favourite cafe, bookshop or hardware store (a favourite hideout for men). But in many intermediate-sized households – especially nuclear family households of three or four people – the emotional spotlight falls with such intensity on each member that they need to find their own space, their own place, their own 'home within the home'. To put it bluntly, they need somewhere to hide from each other when they want peace and quiet.

This is why the members of relatively small households often dream of living in a house that offers many separate and private places: a home entertainment room; private bedrooms for the children possibly with individual study rooms as well; a master suite for the parents that includes bed and bathroom, sitting area and, ideally, space for the parents' own computer and TV set; a shed or garage that's big enough for a chair or two and perhaps yet another small TV set, to which Dad can retreat. 'To be honest,' said one of my respondents in the 2004 Ipsos Mackay Report study, *Australians At Home*, 'I'd rather have a big shed than a big house.' Some mothers even eschew help in the kitchen because they've staked that out as their personal space.

Open-plan living (like open-plan offices) only seems to work well if there are private nooks to which individuals can retreat when the emotional atmosphere in the open area becomes too intense. And if you can't afford to build enough nooks for people to hide in, a set of headphones might do the trick.

I've got one end of the house to myself. No one ever wants to watch what I'm watching. I've got my own recliner and my own TV – it's paradise.

My favourite place is my bedroom. I've got the TV and the computer and I can get away from everything. I can look up the mountain from my window. I like to sneak in there and hide. It's my space. I love it.

Home? I feel more at home in the local coffee shop than anywhere else. They know me there, they know my order – it's the one place I can relax and do a bit of thinking without being interrupted.

It's surprising that property developers and builders (to say nothing of local councils) haven't come up with more imaginative ways of responding to this desire for more private spaces for people in smaller households. The obvious response – build bigger homes – has resulted in the so-called McMansion phenomenon, creating sprawling new suburbs full of large houses on small blocks, churned out as if on a hamburger production line and with backyards barely worthy of the name.

Given the increasing flexibility and transience of our living arrangements, and the inexorable trend towards smaller households, why haven't some of our brightest architects and engineers come up with beautiful and functional ways of creating basic houses with 'options': bolt-on bedrooms, dens, conservatories, home theatres, that can be added or subtracted as the household expands and shrinks? And why haven't we made more creative attempts to adapt the co-housing concept to Australian tastes – letting individual households (including one-person households) occupy small houses clustered around common eating, entertaining and recreation areas to which residents can come and go as they please. It's happened in some places – Canberra, for instance – but has not yet been fully explored as a way of introducing more flexibility into housing for the future. People who've tried it generally love it.

What happens to the herd instinct when it is no longer satisfied by the domestic herd?

Humans are herd animals – social creatures – who seem historically to be most comfortable in herds of around six, seven or eight people.

That used to be the size of a typical Australian domestic herd – either because of the presence of five or six surviving children (in the days before widespread use of effective contraception), because of grandparents sharing a household with parents and children, or because of a generally looser definition of 'family' and indeed of 'marriage'. The historian J.C. Caldwell, in his *Theory of Fertility Decline* (1982), suggested that 'a strengthening of relations between husbands and wives at the expense of relations between spouses and their own parents' in the early years of the 20th century contributed to the falling of the age at marriage and a steady increase in the marriage rate. In other words, a culture shift that loosened the bonds between young people and their parents led to the growing popularity of marriage at a younger age. The same factor led to the rise of the nuclear family and, in turn, contributed to the trend towards smaller households.

That herd of six to eight people also turns out to be the typical size of an effective work group, and of a reasonably cohesive dinner party. It's also about the limit of an effective management span of control. It helps to explain why the backs and forwards in a Rugby team tend to form their own subcultures and why sections of an orchestra express hostility – sometimes mock, sometimes real – towards each other. (You can't have a herd of 15 or 20 or 80, though you can certainly have tribes of that size, which is why even the warring herds within a tribal organisation will unite in their antipathy towards rival organisations.)

There's nothing mysterious about the herd instinct, and there is some elasticity in the size of a functioning, effective herd. But, for most of us, maintaining reasonably close relations with six or seven other people at once is manageable; when the group gets bigger than that, its dynamics change and it becomes harder for people to feel 'at one' with the group. Herd-sized groups tend to foster a comforting sense of emotional security and personal identity that can be even stronger than our individual identity, which is why peer-group pressure is so powerful.

The other thing about herds is that they tend to generate less emotional heat than smaller, sub-herd-sized groups of three or four.

When the size of a household falls below the 'natural' size of a human herd, what happens to the herd instinct? It doesn't wither and die. If home doesn't supply us with a herd to belong to, our herd instinct will drive us to look elsewhere. Given the phenomenon of the shrinking household, this quest for non-domestic herds will ultimately turn out to be good news for the health of our neighbourhoods, communities and even our workplaces.

Book clubs, cooking classes, bushwalking clubs, choirs, adult education courses, wine and food clubs, investment clubs, film societies, bush regeneration groups, informal discussion groups . . . the growing popularity of all these activities is a sign that the herd instinct is finding new outlets.

Our book club is like a real little family. We just love it. But at some point in the evening, someone usually says, 'Don't you think we should say something about the book?'

No doubt there is a growing interest in philosophy, astronomy, Greek ruins, classical music and all the other topics that cram the catalogues of adult education organisations. But the herd instinct is a powerful contributor to the success of many of those courses as well – particularly those that involve travel with a group, or participation in cooking, writing, painting, dancing or drama classes that offer lots of interaction, discussion and 'bonding'.

In many workplaces, work groups become herds that offer much of the security and identity of domestic herds. Unlike friends, but just like families, we don't choose our workmates but have to learn how to rub along with them and this process can foster a particular kind of *esprit de corps* that satisfies the herd instinct. It's no wonder so many workplaces now encourage this process by offering the kind of facilities – coffee shops, gyms, Friday night bars, ping-pong or billiards tables – that blur the distinction between work and social connections.

The easiest way of connecting with the herd is to graze with the herd, which is why the explosion in the number of coffee shops, cafes and food courts has coincided with the rise of one- and two-person households. The growing practice of providing a 'common table' in cafes and restaurants – rather like the 'club table' in traditional clubs – allows lone diners to choose whether to sit alone or to join others for a meal. Such tables typically cater for six to eight diners – the perfect size for a temporary, *ad hoc* herd. Choosing to sit at the common table implies an acceptance of the idea that 'table talk', even with strangers, is an integral part of the pleasure of eating. At the same time, tables laid for one are also increasingly common, to cater for those who would prefer to eat alone (grazing without mooing, as it were) and who are reassured to find that such settings now appear 'normal'.

As households continue to shrink, it is safe to assume there will be still further expansion in the provision of services for people who don't wish to cook their own meals ('Not worth it for one, or even two – we even have breakfast on the way to work now'): more neighbourhood cafes, more takeaway outlets, more home delivery services, more fully prepared meals sold from butchers and supermarkets.

Especially among younger lone householders (and a growing number of two-person householders as well), less home cooking means a changing role for the kitchen. It becomes more of a convenient spot to heat something in the microwave, make a cup of coffee or, perhaps, throw some cereal into a bowl, and less of a work space. It may still serve its traditional function as the focal point for special-occasion eating, where in-home preparation of a meal is a form of entertainment, but the desire to graze with the herd drives the growing demand for flats and apartments with minimal kitchens – rather like the fashionable laundry-in-a-cupboard.

Meanwhile, at the other end of the spectrum, kitchens in larger family and group households are evolving into meeting and eating spaces as well as working areas – rather like old-style country kitchens but with ever more serious stainless steel appliances creating a quasi-commercial, 'bistro' appearance. As in so many areas of Australian life, 'typical' is no longer a word you'd try to apply to a kitchen: more diverse lifestyles, more diverse households, more diverse housing – and more diverse kitchens.

In some inner-urban areas, often catering for the needs of particular immigrant groups, we are seeing a trend towards mini-apartments designed for little more than sleeping and watching TV; everything else happens in the street, the 'village', the neighbourhood. This is likely to be an increasing phenomenon, with suburban commercial developments following the inner-city trend towards the creation of small living spaces above them, on the assumption that the residents will do all their eating, drinking and socialising down in the commercial precinct. There's a long history of this type of living in Europe; the trend towards one- and two-person households is likely to create a growing demand for it here as well.

In Sydney, for example, there's a move back from the suburbs towards the inner city for the first time in 100 years. This is partly a reflection of the fact that, during 2006–7, city apartment prices were falling while suburban house prices continued to rise. But it's also partly due to cultural factors that increase the appeal of inner-city living: a 'cool' sophistication, convenience to work and leisure facilities, lower costs and, of course, easy access to a non-domestic herd.

Even some parents of young children are discovering the advantages of apartment living: lower prices, access to parks, beaches, city-based entertainment; less travel time between home and parents' work; less maintenance; more opportunities for communal living. In *The Sydney Morning Herald* of 24 March 2007, columnist Lisa Pryor listed ways in which architects and developers might attract more young families to this type of living: safe balconies, soundproof walls, a secure parking spot where a car could safely be left with baby equipment in it, ground-level storage for a pram, communal playground areas and perhaps even a children's wading pool.

Eventually, the empty nest

Apart from divorce and bereavement, the most obvious reason for a household to shrink is that the children grow up and leave. Not that they are in a hurry any more: the tendency for adult offspring to stay at home longer is reflected in the fact that 30 percent of Australians in the 20–29 years age group are still living in the family home – including about 45 percent of 20–25-year-olds.

There are many reasons why children stay home longer than their parents did at the same age. The biggest factor is that they are delaying marriage and parenthood. They are also spending longer in tertiary education, often with a HECS debt associated with their course of study, and their parents are therefore inclined to be sympathetic to the need to minimise their living expenses.

But there's another, quirkier reason why young adults tend to stay at home well into their twenties: though their parents complain about it to anyone who'll listen, there's some evidence they are actually pleased by it and may even have implicitly encouraged it. This is the generation of parents who, fearing that their own busyness, their materialism and perhaps their own self-absorption may have diminished their effectiveness as parents, are desperate for signs that they were, after all, good parents in the eyes of their own children. One such sign might be the fact that their children now seem reluctant to leave home. Another may be the oft-quoted claim that 'we are close to the kids'.

Members of this generation of parents have also tended to fill their homes with as many forms of entertainment as they can afford: TV sets and computers, video games, swimming pools, ping-pong and pool tables – the more the home could work like a child magnet, the more the parents would be rewarded by knowing their offspring were safely and contentedly staying at home. To some extent, it has almost seemed as if busy and distracted parents were trying to let the home itself do some of the parenting for them: TV as a babysitter is hardly a new concept, but turning the whole home into a child-centred cocoon takes the concept to a new level, almost as if providing unlimited 'stuff' might compensate for lack of parental time and attention.

So perhaps it is not surprising that a generation of children whose parents tried to make home as nice for them as possible have found it to be very nice indeed. As they've grown into early adulthood, the pattern has persisted: 'I'm very comfortable at home – I've virtually got my own pad – why would I want to move out?'

Although many parents are secretly pleased that their offspring seem reluctant to leave, the living arrangements can be challenging. Homes designed for parents and children do not always lend themselves to the comfortable housing of two generations of adults, each wanting their own space – both physically and metaphorically. (Another reason, perhaps, for larger and/or more flexible houses for our shrinking households.) Parents sometimes take a while to adjust to the idea of sexual partners sharing their 'children's' rooms: meeting a nubile stranger, dreamy and dishevelled, over a bowl of breakfast cereal can be unnerving for parents when it first happens. And the adjustments can be tricky as parents move from their 'our home/our rules' mind-set to the accommodation of two quite different lifestyles.

The offspring find such adjustments similarly difficult, though they tend to take the initiative: many young adults speak of the need to retrain their parents to be more flexible and more relaxed about the evolving arrangements. Money is sometimes a factor in these negotiations: offspring who pay board may feel in a stronger position than those who make no financial contribution at all, though parents seem increasingly indulgent on this point, especially if part of the reason for their children still living with them into early adulthood is to obtain a financial 'leg-up'.

Eventually they do move out, and then what? Homes that have been geared to the pleasure and comfort of children can suddenly seem very empty when they leave. And since many parents tend to regard their children, even as adults, as the heart and soul of the home – the thing that turned a couple into a family and made their home feel more like 'a real home' – it's easy to understand the wrench they feel.

In *Australians At Home*, empty-nesters consistently spoke of their most immediate practical challenge: what shall we do with the children's rooms? Some can't wait to get their hands on the extra space; some try to preserve their offspring's rooms almost as a kind of shrine; many describe the empty space as being symbolic of the emotional space created by the departure of their children.

Parents' responses are usually influenced by the attitudes of the departing offspring themselves. 'Don't sell the bed!' might be interpreted as a sign of a son's or daughter's uncertainty about a new relationship, but it might also be a sign of emotional attachment to the family home. Either way, it's an injunction unlikely to be ignored by parents.

Our kids were horrified when they found we were planning to redecorate their rooms. They seemed to think they could leave all their stuff here forever. We need to have a serious talk, but it's a rather delicate subject. We don't want them to think we are turning our backs on them.

While our daughter was on her honeymoon, I turned her room into part of the lounge, with an arch. Very nice it is, too.

The transition from family home to empty nest sometimes raises the question of moving and, in particular, downsizing – as if this might be an opportunity to make a real break, a real change, to live as we really want to live. The terms 'sea change' and 'tree change' sometimes enter the conversation at this point, though sanity usually prevails: only the most intrepid decide to uproot their lives to establish themselves in an entirely new and strange community. The most likely result of this period of questioning is a decision to fill the existing space – 'At last we've got the spare room we always wanted' – or to move into something smaller, perhaps within striking distance of the family's stamping ground, or perhaps closer to the city.

In other cases, though, the idea of moving scarcely crosses the minds of parents. Some suspect that their adult children, having been members of the stay-at-home generation, will now join the 'boomerang' generation, expecting to be able to return home at short notice, perhaps including wound-licking stays between relationships. Others simply regard the family home as a familiar, comfortable base for continuing family contacts and, in a high-divorce society, a powerful symbol of the family's stability.

When they come home, they say, 'Don't plan anything – we're just going to veg'. Then they hang around and talk and talk. We love it. It really feels like home again.

The whole place lights up when the children come and stay with us. It seems like the full family home, all over again. The grandchildren have added a completely new dimension to it.

For some parents, rich moments of contact with their returning children only emphasise the emptiness of the house the rest of the time, so downsizing can, paradoxically, be used as a way for parents to protect themselves from that experience. It can also be a way of saying, quite unambiguously, 'You're out of the nest and the nest is no more – this is our home now and you're welcome to visit any time, but there's no spare bed.'

Parental reactions to the departure of their children range from the sentimental to the ruthless, often involving a blend of relief and regret. No generalisations are possible, especially when there may be an extended series of departures and returns, each evoking different emotions from all concerned. But the empty nest is a vivid reminder of the irresistible trajectory of life.

'The TV is like my best friend – isn't that pathetic?'

The internet occupies more and more of our time and, especially for lone householders, often acts like a lifeline of contact with the outside world. It can also be the perfect escape for young people seeking refuge from the emotional intensity of the nuclear family. Yet the shrinking of the Australian household has also enhanced the role of the mainstream mass media in our lives.

Radio – especially talkback – comes closer than any other mass medium to creating the illusion of an intimate personal presence. Since the advent of television, radio has reinvented itself several times, but one of its crucial contemporary functions is to serve as a reliable alternative to real-life companionship for people alone in their cars or homes. The best radio presenters have long since mastered the art of talking as if in a one-to-one relationship with each listener, and listeners often feel a strong personal connection with them. Many radio listeners also enjoy being part of an invisible network – a surrogate community – that feels comfortable, reassuring and familiar to them.

Television, the great tranquilliser, is also taking on the role of companion, especially for lone householders. In The Ipsos Mackay Report, *What We Do with Television* (2003), direct observation of TV viewers revealed their tendency to talk to – or even shout at – the screen when they were watching alone or with an uncommunicative companion:

I wouldn't like to get married in a place like that [Fiji]. Spend your money in your own country, you idiot!

Get a haircut!

Answer the question!

Cheerio, Peter [farewelling a newsreader].

Participants in that study spoke of using television as 'a voice around the house' in precisely the same way as committed radio listeners use radio, and the flickering light of the TV screen is now regarded by many people – lone householders and others – as part of the ambience of their homes.

Like radio, but less intimately, TV is generally seen as a friendly presence – helping us by its inflexible schedules to structure our own day, being as demanding or undemanding as we need it to be, stimulating and soothing us by turns, but always, reliably, there (and never offended if we fall asleep mid-sentence). Lone householders routinely speak of their *relationship* with the medium – and sometimes of their addiction to it, as well – and even of the need to institute rules to regulate their TV-viewing behaviour. None of these things is peculiar to lone householders, but their sense of dependency on radio and TV seems understandably stronger than for members of larger households.

Even for the members of three- or four-person households, though, radio and television – and, of course, the internet – can be critical features of the 'hideouts' where people create their own spaces. Bedrooms, the shed, the den, the kitchen . . . all such places are likely to be furnished with a TV and/or computer, partly as a way of creating a less intrusive, less demanding form of intimacy, and partly to create a wall of sound as effective as any closed door.

Mobile phones, iPods, BlackBerries and all the other paraphernalia of the IT revolution can play their part, but the underlying motivation is always the same: we need to feel connected in ways that can't always be satisfied by our living arrangements. It's tempting to argue that if our various social revolutions had not caused the shrinkage of our households, we would not have become so voracious in our consumption of media – both mass and micro. But the opposite might equally be true: perhaps it is the advent of new electronic wizardry that has facilitated our journey towards a less herd-based domesticity.

PART FOUR

The Dreamy Period

'Relaxed and comfortable' or diminished and
disengaged (or all of the above)?

10

Turning away from The Big Picture

How have Australians been dealing with all these upheavals, all these changes, all this uncertainty? How have they adapted to life in Kaleidoscope Nation?

Some have taken it in their stride, exhilarated by the realisation that they are helping to shape a society in transition.

Some have simply resigned themselves to the idea that nothing stands still and have accepted their changed circumstances – personal and economic – with as much grace as they can muster.

Some have adopted a determinedly stoical attitude to whatever life threw at them – retrenchment, divorce, children still dependent in their twenties, debt, drought . . . to say nothing of the threats of terrorism or global warming. 'You just get on with it – what else can you do?'

Some have been so bewildered or even depressed by the sense that life has spun out of control, they have taken refuge in tranquillisers or antidepressants in an attempt to restore some sense of equilibrium to their lives. (Our consumption of antidepressants has tripled in the past ten years.)

Some – especially distressed or disorientated young people – have sought escape into the virtual world of cyberspace, or by altering their perceptions of reality through drugs, including alcohol: the percentage of risky drinkers has risen from six to 13 percent in the past ten years.

Some have become grumpy, constantly railing against the rate of change and wondering why things couldn't just stay the way they were.

Some have paid more attention to their holidays, or acquired holiday houses, in an attempt to create little cocoons of calm, insulated from the pressures of daily life. 'When we're on holiday we feel more like a family,' say some wistful parents. 'We have more time for each other when we're at the beach house,' say some overstretched couples, struggling to protect their relationships from the ravages of busyness. And a common theme: 'When I'm on holiday, I feel more like the kind of person I want to be.'

Some have taken to travel – regular short breaks, overseas trips, or even cramming onto the fleet of cruise ships plying the South Pacific, perhaps seeking the double whammy of the notorious 'booze cruise'. Some have joined the swelling ranks of the so-called Grey Nomads on the highways of Australia, keeping their distance from the problems, irritations and uncertainties of a society in transition. 'Take me away from all this!' has become an increasingly popular cry; 'keep moving' a neat evasive strategy. Whether for reasons of employment, study or travel, about one million Australians are currently out of the country.

Many have taken refuge in out-and-out materialism, consoling themselves with possessions that seemed to signify security, success and perhaps even stability.

•

Australians have not only been responding to the relentless rate of social, cultural and economic change; they have also, over the past seven years or so, been lulled by the sweet talk of economic prosperity. The mining boom has fuelled a period of spectacular economic growth that has offered many of us the consolation of material comfort and the promise of even more.

A further complicating factor has been the ever-present threat of international terrorism, triggered by the 2001 attack on the World Trade Center and exaggerated, many commentators have suggested, to shore up support for the incumbent government. As the distinguished journalist Peter Hartcher wrote in *Quarterly Essay 25, Bipolar Nation: How to Win the 2007 Election:* 'Howard, the necromancer of our national psyche, conjures our fears to frighten us, and then offers to banish them again to soothe us.' Such 'necromancy' has clearly been effective. Hartcher quotes the former chairman of Newspoll, Sol Lebovic: 'If you go back through the history of polling, the peaks in John Howard's approval rating occurred during the guns incident [following the Port Arthur massacre], the Tampa affair and the terrorist attacks of September 11, the Bali bombing, and the war in Iraq.'

So here was a unique combination of factors influencing Australians' attitudes at the turn of the century: a society in flux, with many questions about 'where this is all taking us' still unanswered; a rising tide of prosperity that allowed us the luxury of self-absorption; a background rumble of anxiety about national security. In response, Australians withdrew into a kind of societal trance; they disengaged from the issues that had been preoccupying them; they shut down or, at least, went into retreat. They entered what now looks like the Dreamy Period, and stayed there for the best part of ten years.

Here's how it happened.

The 1996 federal election produced more than a change of government; it marked the beginning of a gradual but profound change in Australia's mood. That election ended 13 years of turbulent economic and cultural reform with Paul Keating its chief architect, first as treasurer and then as prime minister. He and Bob Hawke had forged a formidable political combination based on Hawke's personal popularity and political instincts and Keating's uncompromising economic and social vision.

The Hawke–Keating Labor governments transformed many Australians' view of themselves and the world. They turned our focus more resolutely towards Asia. They shook up our industries and persuaded us that regulation and protection – in everything from banking to manufacturing – were against our long-term interests. Hawke and Keating were passionate advocates of an open, market-based economy, but they also saw a distinct role for governments in attending to the needs of those who might be disadvantaged by the rate and direction of change, and they supported trade union protection of workers' rights. They built on the work of the Whitlam and Fraser governments in deepening our commitment to multiculturalism, paying more attention to the plight of the poor and marginalised, facing some of the uglier aspects of our past treatment of Indigenous Australians and offering increased support to the arts.

This was a period that inspired and excited many Australians, but it disturbed and distressed others. It bewildered some; it angered some. By the end of it, the electorate had turned on Keating and grown weary of the pace of change. They had lost interest in Keating's 'big picture'. In 1996, facing his second election as prime minister, Keating was predicting that all the promised benefits of such a sustained period of reform and restructure would soon flow to the economy and that boom times were just around the corner. But the electorate's confidence had been shaken by the recession of the early 1990s and by stubbornly high rates of interest and unemployment. The voters were no longer listening.

And there, back on top after years of jousting with Andrew Peacock for the leadership of the Liberal Party, and in from his personal political wilderness, was John Howard. In 1996, he seemed tailor-made for the job of reassuring us, settling us down and steadying the pace of change. With no big vision (indeed, 'vision' was to become a dirty word in Canberra for the next decade) and virtually no policy promises, Howard famously articulated his dream of Australia as a 'relaxed and comfortable' society. It was a killer combination: an unpopular government that had done the hard work of economic reform, an electorate suffering from reform fatigue, and an alternative prime minister with the priceless assets of utter familiarity and an air of stolid dependability, promising what sounded like time-off for good behaviour.

The Howard government, duly elected, got off to a poor start: though the voters had modest expectations of Howard as prime minister, they were nevertheless disappointed. By the end of the new government's first year in office, The Mackay Report, *Mind & Mood* (1997), had detected a perception that it was weak, lacked direction and was beholden to certain business interests. Grand claims for improved standards of ministerial accountability had collapsed in the face of several ministerial resignations, followed by a relaxing of the standards themselves. Howard's attempt to draw a distinction between 'core' and 'non-core' election promises further eroded the hope that this would be a government committed to high ethical standards.

On all three of the key criteria by which Australians judge their leaders – strength, integrity, inspiration – Howard was faring poorly and there was a widespread sense of a leadership vacuum. People were disappointed that in spite of the change of government, unemployment was still high and the job market still uncertain. That 1997 report noted that workers were coming to feel like expendable 'human resources' as they began to acknowledge that the prosperity of business might depend on employing as few of them as possible.

Into this rather bleak atmosphere, Pauline Hanson exploded like a firecracker. Though the vast majority of voters never took her seriously, she unleashed our xenophobia and set it roaring around the nation like a wild dog, and her One Nation party tapped into the feeling that both major parties were out of touch with the hopes, and especially the fears, of 'ordinary Australians'. One Nation attracted almost one million primary votes in the 1998 federal election, more than the Democrats and about the same as the National Party.

The prospect of a goods and services tax (GST) was also on the agenda for that election: it was widely opposed and there was a quiet confidence in the electorate that a hostile Senate would kill it.

Hanson and the GST combined to galvanise voters. The mood was hostile to Howard, but recollections of the reasons for unseating Labor were still too fresh in voters' minds to produce another change of government. Nevertheless, the Coalition suffered a swing against it of five percent and lost 19 seats in the House of Representatives.

In the aftermath of that election, voters seemed disillusioned and dispirited, and the early signs of disengagement began to appear. To quote from The Mackay Report, *Mind & Mood* (1998): 'Australia has become a tougher, less compassionate place than it was a year ago. But Australians are not wringing their hands over this: they are looking for ways to insulate themselves from troubling items on the national agenda, and so the focus turns inward.'

The signs of disengagement became more pronounced in reactions to the 1999 referendum on the republic. For most voters, the referendum was practically a non-event: the one thing they wanted – direct election of an Australian head of state – wasn't on offer and they were, in any case, already drifting towards the Dreamy Period. Apathy, confusion and uncertainty, combined with a hostile prime minister and disagreement among the experts, ensured the referendum's defeat.

By then, we were being distracted by the pull of the millennium and, at least in Sydney, the prospect of the 2000 Olympics. Our optimism was rising, but it had nothing to do with politics. Throughout 1999, The Mackay Report was documenting an increasing tendency to disengage from the national agenda and to shrug off the big questions: 'What will be, will be' was becoming our mantra.

You have to make time for yourself. I get up at 6.30 in the morning to watch taped episodes of Days of Our Lives. *It's beautiful. I sit there on my own before the kids get up, and have the first cigarette of the day.*

The key issue: control

By the late 1990s, Australians knew there were many issues still to be addressed – globalisation, Aboriginal reconciliation, youth unemployment, the republic, tax reform, the drug trade, foreign investment, population policy – but it was all starting to seem too much. Too hard. Too daunting.

Too many of these issues seemed beyond their control. Here's a participant in a research project, describing the feeling that, through the 1990s, had led many Australians to yearn for a bit less excitement:

You feel as if you're on a runaway train, speeding out of control. You're too scared to jump off because you know you'll be left behind, so you hang on. But you have no idea where this is taking you.

A sense of powerlessness was beginning to affect the national mood. In 1998, voters had not wanted a GST and thought they had installed a Senate that would vote it down, only to find the Democrats were prepared to support it. (That, incidentally, was the beginning of the end for the Democrats.) Many were shocked to discover that something so unpopular could actually happen.

There were other signs of a mood shift. The subject of Aboriginal reconciliation, for instance, had become confused with the idea that the Aboriginal problem was intractable. Even if they wanted to achieve some form of reconciliation with Indigenous people – or, on a larger scale, tackle the problems of Aboriginal health and welfare – most Australians had no idea how to do it. With the arrival of the Howard government, the issue went conveniently off the boil and became lost in the rhetoric of 'practical reconciliation'. By the early years of the new century, non-Indigenous Australians generally appeared to have lost interest in the whole subject and those who were continuing to promote a national Sorry Day found themselves fighting a losing battle against public indifference. The Aboriginal and Torres Strait Islander Commission (ATSIC) was gone, and there was no longer a clear focus for any lingering concern about Aboriginal issues.

Globalisation was being recognised as a serious challenge, and quite possibly a threat, to many Australian industries and therefore to many Australian jobs. But what could individuals do about it? The evidence of the previous 20 years suggested that inexorable economic forces would exert pressure on the Australian economy, and there seemed little anyone – especially employees – could do to resist it.

The 2001 terrorist attack on New York's World Trade Center and the Pentagon in Washington added to the general climate of insecurity in Australia and created a brief flurry of fear. But the main message was, again, that big events were unfolding on the world stage and we were powerless to do anything about them. Although the federal government tried to orchestrate (and perhaps even to maintain) our fears with its injunction to 'be alert but not alarmed', the events of 9/11 gave us further encouragement to pursue the 'relaxed and comfortable' goal: after all, the easiest way of dealing with a difficult and demanding agenda is to disengage from it and, by the early years of the 21st century, we were mastering the art of the switch-off, aided by the reassuring news of a resources boom that would power our economy for years to come.

When it was proposed that Australian military forces should participate in the invasion of Iraq in 2003, the vast majority of Australians – around 75 percent – opposed it. But the invasion went ahead with Australian troops involved and, once again, we simply shrugged and said, 'It doesn't really matter what we think – all the demonstrations and protests counted for nothing.' Three weeks after the invasion, when US President George W. Bush was claiming victory (a claim that seemed increasingly hollow during the following years of bloody occupation), opposition to the war appeared to have collapsed and Newspoll was registering roughly a 50–50 split between pro- and anti-war attitudes.

Rather than reflecting a sudden and dramatic change of heart, those figures suggested something else: that people were simply losing interest; switching off; no longer taking a strong position either way. Even while we were futilely opposing the war (a symbol of our powerlessness), we were giving higher than ever approval ratings to the prime minister who led us into it ('*he's* in control'). The Mackay Report, *Mind & Mood* (2003), analysed the shifting attitudes to the invasion of Iraq and noted that the level of background anxiety had been raised by the sense that Australia might now be a more logical target for terrorism. That report also explored the reasons for the apparent inconsistency implied by such strong support for John Howard:

> Although the majority of Australians were opposed to the war, Howard's personal popularity has continued to soar – partly because people want to support their leader at a time of crisis and uncertainty, but mainly because their sense of confusion can be most easily resolved through that one simple commitment. In contrast to the complexity of the situation, support for the leader is a straightforward position.

Incidentally, that report noted a growing appreciation of commercial advertising, partly as a mildly therapeutic escape from bad news, and partly because advertising seemed more trustworthy than news of the invasion: 'At least we know what advertisers are up to – their motives are transparent and if they mislead us, we can stop buying their products.' The media, by contrast, were being seen as less transparent and more at the mercy of spin doctors and propagandists:

the idea of journalists being 'embedded' in US combat units raised serious questions in some viewers' minds about impartiality and objectivity.

Revelations about the US's use of torture in secret prisons around the world and photos documenting the humiliation of Iraqi prisoners by American soldiers in the US prison at Abu Ghraib suggested that not all the news is sanitised, after all. We were briefly shocked – the way we're shocked by news of a plane crash – but we had the comfort of knowing 'it wasn't us'. Our faith in America, such as it is, was tarnished by a weary sense of despair about the Bush administration and, among cynics, a reinforcement of existing convictions about the arrogance of US foreign policy and the murkiness of CIA operations.

Later, when the UK and US electorates turned in fury on their political leaders, Tony Blair and George W. Bush, John Howard received no comparable grilling over Iraq from the Australian electorate, nor from the mass media. Why the difference? Some commentators suggested it was simply because there were relatively few Australians deployed in Iraq and, at that time, no casualties. A further explanation might be that neither the UK nor the US was having a Dreamy Period, but we were. Iraq was not making us angry because we had moved beyond the reach of anger.

The same explanation appears to account for the generally low level of reaction to grim news about Australia's treatment of asylum-seekers, to stories of gross maladministration within the Department of Immigration, to the excision of certain Australian islands from Australia in order to create an immigration exclusion zone, and to the so-called Pacific Solution for moving asylum-seekers to other countries, especially Nauru. Even the news that this strategy was costing Australia more money than the maintenance of our own detention centres failed to arouse much interest.

This is human psychology at its most transparent: we want to feel better about ourselves, so we try to ignore or make light of things that might make us feel worse. When our situation feels *generally* stable, settled and positive, we can deal more easily with bits of bad news. But when *all* the news seems to be bad, we insulate ourselves by becoming disengaged from it.

When new anti-terror legislation was proposed, we again paid scant attention to its implications, even though the civil libertarians were trying to engage our attention and the writer Frank Moorhouse, among others, was persuasively arguing (in *The Griffith Review* of November 2006 and elsewhere) that the sedition provisions of the new anti-terror laws were a disturbing symptom of a repressive and authoritarian mind-set. This might all have had the potential to provoke passionate and even angry debate at other times in our social and political history, but in the Dreamy Period the topic was perhaps too alarming or too 'big' for us to deal with, so we insulated ourselves from it by disengaging. When a community is in this kind of mood, governments can expect weaker opposition than usual, even to legislation that might, at other times, strike voters as draconian or at least debatable. Indeed, for many people trying to come to terms with their sense of uncertainty, the more draconian the better, as we'll see later.

When the Work Choices industrial relations laws were introduced in 2006, there was outrage from the Opposition and from the trade union movement who assumed that this was mainly about breaking the power of the unions. But from the community at large? Although opinion poll data suggested that the Work Choices legislation was deeply unpopular, The Ipsos Mackay Report, *Australians At Work* (2006), reported a rather muted, acquiescent initial response.

Even news suggesting the federal government might have deceived us generally failed to arouse much passion in the community, as we moved through the early years of the new century and entered more deeply into the Dreamy Period. Having accepted that they were lied to before the 2001 election, when it was falsely claimed by government ministers that refugees were throwing their children overboard from a sinking fishing boat, voters resigned themselves to the idea that 'they all lie'. Far from being angry about this, they were inclined to shrug. (Of course, some *were* angry: the Dreamy Period was by no means a universal phenomenon, but it had a noticeably anaesthetic effect on the majority.) Three years later, when the Opposition tried to revive interest in the issue, the voters had moved on: the lie was no longer news; it was no longer interesting.

Again, when it was revealed that AWB (the former Australian Wheat Board) had paid an estimated $300 million in 'kickbacks' (i.e., bribes) to the regime of Saddam Hussein in Iraq, in defiance of the conditions of the United Nations' oil-for-food program, the general reaction of Australians was to assume that foreign minister Alexander Downer and trade minister Mark Vaile (and quite possibly the prime minister as well) knew what was going on but chose to turn a blind eye to it. And the electorate's reaction? Subdued, to say the least. People seemed generally to interpret the ministers' denials as yet further evidence for the proposition that all politicians tell lies; their respect for politicians (and for those ministers, in particular) may have been further diminished, but they remained generally disengaged from the deeper issue. When the Opposition foreign affairs spokesman, Kevin Rudd, explicitly accused the prime minister of lying over the AWB scandal, the reaction was one of general agreement but some amazement that Rudd was so worked up about it: 'Of course they knew – now, what's for dinner?'

When a further charge of lying was levelled at John Howard by his own deputy, Peter Costello, over an alleged agreement between them for Costello to succeed Howard as leader, the voters were again largely unmoved. While they assumed Howard had indeed lied over the matter (which only confirmed their existing belief that he, like many politicians, would try to lie his way out of a jam), they were also amused, reading the entire incident as yet another example of Howard's wiliness: he was seen to have outmanoeuvred his deputy in a way that left Costello nowhere to hide from his humiliation.

Such relatively benign reactions were a sign of our disengagement from politics, but they also reflected a widespread sense of powerlessness associated with the belief at that time that the re-election of the Coalition government was a foregone conclusion. Although Labor was ahead in the polls, Kim Beazley was still struggling to assert his authority in voters' minds and there was almost no support for the idea that the polls were actually pointing to a Labor victory in 2007. From the voters' point of view, therefore, there didn't seem much point in getting too angry – or even too interested – in things they could neither control nor change.

Disengagement is easy to confuse with apathy, but it's a quite different thing. In the Dreamy Period, we might have been turning our backs on political and social issues that had the potential to darken our mood, but we were not apathetic: we had simply shifted our focus from the big picture to the miniatures of our own lives. The issue was *control*. When so many issues seemed beyond our control, we began to concentrate instead on the things we could control, and there were plenty of contenders.

We could control our home renovations, which is why we became obsessed with renovations during this period (see Chapter 11). And not just interior renovations: backyards, too, became the focus of new attention as a symbol of our emerging 'backyard mentality'. An elaborate barbecue, a new garden, space for backyard activities, a swimming pool, children's play equipment . . . all these things became the focus of keen attention, because they represented ways we could take control of our own environment.

We could control what school our children would attend, where we would go for our holidays, what we would do on the weekend. We might have lost interest in the Iraq war, but we might be able to agitate for a new pedestrian crossing at the local shops.

We could also take control of our bodies. It is no accident that the fitness craze, the tattoo craze, the body-piercing craze and the cosmetic surgery craze all coincided with the period of disengagement from 'out there' issues and an increasingly narrow, inward and self-indulgent focus. The HILDA research project mentioned in Chapter 4 has reported that, in 2006, the most important thing in the lives of the under-thirties was keeping fit – ahead of education and even ahead of friends. The idea in some upper-middle-class social circles that breast implants might be an acceptable eighteenth or twenty-first birthday gift is perhaps an indication of just how self-absorbed (and, in that socio-economic stratum, how wealthy) we had become.

The home security industry also boomed through the Dreamy Period. Again, the offer was symbolically compelling: we could control our own lives by locking everybody else out and keeping trouble at bay. Our political leaders may believe that national security is at the top of everyone's agenda, but what that means is open to interpretation: the top agenda item, for most Australians, seemed to be 'How can I *avoid* worrying about national security – or national anything? How can I distract myself from all this dark stuff?'

Dead giveaways: viewing and voting

If you're looking for more evidence of the Dreamy Period, look no further than the TV viewing and voting habits of Australians over the past seven or eight years.

This was the era when lifestyle programs came from nowhere to rate their socks off. Around the turn of the century, TV programs like *Burke's Backyard, Backyard Blitz, Better Homes & Gardens, Room for Improvement, The Block* and *Renovation Rescue* showed just how astute TV executives really are: such programs were a projection of what was going on inside our heads. During this period, news and current affairs programs all but dropped out of the Top Ten ratings lists. When we opened our newspapers, similarly, we were more interested in the lifestyle supplements than the headlines.

If it wasn't backyards and renovations, then it was the hermetically closed world of *Big Brother* or the dream of escape to a *SeaChange* hideaway – a little community where life was trapped in a time warp. In each case, the drive was the same: help me keep my mind off what's going on 'out there'; keep me distracted; keep the horizon as close as possible. *Think small* was the aim. As the journalist David Dale has pointed out, this was also the period when we wanted our TV drama to come to us in small, digestible portions. The serial, with its more demanding ambiguities and prolonged tensions, went out of favour and series that consisted of self-contained episodes *(CSI, Law & Order)* were preferred.

An even more revealing story emerges from examination of our voting behaviour. Between 2002 and 2007, every incumbent government – federal, state and territory – was returned to office, in almost every case with an increased majority.

Every incumbent government returned, regardless of its political colour? Did that mean we had arrived at the golden age of political contentment? Yes, it was true that John Howard's shaky start had been all but forgotten as he grew into the job and consolidated his position as a political institution in his own right, increasing his majority in 2001 and again in 2004. Yes, the various state premiers and territory chief ministers were generally well regarded by their constituents. Yes, Opposition leaders around the country seemed to the voters to be an unimpressive, uninspiring lot.

Yet interest in politics was low and falling, and so was our esteem for politicians. Our hearts did not swell with pride when we contemplated their parliamentary behaviour. We were not particularly trusting of governments; not particularly disposed to believe them; uneasy about their capacity for slick and slippery spin. A golden age it was not.

But we kept re-electing them. And the reason was captured by the respondent in one of my surveys who said, on the eve of the 2004 federal election campaign: 'Wake me when it's over, will you?'

Incumbency is always an advantage in Australian politics, especially for federal governments, and the Dreamy Period invested incumbency with even more potency than usual. This has been a period when the electorate has not only resisted change; it has wanted to be left in peace. Voters just wanted to get on with their home renovations and backyard cricket or boules, content in the belief that nothing too radical was going to happen. People still recovering from the queasiness of too much boat-rocking didn't want to rock any more boats. Still feeling powerless and believing the world had become a more hazardous place, they were keen to maintain the status quo. Steady as she goes, please.

To be fair, there was a less dreamy, more hard-nosed factor operating here as well. With a Coalition government entrenched federally, voters quite liked the idea of keeping some tension in the system by re-electing Labor governments in all states and territories. When the Coalition was replaced by Labor federally in 2007, that signalled the likely fall of several state Labor governments, especially in New South Wales where there is a well-established history of voters preferring to have different parties in power in Macquarie Street and Canberra.

If we are in the process of emerging from the Dreamy Period, as suggested in Chapters 15 and 16, no incumbent government will feel as secure as it did during these past several years. Voters who are wide awake tend to notice things that would have passed them by when they were curled up in little cocoons of self-absorption.

The dark side: less tolerance, less compassion, more prejudice

When people are trying to insulate themselves from unwelcome or threatening news, the inward focus is an effective strategy. When so much news seems bad, we look inside ourselves, into our families and into our backyards – but not much further – for encouragement.

We need to know that 'we're okay', regardless of what might be happening beyond the back fence. As a result, we tend to become more insular. We're less sympathetic towards those who seem different from us. In these circumstances, our famous tolerance – our legendary commitment to the 'fair go' – takes a bit of a hammering.

In July 2001, The Mackay Report, *Mind & Mood*, was recording a significant hardening of Australians' attitudes toward Asian and Lebanese migration and, in particular, towards asylum-seekers:

> Just below the surface, there is a high degree of anxiety about Asian immigration, about the idea that Australia's culture is being changed in unexpected ways, and that recent [Lebanese] immigrants are associated with unacceptable increases in crime and violence. Refugees previously described as 'boat people' are now routinely described as 'illegals'.

Though many people were shocked by media exposure of some details about the treatment of 'illegals' in detention centres such as Baxter in South Australia, they soon learned to switch off. In the same way as white Australians are typically unable to face some of the most brutal realities about the plight of many Indigenous Australians, for fear of having to accept some responsibility, we seemed equally unwilling to engage with the implications of the fact that, as a nation, we were treating asylum-seekers more harshly than criminals, simply for having bypassed the normal channels of refugee processing.

The 2001 *Mind & Mood* report documented some of the factors leading us to take refuge in the self-absorption and sense of denial characteristic of the Dreamy Period: we believed the world was becoming a nastier place, and that politicians and other authority figures and institutions – including the church, the media, the banks and even professional cricket (rocked by match-fixing scandals) – were becoming less trustworthy.

You always lock your car at the servo these days.

That comment from a participant in the *Mind & Mood* study identified one small symptom of what many Australians were coming to think of as a deepening malaise: a society in which declining respect for authority was matched by a growing mistrust in the community at large. Even the normal courtesies and decencies of everyday life were thought to be in decline, as part of a general retreat from accepted community values.

When my mother had to be put into a nursing home, a friend warned me to take her engagement ring off and keep it at home. I didn't have the heart to do that and, sure enough, within a week it had gone. It's the staff – they're migrants who don't have the same values as ours.

More stress, more drugs, more crime (the perception typically greater than the reality), too much naked materialism and an accelerating pace of life . . . at the very dawn of the new millennium, these were the issues that caused many Australians to feel disappointment or even despair at the direction their society was taking.

Not surprisingly, they wanted to blame someone, and immigrants – whether of the conventional kind or refugees, especially 'illegals' – were once again the target. The 2001 *Mind & Mood* report:

There is a widespread view that people who have arrived illegally . . . are likely to *behave* illegally once here. Some of the famous Australian tolerance is strained when the subject of 'illegal immigrants' arises. Indeed, some of the most ugly and vicious outpourings of hatred occurred in discussion of boat people/illegal immigrants.

That report also noted that passions aroused by fear of illegal immigration and of Australia being 'swamped' by Asians were so strong, they had the potential to overwhelm factors like the GST in the 2001 federal election campaign. That indeed turned out to be the case: the election result turned on the question of border control. The infamous *Tampa* episode was the clincher for the government. (The story of a Danish sea captain rescuing refugees from a sinking fishing boat, and the Australian navy eventually taking them to Nauru, is fully documented by David Marr and Marian Wilkinson in their 2003 book, *Dark Victory*.)

The 2001 election produced two critical signs of the emerging Dreamy Period. First, in spite of the refugee debate and lingering hostility to the GST, it was a lacklustre affair:

Let's talk about politics. Oh no, it's too boring... Well, I quite like little Johnny Howard – people say he's decent... Who's that fat bloke?... Oh, that's John Beazley... No, I don't think it's John. It might be Tim... Actually, it's Kim Beazley.

That was a snippet of conversation among a group of bright, articulate young mothers in an outer-western suburb of Sydney. Though some conversations about politics in that study were more focused, the general tendency was to avoid the subject:

There hasn't been a lot of political talk in the office of late – surprising, with an election coming up.

259

(Incidentally, a group of quite sophisticated young people in Melbourne, participating in a similar project for Ipsos in 2007, struggled to recall which party John Howard represented, concluding that ALP must stand for 'Australian Liberal Party'. Many voters are less passionate and less knowledgeable about contemporary politics than politicians and journalists might imagine.)

Another noticeable effect of the 2001 election campaign was that from then on, people seemed less inhibited in their expression of prejudice – not just against asylum-seekers, but against any of the favourite targets of community intolerance. It was almost as if there had been official backing for prejudice against a particular group – 'illegals' – and so the dominoes inevitably fell: Asians reported being spat on in the street; Muslim women reported having abuse shouted at them. Aborigines became the target for a fresh round of racist abuse and vile jokes. Lebanese were lumped together in one group – the classic technique of racism – and subjected to widespread contempt, especially in Sydney (where, ironically, the respected and much-loved New South Wales Governor, Professor Marie Bashir, is herself Lebanese). 'The truth is, Lebanese just tend to be criminals,' said one of my Sydney research respondents, without hesitation and without demur from any of his friends taking part in that discussion.

These effects were characteristic of a period marked by declining levels of tolerance and compassion. In the early years of the century, most of the major charities experienced a decline in fundraising income – another symptom of our inward focus.

By 2005, the *Mind & Mood* report had identified a hardening of these attitudes, an increased edginess and a feeling of greater personal vulnerability. The process of insulating ourselves from 'issues' by focusing on more personal, local, immediate concerns was also well advanced by then:

> *I know a lot of people are doing it tough but, to be frank, we're doing quite well. Our kids are at good schools and they will get good jobs. I guess that's just the way it is.*

> *When I watch* Desperate Housewives *I feel like I'm Lynette, but with one child. When she lost it and dumped the kids, I cried for her. I was having a sleep-deprived week, too.*

Some of the racial and religious prejudice so evident during this period was heightened by media reports – in particular, a Sydney rape case involving Lebanese-Australian men, riots at Sydney's Cronulla beach, and cases of Muslim clerics appearing to foment anti-Australian sentiment. But the underlying cause was that at a time like this, when we were dealing with our anxieties and insecurities by turning inwards, we were also more likely to yield to the natural human inclination to resist engagement with 'otherness'.

There's not much point in beating our breasts about the existence of racism in Australian culture. Even more pointless would be any attempt to suggest it isn't there. We are all 'natural' racists because that's the way humans are when confronted by ethnic, cultural or religious groups that seem to challenge our own beliefs, values and practices. Fifteen years ago, when we were more engaged with political and social issues, we were better at keeping such tendencies on the leash. In the Dreamy Period, we let them loose, as a way of keeping our own fears and insecurities at bay.

> *I'm not a racist in any way, shape or form and I don't object to taking refugees. But the minute they play up, they should be sent home.*

They are saying, in effect, 'fuck you' – they have come here illegally and they will do what they like. They are arrogant. There is virtually a race war going on in Sydney between illegal Asian immigrants and the rest of us.

Turn the boats back, is what I say. They come here and stir up their own hatreds.

11

The quest for the perfect bathroom tile

When we narrow the focus and turn it inwards, we can find plenty to engage us and plenty to enjoy. Best of all, life in suburban Australia can seem utterly remote – safely remote, pleasantly remote – from the big, bad world.

Sometimes when I watch the news on TV, it all just seems to be about another world from mine.

Seeing all those images on TV, you think, 'How lucky am I we live here and we're not being bombarded every day, and that's not my child in the hospital.' Everyone here can get on with their daily lives. You can worry about what you're going to eat for dinner tonight and what have we got on this week. Life hasn't really changed – we are still able to buy whatever we want.

The 2003 *Mind & Mood* summarised the mood like this:

Feeling overwhelmed by 'the big picture', [Australians] have shifted their gaze to something smaller and more manageable. In response to tensions created by the invasion of Iraq, this sense of

263

disengagement has actually increased: we are more anxious than ever to escape to the normality and simplicity of everyday life.

Social change might destabilise us; international terrorism might frighten us; more Muslims in our midst might alarm us; the latest wave of immigrants might irritate or threaten us; the prospect of economic uncertainty, lurking even at a time of prosperity and growth, might unnerve us ... but the domestic environment is one place where we can find solace, comfort and a measure of control. There are unhappy homes, of course, and there are busy, bustling homes where peace is hard to find. But when we feel *comfortable* at home – free to be ourselves and to impose our own personalities on the style and atmosphere of our homes – that's about as close to feeling in control as most of us ever get.

In the depths of the Dreamy Period, we were in the mood to embrace our domesticity and to celebrate the idea of ordinariness. The routines of daily life reminded us that Australia is a peaceful country, a reasonably harmonious society and a relatively prosperous place to live. It is almost universally judged to be a great place to raise a family.

The early-century retreat into domesticity has been most powerfully symbolised by our obsession with home renovations. The quest for the perfect bathroom tile can become so engrossing, so distracting and so all-consuming that larger questions – Does our government lie to us? Do we have enough to retire on? Should Australian troops be in Iraq? – can't get a look-in. As suggested in Part One, renovations are a vote for the future, but they are also a vote for the here and now. Nothing locks a householder into the moment like the disruptions and decisions involved in a major renovation: How do I know whether that colour will work until I've seen it on the wall? Where's the plumber? He was supposed to be here at seven-thirty and it's past nine. Look at that – we measured it all so carefully and now the new fridge won't fit in the space.

Impossible to ignore, the renovation process narrows our focus and brings our horizon up close. Like studying for an exam, we go through short, intense periods of knowing all there is to know about wool-blend carpets, sash windows, stone pavers and retractable awnings. We briefly master the dishwasher market, the argument in favour of a double-oven kitchen and the competing claims of chlorine and saltwater pools.

And then the moment passes.

When the renovations are over, 'normality' beckons with its promise of peaceful, reassuring, satisfying routines and rituals. The 2003 *Mind & Mood* report – based on unstructured, unprompted discussion of 'whatever you've been thinking about or talking about in the past few weeks' – described participants going through the dutiful process of discussing the Iraq war, but reserving their most lively and passionate discussions for families, houses and gardens, and the life of the local community. When the conversation turned to offspring, the dynamics of the discussions were transformed, as if this were the moment everyone had been waiting for.

My child was born at the exact moment the deadline for Saddam Hussein to be expelled was up. I've tried to tune out of all that. There's nothing but negatives out there at the moment, but I've just had the most positive experience of my life.

I'm always thinking about my teenagers – driving licences and staying out late are the big things now. I'm still trying to understand their language. 'Going out' doesn't mean actually going out – it means 'he's interested in me'. And 'making out' means kissing…

Oh, yeah? [says a friend, in response] *Who do you think you're kidding?*

Weekends, holidays, cooking, cleaning, eating out, cars, sport, pets, choice of schools, gardening … these are the normal topics of suburban conversation but, in the Dreamy Period, they have also become a strategy for keeping 'the big picture' out of focus. In 2006, symbolically, Australia's No. 1 bestseller was *Spotless,* a book of household cleaning hints. Heavy emphasis on the home, as both cocoon and fortress, became a new, central theme in social research.

In 2004, the *Mind & Mood* report repeated the theme: it described the backyard as the great symbol of Australian security, comfort and control – almost like a private 'village green' for family and friends – and the backyard barbecue not as a platform for passionate debate, as it had sometimes been in the past, but as the Australian way of keeping the world at bay. The emphasis was relentlessly on the personal and the local:

I think we are very lucky to live where we live and how we live. There are lots of little local issues – like when I am going to get the netball newsletter out this week – but really, I look at our family and I think life is pretty good.

'Switch off; shut down; curl up' said one of the chapter headings in that 2004 report, distilling the essence of a period marked by a revival of interest in gardening, pets, sport … and shopping. The term 'retail therapy' gained widespread currency at this time, in self-parodying reference to consumers' realisation that they were, indeed, using shopping as a means of escape from matters that might otherwise invade their space, disturbing or even frightening them. The retail environment has become one of the most powerful symbols of the desire for normality: *Whenever I go shopping it makes me realise that life goes on.* The buzz of a retail environment, like the hiss of an espresso coffee machine, became one of the soundtracks of life in the Dreamy Period.

Reflecting on the results of the New South Wales state election of 2007, columnist and broadcaster Phillip Adams captured the mood perfectly in *The Australian* of 27 March: 'I got the feeling that most voters didn't want to know about climate change. It's too depressing, so let's go shopping. The weather's always perfect in a mall.'

Some commentators have identified this as a time of *dumbing down* in Australian life: the dumbing down of politics, thanks to the sound bite and the spin doctor; the dumbing down of business, courtesy of a new wave of management jargon (as documented in Don Watson's *Death Sentence* and Shelley Gare's *Triumph of the Airheads*); the dumbing down of literature, as reflected in our taste for ever lighter and less demanding novels; the dumbing down of the media, including the once-vaunted SBS television now with commercial breaks and game shows, and the industry-wide drift towards 'soft' stories on current affairs programs; even the dumbing down of the classroom, according to some educationalists concerned by the emphasis on 'outcomes-based' curricula (see Kevin Donnelly's *Dumbing Down*).

The retreat into domesticity is also partly based on a dreamy vision of 'the simple life'. Bewildered by the rate of change and daunted by the issues facing Australia and the world, many Australians love flirting with the idea that it's time to restore their faith in 'simple pleasures': spending more time with partners and children and more time simply being *at home*, being content to 'veg out' in front of the TV, eating out with friends, enjoying *slow* food, taking the kids camping, walking the dog, spending more time in the garden, going on a cycling holiday in France . . . everyone has their own definition of simple pleasures. Some sound simpler than others, and some visions sound more like fantasies than plans, but the underlying motivation is clear: let's get away from it all.

'Laughter is the best medicine' has found its way from the *Reader's Digest* into contemporary folklore. Being able to make each other laugh is often taken to be the mark of real friendship, and laughter is widely regarded as the simplest and most pleasurable of all the simple pleasures: enjoyable in itself, therapeutic, and symbolic of people who are not taking life or themselves too seriously – people who are, in short, 'relaxed and comfortable'. The advice said to have been given to some cancer patients to watch movies that make them laugh has been adopted as a general prescription for a society still suffering from an epidemic of anxiety and still learning how to deal with it.

All the classic forms of media escapism beckon even more appealingly when we are struggling to keep the demons at bay: comedy, romance, crime-drama (good for tension release) and even 'trash':

> *We've been getting all heavy about whether we can believe what the news programs tell us about the war, then we flip open a copy of* New Idea *or* Woman's Day *and you know you can't believe half the stuff, but you lap it up. It's good for a laugh, I suppose . . . trashy is our release.*

12

Yearning for magic simplicities

Our yearning for control didn't only drive us into our own backyards, literally or metaphorically; it led some of us to look for things in the wider community – troublesome teenagers, dodgy corporations, offensive TV programs, irresponsible dog-walkers – that might also be brought under tighter control. The same yearning also encouraged many of us to fall for the reassuring simplicity of black-and-white certainty wherever we thought it might be on offer, from economics to religion.

Although much has been made of 'the politics of fear' in explaining the ascendancy of the Howard government (and, indeed, the Dreamy Period itself), there are two quite different kinds of fear and the difference is important in explaining some apparent contradictions in contemporary attitudes. If we're in shutdown mode, for instance, how come we're so gung-ho about law and order? If we're supposed to have disengaged from the big-picture stuff, why have so many of us flocked to churches around the country?

First, there's *inhibitory* fear that paralyses us into inaction. It inhibits our capacity to react or respond because it is evoked by a threat that seems completely beyond our control. Scared out of our wits, we lose the alertness, and sometimes even the desire, required to deal with the threat. So we try to ignore it.

That's the kind of fear evoked by the vague threat of a terrorist attack. The enemy can't be identified and the attack could come anywhere, any time. It's too big a threat, too mysterious and too unmanageable. So we don't try to manage it; we either give up entirely, curling up into a small ball of blind panic, or carry on as if nothing has happened, or distract ourselves by concentrating on something else entirely. It's the same kind of fear experienced by nervous passengers when an aircraft encounters severe turbulence.

It's also the kind of fear evoked by shock-horror road safety advertising and other propaganda designed to frighten us by presenting us with a dreadful possibility, but with insufficient advice about how to avoid it – 'be alert but not alarmed' a classic example. Too hard to handle; too easy to switch off.

Anticipatory fear, by contrast, results from a threat that seems more manageable – a nasty possibility we might be able to avoid. It's still fear of a threat heading our way, but it offers the possibility of evasive action.

Medical practitioners frightening us with bad news about our health can avoid the switch-off induced by inhibitory fear if they quickly focus our attention on the action we can take to avert some potential medical disaster. As long as the fear is accompanied by the knowledge of what to do to avoid the threat, we can deal with it. It's a warning, perhaps even an ultimatum, rather than the clanging gong of inevitable doom.

The Dreamy Period has produced both kinds of fear. There's the inhibitory fear produced by a sense that things are out of control, the world is becoming a dangerous place, and the individual is powerless. That heightens our anxiety and leads us into escapism and denial – to lose interest in politics, or in questions of social justice, for instance.

But there's some anticipatory fear at work, too. When we think society is becoming more violent, or the crime rate is out of control, or young people need straightening out, we may experience some inhibition, but we're also on the lookout for a strategy to tackle the problem. This is why, as a society, we have ignored some big issues but engaged with others – for example, by our support for a more rigid approach to the sentencing of criminals, with mandatory sentencing prescriptions imposed on judges by governments that realise the community will applaud that kind of toughness.

In their quest for things they *can* control, insecure and anxious people will occasionally look beyond the renovations and the backyard into a society they think would benefit from having more rules, more regulations, more laws, all designed to get things back under control. In other words, people who are feeling insecure yearn for security; people who are feeling edgy and uncertain yearn for certainty. People who are experiencing anticipatory fear may regard tougher legislation as an appropriate form of evasive action.

This trend did not begin with the Dreamy Period, of course. The early signs of an overregulation mentality were described in *Reinventing Australia* (1993): as the tide of anxiety rose, the tendency to regulate society – though not the economy – rose with it.

That tendency has increased and history suggests we may already be overdoing it. Too much regulation usually turns out to be counterproductive in the long run: people who come to feel overregulated will finally rebel at the loss of too many freedoms, though the undoing of regulations is more difficult than the imposing of them. Kids who are bound by too many regulations tend to become loophole specialists ('if it's not actually on the prohibited list, it must be okay'). When tax law becomes too complicated, the lawyers who are best equipped to find ways through and around it are in heavy demand. And Frank Moorhouse has predicted that the sedition provisions of the anti-terror laws will actually provoke more acts of sedition as writers and performers, in particular, react to 'bureaucratic bullying' and mock the excesses of the legislation through satire that deliberately tests the boundaries.

The most serious danger of overregulation as a response to our fear of a degraded society is that it removes many areas of personal responsibility from the moral realm and puts them into the domain of black-letter law. We have less interest in the concept of 'right and wrong' and more interest in 'legal or illegal'. When people insist we should be tougher on this or that aspect of society, they can easily overlook the possibility that too many regulations will stifle our consciences rather than quicken them. Whether it's tougher dog-walking laws, anti-vilification laws, or a ban on TV advertising of 'junk food' until after children have gone to bed, the hazard is the same: by making it appear as if we have solved the problem through regulation, we ease the burden of personal moral responsibility. 'If there are environmentally insensitive products on the supermarket shelf, they should be banned!' said a woman in a research project some years ago. Translation: if they are banned, I won't be tempted to buy them; I won't have to exercise any moral discretion.

Some of those who call for more censorship of the media, similarly, seem to forget that our moral development relies on having the freedom to choose badly – including the freedom to choose what we will watch or read, and the freedom to discover how dreadful some material is. (I am not an opponent of censorship, by the way, especially for the protection of children, but I do oppose the resort to censorship as a substitute for the encouragement of greater personal responsibility.)

While it's true that misbehaviour is disappointing, or worse, there's little evidence that increased regulation will fix the problem: in many corporate boardrooms, the plethora of new regulations has generated a preoccupation with ways of concealing information from corporate regulators.

The fashion for corporate codes of practice is another symptom of the desire to codify, to control and, in the process, to reduce the burden of responsibility on individuals to think about the moral implications of their actions. (Of course, the framers of those codes will tell you their intention is the very opposite.)

Prohibition has proved historically to be a remarkably ineffective strategy against the consumption of alcohol, drugs, pornography, gambling or any other potentially harmful products or services. Nevertheless, as mentioned in Part One, the federal government's sudden and dramatic intervention in the management of a child-abuse epidemic in Northern Territory Aboriginal communities included a number of proposals based on precisely such prohibitions. The government's approach gained widespread support from the electorate – and, in principle, from the Opposition – partly because it seemed strong and decisive but partly also because it appealed to the desire for simplicity: 'The problem is child abuse? Get more police! Bring in the army!' Such an approach carries the danger of confusing the symptom with the disease. Although alcohol and pornography are likely contributors to the problem, they are themselves symptoms of deeper and more complex cultural and social factors, requiring careful and sensitive consultation, negotiation and resolution. 'Get more teachers, nurses and social workers!' might be a more helpful cry in the long run. But a full-frontal, legalistic attack on the symptom sounds seductively like 'the answer'.

One of the things that drove us into the Dreamy Period was the uneasy feeling that we could no longer trust each other – in business, in politics, in the church, in the neighbourhood – as we once did. That's why we've been placing more emphasis on rights, rather than responsibilities: if I don't feel I can trust my employer or my neighbour as I once did, I'll be inclined to resort to a legalistic approach to problems or disputes, and to rely on the idea that the law will redress any wrongs, and insurance – theirs or mine – will pay for the damage.

In this climate, regulatory authorities like the Australian Securities and Investments Commission (ASIC) and the Australian Competition and Consumer Commission (ACCC) acquire heroic status, because we see them as monitoring, on our behalf, the implementation of the laws that will protect us from our own feelings of powerlessness.

It's not only in the pro-regulation mentality that we see the yearning for greater certainty. The rise of fundamentalism – religious and otherwise – is another symptom of the same underlying need to identify some magic simplicities that will save us from too much complexity, too much ambiguity and too much uncertainty: 'Give us *the* answer, and make it simple!' It's no coincidence that at this stage of our social evolution, a self-help book called, quite simply, *The Secret*, is walking off the shelves of the nation's bookshops and a secular version of religious fundamentalism, Landmark Forum, is attracting the kind of attention once given to Scientology.

Religious fundamentalism itself has been on the rise for the past 15 years and is now a dominant force in the religious mainstream. The various branches of Pentecostalism – Assemblies of God, Christian City Church, Hillsong, and so on – attract such large congregations that they have displaced Anglicans from the number two slot on the league table of church attendance (the Catholics being secure, for the time being, at number one).

Many mystics, theologians and psychologists would argue that *doubt* is both the engine and the essence of faith, since it's the doubts that cause you to take the initial leap of faith, and continuing doubts that sustain your faith. That helps explain the current re-emergence of interest in religion and other aspects of the inward journey: when a society is destabilised by change and gripped by uncertainty, religious consolations can be both appealing and comforting.

But for people struggling with feelings of powerlessness and daunted by *too much* uncertainty, there's an extra-special appeal in those branches of religion that offer to sweep all doubt aside in favour of a faith that feels like a certainty. The higher the level of anxiety and insecurity, the greater the appeal of the religious Right with its promise of simple answers to complex questions and a black-and-white, switch-on/switch-off approach to religious faith and salvation: you're either 'saved' by embracing the particular dogma of this or that church, or you're not; one or the other; no grey areas; take it or leave it.

The same yearning for certainty led to the rise of the so-called economic rationalists who preach the gospel of untrammelled free markets. Again, the appeal lies in its magical simplicity. There's only one rule: *let the market decide*. 'There's a problem with the market? There must be too much interference. The forces of supply and demand cannot be denied – left to themselves, they always come up with the right answer.'

It's persuasive stuff, but it relies on a number of questionable premises. One is that people tend to behave rationally – whether as consumers or, indeed, economic strategists – when in fact they rarely do. Humans are, on the whole, more irrational than rational; more driven by emotion than reason; more hormonal than cerebral. So any economic system that assumes an outcome based on rational behaviour is flawed from the start.

But there's a deeper issue. The advocates of free market simplicity usually regard the great Adam Smith (1723–90) as their inspiration. Smith, author of *The Wealth of Nations*, is generally regarded as having advocated a completely free and open market system in which, if everybody would act purely in their own self-interest, everything would come right in the end. But Smith was a moral philosopher, too, and his *Theory of Moral Sentiments*, published before *The Wealth of Nations*, makes it clear he believed in the fundamental benevolence of humans in their dealings with each other. The so-called 'invisible hand' that he suggested would guide the operation of the free market was not only the product of the dynamic relationship between supply and demand, but also of the mutual respect and goodwill shown towards each other by participants in the market. For Smith, the magic of the free market lay in its inherent morality as much as its inherent symmetry.

Smith was writing 250 years ago, when 'market' meant something very different from its meaning today. Personal trust, the binding handshake, the transparency of negotiations are all a far cry from the mass markets of today, where mighty corporations engage phalanxes of lawyers to handle their negotiations with each other, and the consumer is usually the last to know what's really going on.

Some environmentalists and feminists, as well as economic and religious propagandists, have tried to appeal to our yearning for certainty by simplifying their message into just one, black-and-white proposition that explains everything, from global warming to the 'true' meaning of liberation.

The single-factor explanation is alluring, but generally misleading. When medical researchers tell women that the right dose of testosterone will magically restore their lost libido, they overlook the possibility that a woman's level of sexual interest and arousal is likely to be the product of many factors, some physical, some emotional, some relational. When any religion tells us there is only 'one way' or only one answer to life's mysteries, we are right to be sceptical, given the nuances of religious experience and the sweep of human history. There's rarely a single, simple explanation for anything.

In a world that calls on us to live with high levels of ambiguity and unpredictability, the promise of simple certainty is seductive. Even if there isn't a clear answer to some of life's deeper and more troubling questions, those questions might seem less deep and less troubling, at least for a while, if we could embrace something that *felt* like an answer.

13

The inward journey

The Dreamy Period might not have been good for the health of our democracy, but it's been a boom time for retailers and credit providers keen to accommodate our desire for the soothing balm of narcissism. The gambling industry has thrived, too, as Australians have entertained, however fleetingly, the fantasy that they could ease all their financial pain with one big win.

Commercial considerations aside, a period of disengagement – like a retreat – can be a useful time of reflection. An inward focus can set us thinking about the quality of our lives, the ordering of our priorities and the personal goals we might want to achieve.

The self-indulgence that has so powerfully driven our militant materialism often ends up being circular: eventually, it leads us back to the very questions from which we were trying to distract ourselves. For instance, a self-indulgent mind-set can lead us to overeat and/or to eat the wrong kind of food (with an overemphasis on treats and rewards) and, before you know it, obesity is a problem. When it becomes enough of a problem – for an individual or a society – we start thinking about its causes. There are many causes of obesity, of course, but the self-absorption of the Dreamy Period, with its tendency to settle for easy answers and quick-fix solutions (even to deep-seated problems like anxiety and unhappiness) is one of them.

The 'empty feed' – filling yourself up but not getting enough nutrition – is not just a food issue: it's a metaphor for many of the things we do in a consumerist, materialistic society where even so-called simple pleasures often come in a sophisticated, packaged and branded form. We run harder and harder until the need to de-stress overwhelms us and, if we're affluent enough, we retreat to a health farm for a concentrated burst of relaxation – like having a swift inhalation of expensive rose essence instead of taking time to smell, let alone grow, the roses themselves. Or we decide the perfect unwind will be a beach holiday, then choose a resort where we'll first need a new wardrobe to keep up with the style of the place and a subsequent strategy for paying off the credit card.

Gradually, though, our attempts to deal with the stress – or the emptiness – of life on the materialist treadmill may lead us into a more reflective examination of what's really going on and whether it's what we really want. In extreme cases, we may need to suffer some kind of burnout or breakdown that forces us to take stock.

That's why the Dreamy Period has been marked by a dramatic surge of interest in *values*. The serious debate about values has almost nothing to do with old chestnuts like 'mateship' or even the 'fair go'. There may be some mild interest in the airy notion of Australia's distinctive values, but the real question facing us is more personal and immediate: *are we living in harmony with the values we claim to espouse?*

Obviously, that question only arises because so many Australians feel uneasy about the answer. They would like their lives to be lived in accordance with deeply held values, but when they look at how they actually live, they are not sure they like what they see. Who, for instance, would willingly admit that they wish to live by predominantly material values, and to teach their children how to be little materialists, attaching more value to possessions than to loyalty, mutual obligation, fairness or respect for the needs of others?

Many thoughtful Australians are now wondering whether they are living as if materialism is indeed one of their core values, and the one they are most successful in passing on to their children. 'How did the kids get to be such greedy little materialists?' is a question often asked in an uneasy, jokey spirit; the answer, usually unspoken, seems all too clear. 'Why do our kids insist on having the best of everything? When did they become so brand-conscious? Why do they attach so much value to *stuff*?' It's tempting to blame the mass media, of course, and many parents do. (The media are a favourite scapegoat for all society's ills.) But sometimes the parents asking those questions pause and reflect rather ruefully that they know only too well where such values came from.

Similarly, many Australians are coming to realise just how unbalanced their lives are, especially when it comes to time spent at work versus time spent with family and friends. Again, some awkward questions: is this because I've just let things drift, or is it because I'm so committed to making a lot of money that I'm letting that get in the way of my personal relationships? Or is it because I really do place more value on my working life than my personal life?

Though many would say their working lives are very important to them, few would feel comfortable asserting that, yes, they are more attached to their work than their family or friends. Yet when a spouse, say, or a child points out to them that they are rarely home, the remark is bound to feel like an accusation. The reply that 'I do this for the family' may seem hollow to a spouse suffering from feelings of neglect or a family struggling with the absent-parent problem.

'Goodnight, Mummy – see you next weekend,' said a daughter to her mother, one Sunday night. The mother lived at home with her husband and children and wasn't planning to go away that week, so she was puzzled. Her daughter, though, was simply responding to her own perceptions of reality: the mother was a busy professional woman who had been leaving for work before the children were awake and generally arriving home after they had gone to bed. The nanny cooked dinner most nights, and although the wife lovingly prepared the children's school lunches before she left for work, the husband got them off to school each morning. On reflection, she was shocked not only by the implications of her daughter's goodnight, but by the matter-of-fact tone. When she later complained to her husband about such an unfair perception, he simply shrugged.

The gap between *what I believe* and *how I live* feels uncomfortably and even embarrassingly wide to many Australians and some of them are wondering if there isn't some way of narrowing it. Even among the young people so maligned by their parents for being out-and-out materialists, there are signs of interest in 'getting the balance right' – not only between work and family life, but more broadly between material values and the non-material values that are central to the kind of balanced, relaxed lifestyle many young Australians aspire to. They are not about to abandon their preference for branded merchandise or any of the other trappings of a prosperous consumerist society, but they are well aware – and many believe they are more aware than their parents – of the fact that, as one teenage respondent put it, 'there's more to life than Nike'. (He still passionately wanted Nike, by the way.)

Reflecting this interest in non-material values – or perhaps a better term is 'post-material values', since they want to be able to take the material stuff for granted – there is a heightened interest among young Australians in what they are calling 'spirituality'. For some, this refers to conventional religious faith and practice, and many young people are riding the current wave of religious fundamentalism. But others are exploring New Age beliefs, astrology, or Eastern mysticism (especially Buddhism) and some are responding to the increasing prominence of Islam with interest.

Like their parents, though, most young Australians are not drawn to formal religion: for them, the meaning of life is more likely to be found in love and friendship than in religious dogma. The spirituality they are exploring is usually based on a secular, humanistic approach to questions about values and ethics. They are likely to assess potential partners on the basis of their political or social values, in much the same way as earlier generations were attuned to Catholic/Protestant differences. When it comes to employment, many members of this generation will be showing lively interest in the values a potential employer stands for. (This has some obvious implications for employers and managers who will be expected to plug any gaps between the stated values and the actual practice of an organisation.)

For some young people, 'spirituality' has a mainly pharmacological meaning: a heightened sense of wellbeing or tranquillity, for instance, reported by some users of marijuana, alcohol and other depressants, or the range of ecstatic and/or hallucinogenic experiences induced by other drugs.

Though values may be articulated with great conviction, it's not uncommon for people to say, 'By the way, don't look too closely at all this'. In other words, if you examine my life, you might be tempted to think I don't really believe in the values I try to live by. It would be harsh to call this hypocrisy; it's more like a cry for help from people who would like to live more closely in harmony with their view of the good life.

I wish I could slow down, but I keep running faster.

I wish I could simplify my life but it keeps getting more complicated.

I know I should spend more time with the people I love, and I want to, but . . .

Childhood should be a time of freedom and innocence, but that isn't the kind of childhood I'm giving my own children.

We should be less materialistic but we keep buying more stuff.

I wish I could get a better balance between work and the rest of my life.

We should have more 'time out' to relieve our stress.

I envy people who have something to believe in.

That last comment reflects a widespread belief in the value of belief. Even among non-churchgoers and those who have little or no religious faith, and little or no knowledge of religion, there is a persistent view that religion plays an important part in the life of the nation, and that the presence of the church – for all its dark misdeeds, hypocrisy and shortcomings – probably does more good than harm. *I like to see those little groups of people standing around outside churches on Sunday mornings* is a sentimental remark that betrays a lingering sense that some form of religious belief has a beneficial effect on the lives of many people and that believers are lucky to have their faith. Such views are reinforced in times of personal or national tragedy when the institutional church makes its presence felt at funerals or other public ceremonies, providing the rituals and the language that offer comfort.

For some people, the 'inward journey' is not about religion at all: as suggested in Chapter 1, it's about a search for greater moral clarity in the face of an increasingly complicated world. For some, it's a yearning for a clearer sense of life's meaning and purpose. For others, it's a vague sense that 'I should be doing better'. For many Australians, paradoxically, that journey has been inspired by the desire to distract themselves from the very questions that now trouble them. Perhaps that's the inherent value of a retreat.

14

A dream of 'the community'

Another item regularly crops up on that list of ways Australians would like to match their values to their reality:

We should get to know the neighbours – we should try to act more like part of the community.

Many of the changes described in the early chapters of this book have fragmented neighbourhoods and eroded our sense of belonging to a local community. The mobility of the population doesn't help, of course, and neither does the rate of marriage breakdown or the low birthrate. As Chapter 9 suggested, the shrinking household should turn out to be good news for neighbourhoods in the long run, but getting connected is a two-way process that takes time.

'We don't even know who our neighbours are' has become a cliché in some parts of our major metropolitan areas. It may be cited as a symptom of the breakdown of community but it's a remark usually tinged with some disbelief, and sometimes also with sadness or regret. We suspect it shouldn't be like this. The idea of 'the neighbourhood' recalled, perhaps nostalgically, from childhood strikes us as having been a good thing – a sign that the community was functioning the way communities should, giving us a strong sense of place, and contributing to our sense of identity and our emotional and physical security.

There are still plenty of fully functioning communities around Australia, of course. You can find them in brand-new housing estates, in medium-density developments, in the rows of terraces in the inner suburbs of Sydney and Melbourne and pockets of Hobart, Brisbane, Adelaide and Perth, in peninsula suburbs around Sydney Harbour, in villages and towns dotted across rural and regional Australia. But you can also find them where you least expect to – in places some urban designers might regard as suburban wastelands full of outmoded housing stock designed for a different era, and in unprepossessing streets that nevertheless beat with a strong community pulse. A place doesn't have to feel 'nice' to feel like 'my place'.

When we have it, we value it; when we don't, we know what we're missing. In the Dreamy Period, pondering all this (and some of us being in the mood for renovating our lives as well as our houses and our bodies), we sense that the good life we yearn for would ideally be lived in the context of a neighbourhood where we *do* know the neighbours by name and, without wanting to pry into each others' lives, have at least a nodding acquaintance with each other's circumstances. We'd like to think there was enough spirit of reciprocity for us to be confident we'd help each other out in an emergency and notice if a neighbour didn't appear for a day or two.

Perhaps we are on the brink of reinventing the wheel – coming again to realise, as if it's a discovery, that we are social creatures who thrive on the sense of belonging to a community. One motivation for people to re-engage with religion, whether through churches, church-based schools or in other ways, is to connect with a community that has a clearly defined identity.

Although many of us belong to a variety of groups – the workplace, special interest groups, clubs, churches, friendship circles – there's a strong intuitive sense that we also need to feel part of the local neighbourhood where we actually live. The need for *a sense of place* that is both secure and familiar is strong within us; no matter how connected we may feel in other ways, there is a special meaning of 'community' that relies on locality.

That's why some local councils are looking for ways to stimulate the sense of belonging in local neighbourhoods with a *Meet the Street* program that encourages people to get to know their neighbours. Such programs help people feel more comfortable and secure in their neighbourhoods, but they also reduce the risk of individuals or households suffering the problems of social exclusion. Locally based initiatives, like Neighbourhood Watch and Clean Up Australia, can have similar benefits.

Urban planners and enlightened developers are paying more attention to the creation of local neighbourhood spaces that make it easier for people to meet and mingle. Since the car has replaced the footpath as the way most of us get to and from our homes, the opportunities for informal and incidental contact between neighbours are reduced, and so we need other places to bring us together: in the face of the huge commercial push towards regional shopping malls, the revival of suburban strip shops, complete with coffee shops, is one sign of our need to make local connections. With a steady trend towards medium- and high-density living, architectural solutions will also be required to encourage contact between people conditioned by having lived in the privacy of traditional, suburban houses. Though we are herd creatures by nature, it sometimes takes a while to learn how to make contact – even eye contact – with strangers in a lift or car park.

Can we learn from the 'tribal' generation?

The rising generation of young Australians – teens and twentysome-things – is a signpost to our future, and it's beginning to look like a future where our dreams of community might come true. This is a generation not only committed to keeping its options open; it's also remarkably tribal in its attitudes and behaviour. Facilitated by the IT revolution, its members keep closely and almost continuously in touch with each other, sharing information of every imaginable kind.

They've been shaped, of course, by the times. Many of them are the offspring of divorced parents and, at any given time, thousands of them are going through the trauma of watching their parents' marriages fall apart. They've experienced, on a huge scale, the upheavals of 'access visits' to the non-custodial parent and the inevitable disruptions to their own social lives. Many have been burnt by nasty experiences with drugs – or know someone who has. Many engage in binge-drinking – the girls as well as the boys.

By the age of 18, 20 percent have experienced a major depressive episode. They've lived with the reality of youth suicide as a here-and-now issue: unlike their parents, many of them have known, directly or indirectly, someone who has either taken their own life or tried to – 20 percent of deaths in the 15–24 age group are suicides, and estimates of the number of youth suicide attempts each year range upwards from about 40 000. They've grown up with HIV/AIDS on the health education curriculum. They are accustomed to having both parents working (it's so commonplace, we no longer talk about 'latch-key kids' as if they were exceptional cases). They are used to a highly competitive educational system and they know a university degree, if that's what they want, carries a huge price tag.

No wonder their parents so often say, 'I'd hate to be a young person today – it's tougher for them than it was for us.'

In response, something's happened. This is a generation that's decided, intuitively rather than rationally, that the most precious resource it has for coping with life in an unstable and unpredictable world is not education, or technology, or information, or even material prosperity – even though they may value all those things. No, the most precious resource they have is each other.

Faced with the dislocation of so many of their own families, they've quietly set about creating their own surrogate extended families. Their parents and teachers say they are just like tribal creatures – constantly in touch, looking out for each other, tuned into each other's needs and wellbeing. When there's a tragedy, they're all there – gathered at someone's place just like a family. When there's an achievement, they seem genuinely pleased by each other's success. When there's a crisis, the network – the gang, the tribe, the group – swings into action.

Let's not get misty-eyed over this: there are plenty of exceptions. Like every generation of young people, this one has its share of selfishness, cruelty, greed, deception and ugly tribal rivalries. Some of the subcultural groups are as dark and dangerous as any gangs in history. There's plenty of unbridled materialism and as much arrogance to be found among the under-thirties as the over-thirties. Some members of this generation are as self-centred and lacking in respect for authority as any young people ever were. There are plenty of rich kids who never spare a thought for the poor, and plenty of loners who haven't yet found a tribe to join and who may be settling for cybermates to confide in.

But there is a culture shift happening. A teacher at an independent school gave a boy in her class a punishment of three Saturday detentions, working in the school garden. The first week, he turned up with three of his friends. 'Very cute,' said the teacher, 'but he's the one who has to do the work. The rest of you can come back in an hour.'

'No, that's all right,' said the other boys, 'we haven't got anything better to do – give us some work, too.' So she did. And they all turned up for all three Saturdays. One in, all in.

Another teacher noticed two girls locked in an embrace in the corridor outside her English classroom.

'What's wrong?' she enquired.

'Oh, nothing. We're just saying goodbye.'

'Well, you'll see each other again in 40 minutes,' said the teacher. But this, she knew, is the hugging generation – and not just the girls. Boys hugging their friends, male and female, is standard practice. Only their fathers think it odd.

An employment officer arranged an interview for a 16-year-old applying for his first job. He showed up with two mates. 'Which of you is applying for the job?' she asked.

'He is,' said one, 'we just came to keep him company.' Two generations ago, it might have been his father accompanying him to his first job interview. The interviewer felt sure that if she'd given them the chance to share the job between them, they would have jumped at it.

In another company, struggling with a high turnover of drivers, a manager has started recruiting young drivers from among the friends of his existing drivers. His experience convinces him there will be a lower turnover among drivers employed this way.

A mother, unaccustomed to the tribal ways of her teenage son's friends, opens his backpack and doesn't recognise half the stuff in it. Someone else's T-shirt, tracksuit pants and books are mingled with some of his belongings. (Belongings? That's a non-tribal word.) Missing are his new trainers. 'Where are your new trainers?' she asks.

'Oh, Jason needed them for camp.'

'Will he give them back?'

'Mu-*um*. What do you think?'

Take a look at a young couple shopping for an engagement or wedding ring. Chances are, they won't be alone: they'll have a group of friends with them, lending support, advice and approval. It's a big purchase; *ergo*, it's a group thing.

The members of this generation are not yearning for a sense of community – they already have it. They are connected. IT doesn't replace their personal relationships; it augments them. Face to face – clustering – is where they want to be.

Their message to the rest of us is clear: if you want to thrive in this kind of world, *get connected*. And who would disagree? Connectedness is the key to our mental and emotional health.

Does this mean we are approaching the end of the long era of individualism, marked by an intense competitiveness? Is there a new age of communitarianism dawning? How will such a group-orientated generation fare when they start moving up the ladder of organisations designed for a different cultural mind-set? Will they be 'difficult' employees? Will they bring a different style to management? Will our organisations need to change to accommodate their more communal way of doing things? Almost certainly: they'll expect to be more consultative, more co-operative, more casual in dress and manner, less respectful of tradition and convention, and more ready to move on when it suits them. They'll rate the quality of personal relationships – at work and elsewhere – very highly on their list of reasons for staying or going.

You can't raise a generation the way we've raised this one and not expect them to be affected by it.

If our retreat to the cocoon and our quality-of-life reflections have led us to become serious about rebuilding communities, that will have been one of the greatest benefits of the Dreamy Period; it will also be an early sign that we are emerging from it. Once we lift our gaze above the back fence and begin to pay more attention to the life of the neighbourhood and the wider community, we are well on the way to re-engagement.

15

Is the Dreamy Period coming to an end?

Straws in the wind. Hints. Possibilities. Nothing more. But it's hard to escape the feeling that we might be emerging from the Dreamy Period. Sitting up. Taking notice. Politically, there's a new alertness; more generally, a nagging sense that we might need to take another look at the big picture.

The 'lifestyle' craze on television has waned and died. Was that due to nothing more than the fickleness of viewers' tastes, or did it mean we were ready to lift our gaze to a broader horizon?

The New South Wales state election in March 2007 was the first anywhere in Australia since 2002 when an incumbent government did not increase its majority (except in the 2006 Queensland election, where the Beattie government's majority was already so large, it could hardly have been increased). The Iemma government was comfortably returned, but with a significant swing against it and the loss of a couple of seats. As usual, many factors contributed to the result – an unpopular government, an ineffectual Opposition, the intrusion of a federal issue (Work Choices) into the campaign – but the outcome suggested an electorate becoming more engaged. This time, voters were not simply saying 'wake me when it's over'; many had changed their minds since the last election. That may be the beginning of a trend in which, for the next few years, incumbency will lose some of its potency.

Anyone tracking the Dreamy Period would have wondered what might one day cause us to emerge from it: a terrorist attack? A bird flu epidemic? A crash in commodity prices that would burst our economic bubble? A painful hike in interest rates? If the Dreamy Period is, indeed, coming to an end, our emergence from it has not been the result of a single, sudden crisis. Several unrelated developments point to a mood shift, but they may be signs or symptoms of it, rather than its causes.

The environment: This is the big one; the list-topper; the barbecue-stopper. Not since the late '80s has there been such widespread openness to the possibility that the planet is sending us a message. A drought that seriously threatens the water supplies of our capital cities, bushfires that rage out of control for months and have seasoned experts shaking their heads, and the mounting evidence of global warming all suggest there's an issue here we can't ignore.

Even some sceptics who see climate change as part of the inexorable swing of the global pendulum are now wondering whether this latest swing might have been accelerated by human activity. In everything from water and electricity consumption to the use of our cars, we are starting to engage with the idea that tough restrictions might one day be called for – though, it must be said, there's no sign of any immediate, spontaneous change in our behaviour, especially as drivers.

The nuclear debate: A spin-off from the issue of global warming is the re-emergence of serious discussion about nuclear power. Many people who would previously have dismissed it out of hand are becoming more open to the argument that it may be the lesser of two evils (the other being coal). Do the advantages of a 'clean' source of power offset the costs of producing it and the hazards associated with the process, including the storage of radioactive waste? Such questions will exercise our minds for some time, but the point is that we have started paying attention to them.

'Values': Right through the Dreamy Period, we have been quietly pondering the whole idea of values and priorities. The subject came into sharper relief with the March 2007 release of the Relationships Forum Australia report, *An Unexpected Tragedy*. That report, summarised in Chapter 4, tapped a rich vein of interest: extended media analysis of its contents reflected its relevance and timeliness. As we have seen, it's not so-called 'Aussie values' that are engaging our attention, but deeper, more personal questions: have we become too materialistic for our own good? How can we lead more balanced lives? Can we revive our communities and our sense of belonging to them?

Rethinking multiculturalism: Any signs of ethnic tension – including the unleashing of anti-Islamic prejudice – rattle us and remind us that multiculturalism is a fragile edifice that requires commitment, goodwill and a healthy curiosity about our differences. Events like the 2006 Cronulla beach riots in Sydney, ethnic violence among spectators at the 2007 Australian Open tennis tournament in Melbourne, the news that the New South Wales regional city of Tamworth had turned its back on a group of Sudanese refugees, and occasional outbreaks of anxiety about the 'hidden messages' of Islamic preachers in Australia have all forced us to think again about multiculturalism. (As usual, we're more likely to focus on what we really think when it feels as if we're being asked to change our minds about something.)

David Hicks: A change in our attitudes to David Hicks looked like another symptom of a mood shift. Hicks, an Australian citizen, was captured by US forces in Afghanistan (where he was apparently training with the Taliban) and taken to the infamous Guantanamo Bay prison in Cuba. There he languished for five years without trial, the one attempt at charging him having failed because the charges were judged unlawful. He finally entered into a plea bargain in March 2007, in response to a vague charge of giving support to a terrorist organisation, and was repatriated to serve a short sentence in Adelaide's Yatala jail.

Towards the end of Hicks's fifth year in prison, an authoritative Newspoll survey revealed that 71 percent of Australians thought he should be brought home. Six months previously, it's doubtful if most of us were paying enough attention to have an opinion, but perhaps a flurry of media activity marking the fifth anniversary of his incarceration without trial jolted us. While most Australians assumed he was guilty of something, questions about the fairness and justice of his treatment came to seem, in the public mind, larger than the question of what he had actually done.

The Iraq war: Following the Baker-Hamilton Report's grim assessment of the US-led occupation of Iraq, the subsequent decision by the Blair government to begin withdrawing British troops and the US Congress's determination to set a deadline for the withdrawal of American forces, our own involvement in Iraq began to attract more critical interest.

GetUp: With well over 100 000 online contacts, and growing by the day, GetUp has established itself as a potent lobby group of

Australians who are keen to speak up on a variety of political and other issues, including global warming. In May 2007, GetUp was claiming it had garnered over 25 000 signatures to a petition protesting against legislation designed to close the electoral rolls on the very night the federal election is called. It also claims to have delivered 8000 messages to Labor's 2007 Summit on Climate Change. These are tiny numbers in the scheme of things, but the very existence of GetUp is possibly another sign, another hint, that the Dreamy Period is drawing to a close.

Hip-hop activism: Though young Australians are often criticised for their apathy, some young people regard it as cool – *de rigueur,* in fact – to maintain the appearance of apathy. Below the surface, and especially below the surface of their music, are signs of strong engagement with political themes and issues. Groups like The Herd – 'Burn down the parliament' – could hardly be more explicit; others wear their political colours as T-shirts. Others, like True Live, refuse to label their work as 'political', though they sing about better futures and the ways society must change. Online forums, networks and 'zines are also providing outlets for young Australians' political expression that flies below the radar of conventional media.

The reappearance of Paul Keating: During 2006–7, the former prime minister began to appear in the media to comment on selected issues – new media ownership laws, superannuation, a fleeting fracas concerning Labor leader Kevin Rudd's meetings with the disgraced former premier of Western Australia, Brian Burke. Keating's trademark acerbic style (Peter Costello, 'all tip and no iceberg'; Brian Burke, 'the Arthur Daley of the West') reminded his former supporters of what they had been missing and brought what sounded, in a more conservative era, like a fresh, fearless voice to the political debate.

In a 2006 interview about media ownership with ABC TV's *Lateline* presenter, Tony Jones, Keating was asked why the points he was making had not been made – or made with such clarity – by anyone else. Keating replied that 'passion' was what was needed, a remark that sounded like a wake-up call not only to Labor politicians but also to the electorate. (The sustained sell-out success of the musical *Keating!* is partly a tribute to the show itself, and partly a sign of nostalgia for the spirit of political engagement associated with the Hawke–Keating era.)

New Labor leader: Kevin Rudd's accession to the federal Labor leadership at the end of 2006 appears to have added some momentum to the process of re-engagement. With a federal election looming at the end of 2007, the political contest suddenly became more lively (and uglier, with mud-slinging an early sign of desperation in government ranks). Regardless of their party preferences, voters became convinced a serious contest was under way.

Work Choices: Although initial responses to the federal government's Work Choices legislation had seemed muted and even acquiescent, largely because of a widespread belief in the robustness of the economy, the first anniversary of the Act in March 2007 provoked fresh discussion and some increased uneasiness about its long-term implications. It also became an issue in the New South Wales state election campaign at that time, raising questions about whether the Coalition, if elected to government, would hand over too many industrial relations powers to the federal government. The debate was further fuelled by a front-page report in *The Sydney Morning Herald* on 17 April 2007, revealing that 45 percent of Australian Workplace Agreements (AWAs) negotiated under the Work Choices legislation had stripped away all the award conditions the government had promised would be protected by law. The newspaper also claimed staff at the Office of the Employment Advocate believed as many as 28 percent of AWAs may have broken the law by undercutting legislated minimum employment entitlements.

In the face of rising community concern about AWAs, the commitment by Labor to abolish them if elected to office, and a sustained advertising campaign by the ACTU, the government announced in May 2007 that it would modify its Work Choices legislation by adding a 'battlers' clause'. All workplace agreements covering employees earning less than $75 000 a year were to meet a new test designed to ensure fair compensation in return for giving up penalty rates, overtime and other award entitlements. (The government also quietly dropped the use of the term 'Work Choices' though that remained, of course, the title of the Act.)

Labor continued to insist the legislation gave too much power to employers, and the ACTU claimed the abolition of collective bargaining provisions contravened internationally recognised human rights. Although Labor's determination to abolish AWAs was heavily criticised by sections of business – the mining industry, in particular – polling in mid-2007 suggested a firming of voters' support for Labor's position. On this issue, if on no other, voters were able to discern clear – and quite traditional – distinctions between the major parties as they approached the 2007 federal election.

Taken together, the items on that list suggested that, by early 2007, we were emerging from the Dreamy Period. But were they causes or effects? Did they jolt us from our torpor, or did we attend to them because we had, for other reasons, woken up?

Some factors, like the threat posed by global warming or alarm over AWAs, might well have been wake-up calls. Or would ten years of out-and-out materialism inevitably lead us to re-engage with the idea of Australia as a society, rather than merely an economy?

Or could there have been a larger mood cycle operating that's hard to track while we're in the middle of it? Perhaps there are national mood swings that just happen. (This is certainly the rather eccentric view of Robert Prechter in his 1999 book, *The Wave Principle of Human Social Behaviour and the New Science of Socionomics*.) We might have been coming out of the Dreamy Period simply because it was time.

If that's what is happening, whatever the cause, the 'big picture' will once again come into focus and we will be prepared to listen more attentively to the voices of activists, artists, provocateurs, commentators and politicians (to say nothing of charities) whose messages, these past seven or eight years, have been only faintly heard. We might also find that home renovations have not, in the end, satisfied our quest for the meaning of life. By mid-2007, 'who do you think will win the election?' had challenged 'I think I've found the perfect bathroom tile' as a topic of conversation at dinner, but it was hard to be sure whether that was a sign of re-engagement or natural curiosity. A more reliable indicator was this: by the middle of 2007, news and current affairs programs had stormed back up the TV ratings ladder, regularly accounting for four or five of the top ten programs.

As politically astute as ever, John Howard summed up the situation in mid-2007, when his government was trailing Labor in the polls and when he himself was being eclipsed by Kevin Rudd in Newspoll's measure of preferred prime minister. His impression was that the voters had not stopped listening to him in the way they stopped listening to Paul Keating in 1996, and in that assessment Howard captured the essential difference between the beginning and end of the Dreamy Period. When they are newly alert after such a prolonged period of disengagement, voters are certainly listening, but what they hear is not only the clatter of day-to-day politics but also the thrum of memory.

16

Re-engagement, or euphoria?

A few weeks before the 2007 federal election, when the Coalition was facing certain defeat, John Howard issued a stern warning. Echoing the words of Paul Keating in 1996, he told voters: 'If you change the government, you change the country.' In that one remark, Howard revealed just how significantly his political skills had deserted him, and how out of touch he had become. Didn't he know that the country had already changed, and that's why his government was trailing so badly in the opinion polls and Kevin Rudd was riding so high? It wasn't that Rudd had struck some magically responsive chord in the electorate; it was that voters had, as suggested in the previous chapter, begun listening to memories that had, in many cases, lain dormant for several years. On reflection, they wondered why they hadn't made the change long ago: Rudd as Opposition leader simply offered an extra incentive to do so.

Conventional political wisdom says that Oppositions don't win elections; governments lose them. That was certainly the case in 2007, so it won't be until 2010 that we will know whether Labor under Kevin Rudd can win an election, as opposed to benefiting from the Coalition's drubbing at the polls.

The change of federal government did not prove that Australians had re-engaged with the political process – or, more generally, with 'the big picture' of social, political and economic issues – but it was consistent with the other signs suggesting that the Dreamy Period might be coming to an end. All the factors identified in Chapter 15 played their part in this turning of the electoral tide.

The underlying problem for the Coalition was that it had accumulated too much baggage of a particular kind, over too many years. Iraq, Tampa, 'children overboard', AWB kickbacks, Work Choices, Aboriginal reconciliation, asylum-seekers, the erosion of civil liberties in the name of the 'war on terror', the five-year incarceration of David Hicks, the 'rendition' and detention of Mamdouh Habib, the unlawful detention of Cornelia Rau (a German citizen with permanent residency in Australia) and of Mohammed Haneef (an Indian doctor on the Gold Coast, wrongly linked to a terrorist act in the UK), refusal to engage with the challenge of climate change . . . the weight of all this memory was too much to bear, especially as each of these issues was laden with moral freight.

While apologists for the Coalition tried to suggest the looming electoral defeat was merely a case of the 'it's time' factor – as if we were ready for a new political hairstyle or a clean political shirt – the truth was quite different. This was the election when morality eclipsed economics as a central, if largely unspoken, issue.

As the election approached and the opinion polls pointed to an intractable swing to Labor, some commentators became mesmerised by one particular set of Newspoll figures showing the Coalition well ahead of Labor for 'good economic management'. They stroked their chins and wondered if this would prove to be Labor's Achilles heel.

'You wait,' they said, 'the voters will get into that polling booth, break into a nervous sweat and decide it isn't worth the risk.'

Their view meshed with conventional political wisdom that says, come voting time, the hip-pocket nerve always twitches and self-interest takes over. As Bill Clinton famously remarked, 'It's the economy, stupid'. In other words, whatever other issues you might think are motivating the voters at the time of an election, one factor always prevails: the economy.

The 2007 election didn't disprove the Clinton theory, but it certainly looked like an exception to the rule. In spite of the persistent efforts of the Coalition to make economic management the primary focus of the election campaign and to portray Kevin Rudd, Wayne Swan (the shadow treasurer) and the Labor Party as inexperienced and even naïve on economic matters, the voters remained unmoved: the economy simply wasn't front and centre in their minds.

One reason for that may well have been that, thanks to the resources boom, voters perceived the economy as so robust and stable, they had the luxury of being able to focus on other things.

But it's equally true that those 'other things' had themselves become increasingly important. The essence of the shift in the mood of the electorate was this: voters had begun thinking more about the state of society than the state of the economy: 'what kind of society are we becoming?' had become a more pressing question than 'how big will the budget surplus be this year?' Perhaps the single most compelling piece of evidence of this shift was in voters' reactions to the massive income-tax cuts promised by both sides of politics in the first week of the 2007 election campaign.

John Howard and Peter Costello got in first, announcing proposed tax cuts of $31 billion over four years, to a chorus of cheers from sections of the media (*The Australian*, in particular), suggesting this was the 'king hit' that would put Labor out of the race; the definitive bold stroke that would place economic management firmly back at the top of the political agenda.

Among voters, however, the response was more muted and more sceptical – even cynical. Conditioned to a steady program of Coalition tax cuts, year after year, voters perceived this as 'more of the same', rather than a 'king hit'. They also wondered why the Howard government was persisting in its policy of squandering the benefits of Australia's resources boom on tax handouts, rather than seizing the opportunity to take some nation-building initiatives (a national high-speed rail network, for instance, or an attack on the management of water resources) as well as addressing the parlous state of Australia's public hospitals and schools. While some of these matters were acknowledged to be the responsibility of the states, the electorate was growing weary of a situation in which it appeared as if Canberra's coffers were overflowing, while the states were struggling to fund some of their programs, often having to borrow money to do so.

During the days following this announcement – when Rudd and Swan were said to be closeted with their officials, working out their response to the Coalition's tax 'strategy' – the widespread expectation in the electorate was that Labor would decline to engage in a tax-cut contest and would, instead, emphasise the need to invest heavily in infrastructure development, alternative energy sources and public health and education. That expectation was based firmly on voters' wish that a federal government would indeed start using our new-found national wealth to address precisely those issues: 'Why is anyone talking about tax cuts for the rich when our public schools and hospitals are crying out for more money?'

At the end of that week, Labor announced that, broadly speaking, it would match the Coalition's tax-cut promises, though with a delay in concessions to the rich.

The reaction in the community at large was one of incredulity. While Labor's response might have, in strategic terms, 'neutralised' the Coalition's tax promises, it also raised the worrying prospect in pro-Labor voters' minds that Rudd Labor might not be quite as bold and imaginative as they had been hoping. As voters got their first real inkling of what 'fiscal conservative' might mean in a Rudd government, the tax-cut episode positioned Labor as almost indistinguishable from the Coalition on this issue.

On other issues, as well, Rudd and Howard seemed, throughout 2007, rather like a pair of match-race yachts engaged in a tacking duel, each trying to cover the other. As Phillip Adams had put it in *The Australian* on 17 April 2007: 'I wish Rudd wasn't so quick to open the gap on Howard by closing the gap on policy differences'. In the end, of course, none of it mattered: when the electorate has made up its mind so far ahead of an election, the many millions of dollars spent on campaign advertising and the careful crafting of every phrase to be uttered by the contenders make no perceptible difference to the outcome.

After the election was lost by the Coalition, the economics editor of *The Sydney Morning Herald,* Ross Gittins, among others, pleaded with the new Labor government to break its tax-cut promises, on the grounds that proceeding with such generous cuts would be reckless rather than conservative. But the May 2008 budget delivered, on schedule, the cuts promised in the election campaign – though, to be fair, the budget also delivered the hoped-for major spending initiatives in the areas of health, education and infrastructure.

If reactions to tax cuts were a sign of a shift in voters' priorities, so was the storm gathering around the Work Choices legislation. As Chapter 15 suggested, Work Choices was one of several factors that seemed to have woken voters from their political torpor. By the time of the 2007 election, it had become a powerful symbol of the clash of ideologies: the Coalition as determined as ever to smash the power of the unions, and Labor as determined as ever to abolish Australian Workplace Agreements and restore the possibility of collective bargaining to the workplace. In pro-Labor voters' minds, Work Choices had come to seem like an assault on the security and the culture of the workplace: the potential for exploitation of employees had turned this into a moral issue.

Even with their vision blurred by the blizzard of multi-billion-dollar election promises, voters were still able to discern some other moral issues that had remained unresolved for years: the treatment of asylum-seekers, for instance. Australians knew, but didn't want to know, that the Howard government had presided over a system of such brutal treatment of asylum-seekers in our detention centres that, in 2004, the eminent psychiatrist, Dr Louise Newman, in evidence to the Human Rights and Equal Opportunity Commission, had described it as 'State-sponsored torture and child abuse'. In a similar vein, Senator John Faulkner had quizzed a senior public servant at a parliamentary enquiry about the deliberate dehumanisation of detainees (for example, by prison guards' refusal to use their names), and the official had confirmed that dehumanisation was 'policy'.

Though voters had buried their heads in the sand for some years over just such revelations, the 2007 election campaign brought them back into a kind of half-consciousness – not as core election issues, but as part of a general sense that the Coalition had presided over a period of moral decline and political sleaziness, in which material prosperity was sometimes perceived as the reward for not paying too much attention. All these factors – Iraq, AWB kickbacks, detention-centre operations – had lingered in our memories as disturbing but unresolved moral issues, because each of them reflected on our integrity as a nation. How, for instance, could we complain about human rights abuses in other countries when abuses were taking place in our own backyard?

When Kevin Rudd committed a Labor government to the withdrawal of Australia's combat troops from Iraq, many voters began to think again about their initial reservations about the invasion, and an old question was revived: why did the Howard government commit Australian military forces, for the first time in our history, to a 'pre-emptive' invasion, in the face of huge public resistance and an absence of any direct threat to us or our allies? Although the answer given by most Australians at the time was, 'Because George W. Bush wanted him to,' there was still an uneasy sense that our participation in that invasion had fundamentally contradicted the concept of 'defence' forces.

Dr Hans Blix, former US weapons inspector and winner of the 2007 Sydney Peace Prize, had been reminding us that there was no evidence of weapons of mass destruction in Iraq, that al-Qaeda was not present in Iraq until after the US-led occupation, and that the legacy of the invasion has been anarchy, not democracy. Yes, the evil Saddam Hussein was deposed, but in Blix's view, there were two primary reasons for the invasion: to protect US access to Iraqi oil reserves, and to provide an alternative land base for US troops then stationed in Pakistan.

Added to such acute moral issues was the frustration over our chronic failure to make more substantial progress on Aboriginal reconciliation (including the long-awaited symbolic apology to the Stolen Generations). Even the threat posed by global warming was being seen as a moral rather than an economic issue ('It's the ecology, stupid'), having been identified by Kevin Rudd as 'the great moral issue of our time'.

All these were signs of a yearning for something more than tax cuts and budget surpluses. This time, we were more interested in national pride than fatter wallets. It was a mood-shift bound to unseat any government that continued to set so much store by economics, when the voters' agenda was open to many more possibilities.

The 2007 election was an emphatic defeat for the Coalition and for John Howard, who became only the second prime minister in Australian history to lose his own seat. In the aftermath of the defeat, the Liberal Party seemed understandably dispirited, but also disorientated and, by some accounts, almost broke. The process of coming to terms with their defeat was made more poignant than it might otherwise have been by the decision of Peter Costello – for so long the man assumed to be waiting in the wings – not to contest the leadership of the party. In that moment, Costello confirmed the feeling lurking in the minds of many voters that he had never really wanted the job, anyway. Writing in *The Weekend Australian* of 15 December 2007, Paul Kelly noted that 'Costello had neither the numbers to force Howard out nor the ability to persuade him. The Liberal Party's tragic mishandling of the leadership issue over the 2004-6 term is that Howard stayed too long but his deputy never found the mechanism to remove him, by charm or threat. The reality, however, is that Costello's flaws cannot excuse Howard's misjudgment.'

In *The Australian Financial Review* of 11 December, Pamela Williams's analysis of Howard's chaotic election campaign strategy led her to a similarly melancholy conclusion for the Liberals: 'In the end, Howard's strength was proved ephemeral. The man who played the electorate so badly did not even have the membership ticket to vote for a new party leader. The man who believed he could hold the vote around the whole country could not even hold his own seat. And when he fell, he took the party with him.'

Howard's legacy was a Coalition in disarray, struggling to find a new direction and new leadership and finally, perhaps temporarily, settling for Brendan Nelson over Malcolm Turnbull. As policy after policy was ditched, it was clear the party was keen to distance itself, quickly and decisively, from the Howard era: Work Choices – gone; opposition to ratification of the Kyoto Protocol on climate change – gone; resistance to the idea of a formal apology to the stolen generations of Aboriginal children – gone.

Historians will ultimately assess Howard's prime ministership in political, economic social and cultural terms. As the electorate emerged from the Dreamy Period, though, it looked as if removing Howard was an important symbolic act. Gone was the feeling expressed by many 'small-l' liberals over the previous seven or eight years, that they had begun to feel embarrassed or even ashamed to be Australians; gone was the sense of a government playing on our fears for its own political ends; gone, too, was the uncomfortable feeling that Australia was becoming a foreign policy lackey of the US.

From Howard's own point of view, perhaps his greatest legacy might have been the two pieces of legislation dearest to his heart: a GST that fulfilled his long ambition of shifting the tax emphasis somewhat away from income to consumption (though, like all consumption taxes, it was inherently regressive), and the Work Choices laws designed to strip the trade unions of their remaining power. To see that industrial relations legislation not only repealed but repudiated by his own party must have been almost as bitter a pill for Howard to swallow as the loss of office.

Three big symbols of a fresh start

Kevin Rudd assumed the prime ministership, buoyed by an ocean of goodwill. At least in the short term, re-engagement with politics seemed to have involved a significant emotional investment in the idea that this new government was more than 'just' a new government: Rudd and his new crew were seen as having the potential to effect rapid and significant cultural change. For many voters, jubilant over the result, it seemed as if Australia had, at one stroke, shifted its gaze from the past to the future.

In the days and weeks following the election, the most common emotions being expressed in the community were relief and hope: relief that a rather dark period was behind us – the period described in Chapter 10 – and hope that the new government would set us on a new course towards becoming a prouder, less troubled society, prepared to take bold initiatives to set right some past wrongs and to shift our gaze to a broader horizon.

Three early initiatives of the Rudd government tapped into this euphoric – perhaps even rather hyperbolic – spirit of hope: first, the ratification of the Kyoto Protocol on climate change; second, a formal apology to the so-called Stolen Generations (Aboriginal children forcibly removed from their parents between the 1930s and 1970s, on the promise of a better life); third, the staging of the 2020 Summit.

The ratification of the Kyoto Protocol was almost the first act of the new government, and its symbolic effect may well have been greater than its actual political significance. Even among those who didn't understand the point – let alone the nuances – of the protocol, its ratification said that 'Australian is back in the world community . . . we're no longer slavishly following the US . . . we can take our place at the negotiating table not only for the climate change debate, but for anything at all.' In the bracing climate of post-election enthusiasm, the very word 'Kyoto' became code for 'back in the game'.

The symbolism of Kyoto was important at another level, as well: it gave 'green' voters grounds for believing the Rudd government would be bold and even revolutionary in its approach to tackling such challenges as the development of renewable sources of energy. Indeed, the ratification of Kyoto raised expectations about the government's approach not only to environmental issues but to a new agenda more generally: it certainly fuelled the euphoria of those who seemed to be placing so much faith in the new government that they were half-expecting it to wipe the public policy slate clean and start again: 'Today, Kyoto; tomorrow, *everything!*'

The apology to the Stolen Generations of Aborigines took many Australians by surprise by its suddenness – it occurred on the very first day of sitting of the new parliament. Again, there was symbolism at work that seemed to go well beyond the scope of the act itself. The apology unleashed a powerful emotional response across the nation: many people reported having been reduced to tears by the prime minister's speech, and even some sceptics found themselves unaccountably and even reluctantly drawn into the emotion of the moment.

Why was the reaction to the apology so intense when, to be frank, Aboriginal affairs have never been anywhere near the top of the nation's agenda of issues? There are at least two plausible explanations, and both probably played a part in generating a response that seemed almost cathartic in its intensity.

First, there's the controversial possibility that the apology tapped into a deeply buried sub-stratum of almost unconscious, collective shame. The appalling history of European settlers' treatment of Aborigines is firmly lodged in this nation's psyche, and our frequent reluctance to confront or admit it, and our virulent prejudice against Indigenous Australians (reserving, for instance, our vilest racist jokes for them), have always looked like classic symptoms of repressed shame, as opposed to guilt. The novelist Drusilla Modjeska drew a useful distinction between guilt and shame in her address at the 1997 NSW Premier's Literary Awards:

> Guilt ... operates in the realm of personal breach. Shame, on the other hand, operates in the realm of honour and dishonour, responsibility and our common humanity. A nation can be shamed, or a family, or a child ... While guilt is often limiting in that it draws down onto individual acts of wrongdoing, shame can be a

spur back into a common humanity, if not community, by the recognition of force much greater than our small guilty selves.

While many people, including John Howard, have wanted to reject the idea of 'collective guilt' for actions we didn't personally commit, the concept of 'collective shame' does, perhaps, make sense. It would certainly help to explain the intensity of emotion on the day of the apology.

Second, while the main force of the apology was that it did address an unresolved issue in relations between Aborigines and the Australian government, it also seems fair to suggest that reactions to this historic event were so strong and so widespread that they might not have been confined to the 'stolen generations' issue, nor even to Aboriginal affairs. The apology, like Kyoto, served as a symbol of something more, providing a rallying point for those looking for a way to celebrate the 'new order'. In this way, perhaps, it served as a sign that 'anything is now possible'. On this interpretation, the response to the apology can be seen as part of a broader response to the new government itself, and to the possibility of politics being handled in a more compassionate and more bipartisan way.

Had a similarly powerful symbol been created in a different context entirely (a radical attack on poverty, for instance, or some other initiative that implied a more human, less adversarial approach to federal politics), it, too, might have evoked a strong emotional response. This was an electorate – a community – looking for reassurance that something new, perhaps even revolutionary, was indeed happening: from that point of view, the timing of the apology could not have been better. But these broader, contextual interpretations do not deny the central fact that, as a specific act of apology (lacking only a corresponding act of forgiveness), Kevin Rudd's historic speech opened up the possibility of fresh progress in relations between black and white Australians.

The 2020 Summit was less an initiative than a response to the pent-up demand among many Australians for a 'national conversation'. Before the prime minister announced the terms of the Summit (1000 of Australia's 'brightest and best' to spend a weekend exploring ten subject areas), summits, round tables, conferences and debates had begun springing up in all kinds of contexts. Indeed, the emergence of a new zest for 'conversation' must rank as one of the markers of our emergence from the Dreamy Period.

Common Ground, Intelligence2, Deliberative Polls ... such high-profile initiatives were well under way before the 2020 Summit, as were a growing number of informal 'think-tank' events, ranging from education and health forums to debates about multiculturalism and democracy itself. By the beginning of 2008, Australia was engaged in a veritable talkfest: some of these events, following the classical debating model, seemed destined merely to reinforce prejudices; some offered opportunities for the community to become better informed about particular topics; some were designed to establish points of agreement and common purpose among those of differing points of view. ABC TV, following the sustained success of SBS's *Insight* program, launched *Q & A* at just the right time to tap into this growing need to gather and talk.

The 2020 Summit was part of the trend. Some commentators were critical of the selection process, believing a greater effort should have been made to avoid 'the usual suspects' whose views were already well known or who had ready access to the media. They felt greater representation should have been given to the rising generation of young thinkers, bursting with fresh ideas and eager to find a forum in which to express them.

To some extent, this criticism was addressed by the conduct of a Youth Summit, one week before the 2020 Summit (though some of the 100 young people selected for the Youth Summit complained of feeling as if they'd been invited to a wedding and then seated at the 'children's table'). In the weeks leading up to the 2020 Summit, 'summits' were also conducted in over 500 primary and secondary schools around the nation. These in-school events encouraged pupils to identify key issues facing Australian society, and to propose solutions to be submitted to the government. Submissions came in all shapes and sizes, via all imaginable media, and focused particularly on population, sustainability, climate change and water. Recommendations ranged from installation of shower heads with in-built timers to the invention of classroom-managing robots 'with hearts of steel'.

The 2020 Summit itself attracted a great deal of interest from the media, though it was difficult to gauge the level of interest in the community-at-large. The ten subjects explored by participants (who came to be known as 'summiteers') were: productivity, the economy, the environment, rural issues, health, families, indigenous issues, the creative arts, governance and national security. The strongest immediate recommendation to emerge from the Summit was that Australia should move decisively towards becoming a republic – hardly a revolutionary proposal, since a large majority of Australians have held precisely that view for many years.

Some cynics dismissed the 2020 Summit as an exercise in legitimising existing Labor policies, and others felt it was a kind of 'Kev-fest': in *The Sydney Morning Herald* of 21 April 2008, Annabel

Crabb wrote that 'the entire program was suffused with Kevinism, as delegates tried each in their own little way to achieve the ultimate state of grace, or Kevin on Earth'. The government undertook to respond to all recommendations by the end of 2008, but the symbolic work was done by the event itself: the Summit positioned the new government as being interested in the big picture, not afraid to confront issues, and prepared to listen to voices outside the parliament and public service.

Nevertheless, the 2020 Summit did create expectations of specific action on many fronts – from a major overhaul of the tax system to a plan for students to be able to work off their HECS debt through community service – and the government's response to Summit recommendations will finally determine its substantive, as well as symbolic, value.

Other symbols emerged from the early months of the new government that sent encouraging messages not only to the Labor faithful, but to a community looking for signs of a 'new order'. The strong representation of women among the ministers and parliamentary secretaries of Labor's new government was one such symbol: Julia Gillard (Australia's first female deputy prime minister), Penny Wong, Nicola Roxon, Jenny Macklin, Tanya Plibersek, Kate Ellis, Maxine McKew and Justine Elliot gave the Rudd government a distinctly more female tone than any previous government from either side of politics. (Whether this feminisation of the government will do what voters have always hoped it might – make politics less aggressive, less adversarial, more courteous and less 'blokey' – remains to be seen.)

The prime minister's announcement of the appointment of Quentin Bryce, Governor of Queensland and former Federal Sex Discrimination Commissioner, as the next governor-general drew widespread praise. Again, there was an element of 'the new order' in the appointment: Bryce (like Rudd, originally hailing from rural Queensland) became Australia's first female governor-general, but she was also widely tipped to be Australia's last governor-general and, as part of the process of transition to a republic, Australia's first Australian head of state.

During his first visit to London as prime minister, Kevin Rudd encouraged such speculation by his carefully-timed remarks about the republic on 8 April 2008, the day before his first audience with the Queen at which he recommended Bryce's appointment. 'Once a republican, always a republican,' he announced to the media. While declaring that a referendum on the issue was not a priority, he added that 'it's absolutely clear in the Australian Labor Party platform that's where we intend to go'. Labor's platform is indeed explicit on the issue: the 2007 election manifesto stated that 'Labor believes the monarchy no longer reflects either the fundamental democratic principles that underpin the Australian nation or its diversity.' (See Chapter 19: The Monarchy.)

Now for the long haul...

Before the 2007 federal election, several economic commentators had been suggesting that this would be a good election to lose. With world financial markets in disarray (partly in response to the collapse of the US sub-prime mortgage market), Australian share prices tumbling, oil prices soaring, house prices levelling off or falling, interest rates rising and unemployment creeping back up again, 2008 certainly turned out to be a challenging first year for the Rudd government.

Even so, nothing is harder for popular politicians than to keep their feet on the ground. And nothing is harder for voters swept up in the euphoria of a new government than to remind themselves that no government can work miracles, all politicians have feet of clay, and symbols, however powerful, are no substitute for substance.

Starting out as one of the most popular prime ministers in recent Australian history, Kevin Rudd faces the special challenge of not yielding to hubris, and not falling into some of the other traps that finally brought John Howard undone: exploiting the community's anxieties and insecurities for his own political ends; reinforcing darker impulses (such as prejudice) that eventually come back to haunt us; ignoring the will of the people: making unsustainable undertakings (for example, about interest rates); failing to judge the right moment to leave the stage.

For both government and people, post-election euphoria carries hazards, not the least of which is the temptation to yield to the seductive embrace of the nanny state and to fall for the trap of thinking that more rules and regulations will make us feel secure and 'in control'. For any new government, there's the risk of cashing in too much goodwill with over-zealous regulation that responds to the concerns of special-interest groups about various recurring issues – gambling, drinking, parenting, media content – and an associated desire among activists to have the government 'do something'. For the community, there's the mirror-image hazard: pinning too much faith in a new government and assuming that all its actions will be well-intentioned and wise.

There's also the hazard, particularly for Labor governments, of using the prosperity of a booming, market-based economy to fuel ever-more generous welfare arrangements, so that not only the poor, disadvantaged and marginalised are cared for, but 'middle-class welfare' is also encouraged (as it was, to some extent, by the Howard government's failure to means-test things like the baby bonus and grants to first-home buyers). In an unusually philosophical speech to The Sydney Institute on 12 June 2008, Dr Craig Emerson, Minister for Small Business, used the term 'market democrats' to describe the new Labor government's approach to the need for balance between free markets and compassion for the genuinely disadvantaged:

> Market democrats support opportunity for all in a market economy. They see the role of government not in fettering the market but in harnessing the power of the market for the public good . . . Market democrats are the champions of competition and compassion.

Perhaps the surest sign that we have entered a period of re-engagement (rather than mere euphoria) will be when Kevin Rudd's poll ratings dip significantly, and voters' enthusiasm is replaced by a more measured critique of what the government is actually doing. By mid-2008, that critique was starting to happen, though the prime minister continued to enjoy stratospheric ratings in the polls.

The most strident criticism, predictably, was coming from the Opposition. Six months after the prime minister announced, as part of his formal apology to the Stolen Generations, that he was setting up a task force on Aboriginal health and welfare to be co-chaired by himself and the Opposition leader, Brendan Nelson complained that nothing more had been heard of this. Dr Nelson similarly complained, as the parliament rose on 26 June 2008 for its mid-winter break, that in its first seven months in office, the Rudd government had set up 137 enquiries or committees – the clear implication being that there was more talk than action.

Writing in *The Sydney Morning Herald* of 14-15 June, Matthew Moore highlighted the failure of the Rudd government to show any sign of honouring its promise to reform the Freedom of Information laws, in sharp contrast to the impressive FoI reforms in Queensland that had occurred under its new premier, Anna Bligh.

Other grounds for criticism of the government's performance were also beginning to emerge.

In June 2008, the Minister for the Environment, Peter Garrett, attended a meeting of the International Whaling Commission in Santiago, Chile, intent on persuading the IWC to ban Japan's scientific whaling operations, and accusing Japan of using 'research' as a mere cover for killing. Before the meeting, Garrett had declared that there was no room for compromise on this issue but, in the event, no vote was taken and Australia's position did not prevail. While Greenpeace and the Opposition were highly critical of the outcome, Garrett had always conceded this would be a long process and that more diplomacy was required before any resort to legal action. Nevertheless, reports of the IWC conference provided ammunition for those inclined to criticise the government for 'too much talk, not enough action'.

In the same month, the Minister for Energy, Martin Ferguson, was sent to a conference in Saudi Arabia to 'apply the blowtorch to OPEC' (in Kevin Rudd's words) in an attempt to persuade the oil producing nations to lift production as a way of easing oil prices. In the event, no 'blowtorch' was applied: Ferguson was reported to have praised Saudi Arabia for helping stabilise the oil market and prevent damage to the global economy. And while he called for more investment in oil production, a more transparent market and for developing countries to cut their subsidised fuel programs, he did not specifically seek an increase in OPEC's production levels, claiming later that Australia's position had already been made clear.

The looming challenge of petrol prices

Martin Ferguson's visit to Jeddah came at a time when the issue of petrol prices was beginning to dog the Rudd government, partly because the prime minister was widely believed to have promised to bring petrol prices down (a belief reported by Newspoll to be held by 51 percent of voters). The immediate issue of price at the retail pump was being clouded by confusion about whether the government's proposed carbon emissions trading scheme would add to the upward pressure on the price of petrol. At the end of June 2008, *The Sydney Morning Herald* reported a cabinet assurance that its carbon trading scheme would not add to the net price of petrol: either petrol would be omitted from the scheme or, if it were included, the excise would be reduced to offset the increase caused by the imposition of a carbon tax.

Inevitably, this raised large questions about what the government could – or should – do in response to petrol prices that were predicted to keep rising steeply for the foreseeable future. Any attempt to artificially hold down the price of petrol would be likely to enrage environmentalists and others who believe that rising petrol prices are a blessing, because they create a financial spur to changed behaviour.

How, they wondered, could a government say it was serious about reducing carbon emissions – and oil-dependency generally – while trying to find ways of making petrol cheaper?

While the ACCC was implementing its petrol price surveillance system in the hope of ending opportunistic pricing by petrol retailers, rising petrol prices nevertheless gave the Rudd government the perfect opportunity to offer leadership about the need to accept some short- and medium-term pain and disruption as society moves to a less oil-dependent approach to living, especially in the area of transport. As Alan Fels and Fred Brenchley wrote in *The Sydney Morning Herald* of 28-29 June 2008: 'The transition to a low carbon economy will certainly redefine political courage.'

In a *Herald* article about global inflation published two weeks earlier, Peter Hartcher had noted that 'Rudd was carried into power with the expectation that he could somehow stop prices from rising. To adapt Winston Churchill, these expectations are a tiger that, so far, he has dared not dismount. This is the time to attempt a dismount. He should treat the Australian people as adults; take us into his confidence, point to the great wave of global inflation, and explain that he can help manage it, but that he cannot single-handedly turn the tide of global history... Rudd should not pose as the King Canute of Australian politics, ludicrously ordering back an unstoppable tide. He should dare Brendan Nelson to snatch that crown.'

Hartcher's reference to Brendan Nelson was a response to the Opposition leader's demand that the government should immediately reduce the petrol excise, regardless of the implications of its proposed carbon tax, as a way of holding down prices at the pump.

On both sides of politics, the question of petrol prices could not be avoided: by the middle of 2008, this had become a major community concern – not only because of the cost of filling the tank of the family car, but also because of the obvious connection between the price of petrol and the price of food and other commodities whose retail prices are hostage to transport costs.

While some opinion polls were showing that motorists would like the government to do whatever it could to hold petrol prices down, the deeper truth emerging from exploratory qualitative research was that this was a community ready to fight the environmental enemy in whatever theatre of war governments might choose: water use, car use, electricity use, plastic bag use . . . all such areas were perceived to be 'fair game' for tougher regulations and restrictions. By early 2008, the community's concern about the future of the planet had been tuned to a higher pitch than ever before, which meant that a high degree of compliance with any new regulations was likely, as demonstrated by the impressive level of compliance with domestic water restrictions around the country.

An absence of bold leadership on such issues almost guarantees they will drop off the community's list of top priorities. Since comfort and convenience tend to win over responsibility and restraint, the window of opportunity for leadership is actually quite small: 'If the government isn't encouraging us to change our ways, the problem can't be as serious as we thought' – that pretty much sums up the danger of inadequate or laggardly leadership. The NSW government's decision in June 2008 to relax water restrictions to the extent of allowing people to wash their cars was a case in point. Given that Sydney's Warragamba Dam was still only two-thirds full, that decision, though welcome, raised inevitable doubts in the community's mind about whether 'the water crisis' was a crisis at all, especially as an unwashed car had by then come to seem like a badge of environmental sensitivity.

Engaged consumers, too

If Australia is indeed waking from its Dreamy Period, politics won't be the only focus of its attention, though it's fair to suggest that with a freshly engaged electorate, incumbent governments – federal, state or territory – will feel less secure over the next five years than they might have over the past five. Voters at every level of government will be more alert, more critical, more demanding and less acquiescent.

The same goes for consumers. In a period of re-engagement, consumers will be less forgiving of any sign of exploitation, manipulation or deception on the part of advertisers, marketers and retailers. Greater transparency will be expected; greater honesty; greater frankness; greater attention to value-for-money and, indeed, to the values a brand stands for. Consumers will be more ready to criticise and complain; more open to the idea of 'shopping around'.

During the Dreamy Period, consumers were more relaxed, more acquiescent and more accommodating. The consumer marketplace was one of our favourite escapes: the colour and movement, the buzz, the allure of sophisticated packaging and display . . . all this was the stuff of retail therapy, and we soaked it up with more than usual enthusiasm. Our record levels of personal and household debt showed just how keen we had become on acquiring the trappings of prosperity; just how self-absorbed; just how self-indulgent.

There is no real sign of a retreat from the rampant materialism of the past decade, but the level of debt is taking its toll (especially as interest rates creep up) and more Australians are questioning whether they went a bit too far in the direction of extravagant self-indulgence – and, indeed, whether they were setting a sufficiently sensible example of restraint to their children. As the pain of sustained debt registers, consumers will be inclined to be more cautious about their spending and more selective about their indulgence.

No one would ever suggest that advertisers and marketers will be more successful if they become less emotional and more rational in their brand campaigns. But in the new era, consumers of everything from luxury cars to packaged food will be looking for the reassurance of some rational underpinnings of emotional appeals. The 'sizzle' is as important as ever but perhaps a bit more attention is now going to be paid to the 'sausage' as well.

Will the luxury/premium segment of consumer markets wither in this more restrained, more alert environment? Probably not: when belts need to be tightened and the threat of inflation and/or recession is looming, people still like to indulge themselves either as an antidote for the pain, or as a form of consolation, or, for the rich, as a way of demonstrating there is no pain: 'Downturn? What downturn?'

Such economic aloofness is reflected in the generally abysmal level of philanthropy among rich Australians, compared with their overseas counterparts: in the past ten years, while the average household income of affluent Australians has risen by 36 percent, their charitable giving has gone from 0.36 percent to 0.45 percent of their income, according to research undertaken by Daniel Petrie. This compares with 3.8 percent of income given to charity by affluent people in comparable countries to ours – especially the US.

In tighter economic circumstances, of course, the demand for charitable services increases. David Knowles, head of philanthropic services at Perpetual, told the *Australian Financial Review* of 14 May 2008: 'In economic terms, I would boil it down simply to say: demand is up and supply is down.' Knowles's view is confirmed by several charities who note that giving tends to dry up at precisely the time when generosity is most needed.

So, with some spectacular exceptions, it appears that tough times increase the tendency of wealthy Australians to attend to their own needs. Even among those who struggle to make ends meet, the self-indulgence of occasionally 'splashing out' feels like a welcome consolation in a tough economic environment: 'Look, I bought myself this cute little bag – I didn't need it, I can't really afford it, but I just felt like giving myself a treat.'

In media consumption, the shift back towards news and current affairs appears to have stalled, while *Domestic Blitz* and *Better Homes and Gardens* have strengthened their grip on the mass audience. Could this mean the change of government was not a sign of genuine re-engagement, but only of dissatisfation with the Coalition? Could it be that we are seeing the beginning of the Dreamy Period – Stage 2? Given all the other evidence of a re-awakening, that seems unlikely (and there is, after all, never just one trend). The mass media have always primarily been a pastime – literally, a way of passing the time – and the mass audience generally seeks entertainment rather than education, especially when it comes to television. In fact, whether we've re-engaged or not, a tougher economic environment invariably stimulates the appetite of the mass audience for escapism.

A new optimism, tinged with anxiety

Beyond politics, beyond consumerism, beyond the media, the new era of re-engagement will be marked by more vocal and more determined activism. From local community groups to trade unions and even to online networks like GetUp!, Australians are finding their voices and rediscovering the sense of empowerment that engagement and participation can bring. Encouraged by the demise of Work Choices, but also in response to a tougher economic environment, trade unionism will increase its appeal to workers, not only as a powerful voice on their behalf, but also as a source of emotional comfort and tribal identity. The sense of powerlessness is beginning to recede (though there are still plenty of disadvantaged and marginalised Australians, including the estimated 100 000 homeless, for whom that is obviously untrue).

As Australia headed into the second half of 2008, various surveys pointed to falling consumer and business confidence. Paradoxically, that might have been a good sign, when taken in the context of the general sense of optimism and hope that accompanied the change of federal government. While consumers were adapting to the prospect that life might become tougher, and business leaders were starting to feel the chill of an economic downturn, there was persistent confidence in the idea that some of our biggest challenges might now be addressed. Whether we were talking about climate change, the public hospital system or poverty, there was an emerging sense that change is possible and that we ourselves, as individuals, could and perhaps should act (see 'One small step . . .' at the end of the book).

Such optimism represents a significant opportunity for governments at every level to harness the energy of a newly alert, freshly engaged society. In such a climate, a failure of political will would be more than usually disappointing to Australians hoping for a new, more visionary style of leadership – more inclusive, less divisive; more noble, less mean-spirited; more independent in foreign policy; more reflective of a diverse, open and civil society.

PART FIVE

We need to talk about . . .

Global warming
Politics
The Monarchy
Public education
Poverty
Arts funding

17

Global warming: Are we serious about renewable energy?

No one could say we weren't warned.

The debate about climate change has been raging for years, with furious disagreement among the experts over the extent to which human activity has interrupted the long, long cycles of our planet's climatic and ecological history. There was, after all, a time when the Earth was virtually a snowball; another, when the temperature at the iceless North Pole was a balmy 23 degrees; another, when sea levels were so low, vast land bridges connected land masses that now appear as separate continents.

Through all the talk, most of us haven't known quite what to think, but 2007 has been a turning point. Books like Tim Flannery's *The Weather Makers* and James Lovelock's *The Revenge of Gaia* have impressed many previously sceptical readers. Al Gore's film, *An Inconvenient Truth*, had us flocking to cinemas to catch the bad news, and Nicholas Stern's report, *The Economics of Climate Change*, persuaded even the most reluctant politicians in our midst to sit up and take notice. Perhaps it was that word 'economics' that finally did the trick, where 'ecology' and even 'morality' had previously failed.

So now we know the planet is warming again, and we're pretty sure human activity is accelerating the process. Even if you're still sceptical about that, it's clear we have been behaving recklessly towards the planet that sustains us and the threat of global warming has been a timely wake-up call.

Whether the pumping of greenhouse gases – especially carbon dioxide – into the atmosphere is a major or minor contributor to global warming, it's obviously a horrible thing to do and we have to find ways of giving it up. Until we do, blue skies will seem like a picture-book fantasy to millions of people in parts of the world where pollution from the burning of coal permanently blackens the sky.

Being Australians, we'd like to be able to claim that we're such small players in the scheme of things, it hardly matters what we do. Yet we see daily evidence of our own recklessness and the fragility of our own immediate environment, especially in our water shortages but even in the brown smudge that, for years, has hung menacingly in the sky above our two major cities.

There are personal responses to all this; there are national responses; there are global responses. They are all necessary. Obviously, we've got to junk gas-guzzling vehicles, drive less, use public transport more, fly less, conserve water religiously, use less electricity, recycle everything we can . . . in short, become utterly planet-conscious in everything we do. Individual actions like those are respectful towards the environment, and that's a good way to live, crisis or no crisis. But low-emission light bulbs and bicycles, virtuous as they are, aren't going to solve the planet's woes.

To suggest that Australia shouldn't be taking drastic national action to cut its own carbon emissions because the rest of the world – China and India in particular – is continuing on its merry way is to miss the whole point of the crisis. Brilliant new technology is urgently needed; creative solutions are urgently needed; leadership is urgently needed: why not from us?

In any case, we have nothing to be smug about. Per capita, we are second only to the US as the world's worst emitter of carbon. In the past 25 years, we have been increasing our emissions at twice the world average rate. If we are on the brink of developing clean-burn coal technology, as coal industry advocates assure us we are, we'd better get on with it – not only for the good of our own skies and lungs, but for the contribution such technology could make to the global reduction of carbon emissions.

Wherever we send our coal to be burned, our moral obligation goes with it, since we are selling a product that has the potential to damage the health of millions of people. (If tobacco companies are morally responsible for the sale of unhealthy products, why aren't we?)

As soon as we've worked out how to burn coal more cleanly, that obligation extends to making the provision of clean-burn technology available to anyone who buys our coal – or, indeed, anyone who burns coal from anywhere. If our research scientists have the brains and we give them enough financial backing, we could make the world's biggest leap towards addressing the problem of coal. But that's only a short-term solution: coal is still a non-renewable fossil fuel.

'Carbon neutral' is the new buzz. Professor Peter Newman, director of Murdoch University's Institute for Sustainability and Technology, wrote in *The West Australian* of 28 April 2007 that on a recent round-the-world air trip, he paid an extra $80 to ensure 33 trees were planted, making his trip carbon-neutral. He argues that by adding realistic costs to activities that involve the use of fossil fuel – in power generation and transport, in particular – carbon-neutral policies will generate the funds to accelerate research into clean and renewable energy sources.

Now, what about solar? Germany produces more solar-powered electricity than we do. Spain is experimenting with huge (and beautiful) solar power towers. Our very own Commonwealth Scientific and Industrial Research Organisation – the CSIRO – already knows how solar power could generate all the electricity we need. CSIRO scientists have developed the technology, based on solar panels covering an area 25 km by 25 km (though not necessarily all in one place): they still have to solve the problems of overnight battery storage and long-range transmission of power but, given a generous research and development budget, the CSIRO believes solar power could generate all Australia's electricity needs by 2020.

So here we are, on the world's driest continent, with vast tracts of arid, sun-drenched open space and the technology to harness the power of the sun, talking about . . . *nuclear* power? *Really?*

Yes, nuclear is a zero-emission power source, though it consumes a great deal of energy in the mining, transport and processing of uranium ore, and in the processes of enrichment, storage and waste disposal. Manufacturing solar panels also consumes energy, of course, but the CSIRO says they pay for themselves in savings on the cost of power generation within three years, and those being produced today have a life span of about 20 years.

Uranium is not a renewable source of energy, the risk of a catastrophic accident is ever-present (as it is with underground coal-mining), a nuclear power industry is vulnerable to pressure to develop nuclear weapons, and the problem of safe storage of radioactive waste for a millennium or two is still far from being solved. Even countries that already have a nuclear power industry, like the UK, will inevitably be turning their attention to renewable energy alternatives (especially solar and wind) for all the obvious reasons – the most compelling being that they are free of ecological hazard.

The implementation of an Australian nuclear industry would be at least 15 years away, even if we decided to do it today, and the cost of its electricity would be between 20 and 50 percent higher than for coal. By then, clean-burn coal will have been established as a viable short-term option, solar and wind power will have become the goal of every sensible nation on earth, and we could be world leaders in those fields.

May I state the obvious? The global warming crisis is all about the future – including our grandchildren's future and their grandchildren's future. We are laying the groundwork now for that l-o-n-g journey. Hands up all those who know a fail-safe way of generating nuclear power and storing nuclear waste, come what may.

But solar? Keep replacing the panels as they wear out. Add a few square kilometres to the panel installations, as required, or develop even more efficient solar towers. If the sun stops shining, then every prediction was wrong and we're all history. If it doesn't, we'd have power forever, with no emissions, no mining, no risk to the health of future generations.

It's hard to see the objection.

But we shouldn't be embracing a single solution. In the same way as drought-proof cities will have to rely on a combination of water storage, recycling, desalination and underground aquifers, so our power will need to be generated from as many renewable energy sources as possible.

Wind power is good. So is wave power. And we have plenty of wind and waves around our vast coastline. We're also well endowed with hot rocks from which to generate some geothermal energy.

Where to from here?

First, let's get on with the development of cleaner coal technology to tide us over and help our global neighbours out of a jam. But let's also assume we'll be phasing out of coal altogether, probably over the next two decades, as renewable energy sources – solar, wind, wave, geothermal – come on stream.

Second, invest whatever it takes to develop the technology for efficient storage and transmission of solar-powered electricity and share that technology with the world.

Third, ask the CSIRO to start planning, right now, for the location of large solar installations in uninhabited regions of every state.

It's always awkward when a moral imperative, like the health and wellbeing of future generations, collides with an economic imperative, like profit. We have a long history of letting economic imperatives prevail. This time, it looks as if the moral imperative won't be denied. If we ultimately had to choose between material prosperity and survival, which way do you think we would jump? If we know the answer, why not act now, so we never have to face that choice.

18

Politics: Can we improve the system?

'Parliament is an inherently unhappy place,' I once heard former New South Wales education minister Rodney Cavalier say at a seminar. 'Members of the Opposition want to be in government, backbenchers want to be on the front bench, junior ministers want to be in cabinet and half the members of cabinet want to be premier.'

Perhaps the electorate is an inherently unhappy place, too, since only about half the voters ever get the government they want. In fact, the two-party system strikes many voters as being a bit redundant in the present political climate. Politicians on both sides disagree with that assessment, of course, but the voters often find it difficult to imagine what difference a change of government would make. Occasionally, an issue pops up – like workplace reform – that revives traditional differences, but policies are rarely seen as naturally belonging in one camp or the other.

The overwhelming emphasis on leaders ('Who are you going to vote for – Howard or Rudd?') exacerbates the problem. In fact, the rise of personality politics is one of the most convincing signs that yesterday's Right/Left distinctions are losing their relevance in modern politics.

We're obviously not going to overhaul the party system for the foreseeable future. But esteem for politics and politicians is so low – partly reflected in declining membership of political parties, and partly in scathing attitudes towards politics in the wider community – that something needs to change.

Bad parliamentary behaviour, for a start. Mud-slinging, personal abuse, excessive rowdiness. Australian politics has a well-earned reputation as a bruising, brutal business, both in the parliamentary chamber and behind closed doors. The factions within the major parties appear to hate each other even more than they hate their political opponents.

If we were to clean up the parliamentary process, perhaps we should start with Question Time. To be blunt, it's a farce, a charade, a Punch and Judy show. Many Australians suspect that parliamentarians must feel the same way which is why it so often seems to be treated like a game. No one assumes this is where the work of the parliament is done: it's a kind of public relations exercise designed to rally the troops and create a fleeting impression of winners and losers, presumably to impress the politicians themselves and a few journalists. Yes, it occasionally unearths something we need to know; it occasionally embarrasses a politician on one side of the chamber, to the accompaniment of childish hoots of glee from the other. Voters occasionally find it entertaining, usually for the wrong reasons – verbal violence can be fun to watch for ten or 20 seconds on the evening news, but it only adds to the deep-seated sense of despair about the futility of it all.

Couldn't Question Time be turned into a more useful exercise? Suppose questions could only be asked by non-government members: that, at least, would eliminate the farcical use of so-called 'Dorothy Dixers', asked by obedient government backbenchers of ministers who want to use Question Time to make mini-speeches – either to brag or to score points off the Opposition or simply to waste time so the Opposition can't get on with it. Get rid of all that, for a start.

Another constructive step would be to limit Oppositions to one question on any one topic per session, with a possible supplementary question that clearly arises from a minister's answer. It's time to put an end to the nonsense of an Opposition taking up an entire Question Time endlessly trawling through one subject. Politicians may say this is all good sport and 'puts pressure on the government'. Voters simply say, 'Could you all please grow up? Could you please ask questions that get us somewhere? Could you please treat the parliament – and each other – with a bit more respect?'

While we're at it, why not examine the feasibility of appointing an independent speaker, as the British House of Commons does, rather than plucking an elected MP out of the system and hoping for the best – often with disappointing results. The British example of five-year terms also warrants some consideration. Our three-year terms seem faintly ridiculous when you consider the cost of elections, the short planning horizons they impose on governments and the fact that the third year in office often amounts to a year-long election campaign.

The rigidity of the two-party system needs some attention, too, especially given the blurring of traditional philosophical distinctions between the parties. It has not escaped voters' attention that the quality and seriousness of parliamentary debate is immeasurably lifted when there's a so-called 'conscience vote' – in other words, when members of parliament are speaking their minds and airing a topic thoroughly, unconstrained by what their party has instructed them to say. On such occasions, voters have even been heard to express pride in the intellectual capacity, courtesy and fairness of our MPs.

'Why can't all votes be conscience votes?' is a question often asked at such times. Perhaps the answer is that it would be too cumbersome or too time-consuming, but voters are entitled to raise that question and they'd like to hear the answer. As things stand, they feel as if the inherently adversarial nature of the system means that MPs and senators represent their parties, not the people in their electorates. When Queensland senator Barnaby Joyce first entered the Senate in 2004 and spoke as if he were indeed going to represent the people of Queensland, he was sharply rebuked by a prime minister who was in no doubt that all MPs' first responsibility is to the party they represented when they stood for election.

It's a thorny issue, especially in the case of the Senate, which is supposed to be charged with the responsibility of protecting the states' rights. (Whatever happened to that idea?)

The voters are in no doubt: the whole party discipline thing needs to be loosened, not tightened. Their main plea is for a more united sense of purpose ('the good of the country'), less point-scoring, less rigid adherence to the party line, more seriousness, more dignity. Though many MPs are praised for their integrity, their idealism, their hard work and their sensitivity to the needs of their own electorates, they are thought to be compromised by a parliamentary process that diminishes them all.

It goes without saying that voters are appalled by ministerial impropriety (though, in the Dreamy Period, they didn't care as much as usual). They mistrust a system that leaves such matters in the hands of a prime minister or premier and would love to see higher standards set, with some independent assessment of whether those standards have been breached.

And the states? A reflex response among many Australians is that 'we don't need the states'. This is partly a reflection of the general belief that Australians are overgoverned: do we really need 15 houses of parliament to govern 20 million people? (By the way, we could eliminate five of those houses of parliament at one stroke, simply by bringing all the states into line with Queensland and doing away with their upper houses.) But it's also due to genuine confusion about who is responsible for what – especially in areas like health and education. And when the Commonwealth takes over state powers – as in the 2006 case of industrial relations laws – voters wonder whether we are heading, inexorably, for a more centralised system.

On the other hand, they quite like the inherent tension in a system that has federal and state governments, sometimes of different persuasions, needing to work together. That provides some of the 'checks and balances' voters would like to believe in.

One day, perhaps, we'll do what some voters dream of: create two tiers of government by replacing state and local government with a number of provinces. But there's no pressure in the system for such a change. In the meantime, can't we refine the current system, starting with the parliamentary behaviour of politicians themselves?

19

The Monarchy: Aren't we over it yet?

The monarchy? *Us?* Yes, that's what we still are. We are part of a unique thing called a 'shared monarchy' which means we borrow someone else's head of state for special occasions and, the rest of the time, get by with a *vice*-regal figure we treat as our quasi-head of state. We share our monarch not only with the UK, but with 14 other countries including the Solomon Islands, Grenada, Canada and New Zealand. It's a relic; a carry-over from the time when we were a colonial outpost of the British Empire, before Britain lost its imperial clout.

You could say it's quaint – and so it is. You could even say it works – and so it does, in the sense that we don't have Britain's Queen telling our governor-general or government what to do. (Mind you, she wouldn't dare tell the British government what to do, either.) But it doesn't work if you think a strong, independent nation needs the symbolism of its own head of state. The British royal family presumably chuckles, whenever it occurs to them, about our tardiness in cutting this anachronistic apron string and standing, finally and fully, on our own two feet.

Most Australians want an Australian head of state, though some think the governor-general is near enough and, in any case, most of us lost interest in the subject during the Dreamy Period. When we force ourselves to think about it, we're still a bit nervous about the word 'republic' and perhaps even about the word 'president' (the world having seen too many ugly versions of both). The labels don't matter, of course. We can call our head of state whatever we like – including Governor-General. In fact, if we wanted to have our very own monarchy, we could even do that.

We wouldn't have to found a hereditary monarchy – that wouldn't be our style, and it wouldn't be consistent with our anti-elitist culture (anti-elitist in everything but sport, that is). But we could easily elect a monarch, and let him or her serve until a pre-determined age – say 70 or 75 – and then elect someone else to take over. Pick the right person at age 50, and you wouldn't have to worry about it for another 20 or 25 years.

A republican system would be a simpler, less controversial idea, but let's not change our name. We can still call ourselves the Commonwealth of Australia.

Australians don't only want their own head of state; they want a say in who it should be. They want an election, and they should have an election. What possible objection could there be to the people choosing their own head of state? The only issue is: how can we organise an election that is appropriate to the dignity of the office, isn't subject to the rough-and-tumble of a conventional election campaign, and isn't at all political.

Here's what I'd do.

Invite all our state premiers and chief justices to submit nominations to a federal parliamentary all-party committee, perhaps chaired by the chief justice of the High Court, which works its way through the list of nominees and then submits a short list (maximum of seven names, at least two women and at least two men) to the federal parliament. The parliament is charged with the responsibility of coming up with a final list of three nominations, including at least one woman and at least one man. There is no unseemly parliamentary debate about the merits of the candidates: members and senators debate as much as they wish in private, informal discussion and then vote by secret ballot (by some suitable version of our much-loved preferential system) to obtain the three names.

Those three names are then put to the people in an election. The candidates will probably be well known, and, in any case, biographical notes about them would be widely circulated. The media would be involved, so there'd be plenty of information in the public domain in the weeks leading up to the poll.

Advertising would be banned (the sort of candidates we'd want wouldn't have a bar of electioneering). So would the publication of opinion polls. This must have none of the trappings of a political election, though it would be impossible to stop the experts pontificating and the commentators commenting.

Personally, I'd elect this person for a very long time. As with the fanciful idea of an elected monarch, we could simply set a retiring age of 70 or 75, which would automatically determine the length of service. (Obviously, we'd need a mechanism for terminating the appointment in case of obvious signs of madness or incapacity.) This is a figurehead, remember; a largely ceremonial figure; a wise counsellor to the prime minister, perhaps, but not an active player in the political process. We need a skilled orator, a dignified presence, a focal point for the nation in times of tragedy, crisis, triumph or adversity as well as someone equipped to do the formal work of signing bills into law, chairing meetings of the Executive Council, and so on. So it's appropriate that he or she serve for long enough to become something of an institution, the way a monarch does.

As for the precise codification of the head of state's powers, I imagine it would take the chief justice of the High Court, the governor-general and a couple of suitably equipped frontbenchers from both sides of politics a week or two to nut that out, their proposals to be considered by the federal parliament as part of its debate on a bill to establish the position of head of state.

And the states? For as long as we have state governments, we'll need state governors (which is a good reason to continue calling our head of state 'governor-general'). There's no call for their popular election, so why not continue to appoint them the way we do now, except that each state premier's recommendation would need to be approved by our very own, exclusive, head of state rather than by England's Queen.

There – was that so hard?

20

Public education: Do we really believe in it?

Our school education system is becoming increasingly polarised. Governments – federal, state and territory – fund public schools, but 22 percent of their total budget is spent on subsidising private (mostly church-based) schools where parents have to pay fees as well. Some private schools are wealthy enough to survive on their own (though we don't ask them to: our present system provides subsidies to *all* private schools) but most are really hybrids that couldn't survive in their present form without state funding.

In an interview televised on ABC's *Stateline* in New South Wales on 18 May 2007, John Howard put all this into perspective by noting that governments spend, on average, $6000 per student in private schools and $11 000 per student in public schools.

It wasn't always like this. Until the mid-1960s, we had a state-funded system of public education, and a parallel system of self-funded private schools – most of them Catholic schools that only existed because the Catholic church wanted to educate its young in its own way. Other churches also had their own schools, and there were a few fully independent private schools as well (like Sydney, Melbourne and Brisbane Grammar schools). In those days, public schools were highly regarded and well resourced, because that's where most parents sent their children. Indeed, children sent to private non-Catholic schools were sometimes regarded as not quite up to scratch academically – as indeed were many of their teachers – and the private school was supposed to compensate for that by providing extra polish and, of course, the cachet of the old school tie – a relic of the English 'public school' (i.e., private school) tradition. Many private schools had strong family connections running through several generations, and they were also where wealthy business and professional people sent their offspring, so the networking benefits were often judged to be worth the fees.

'Private school snob' was a standard insult in those days, though private schools certainly produced more than snobs: some of the 20th century's most outstanding scholars, politicians, and leaders in business and the professions were educated in private schools. The point is: those schools did what they did without money from the state, and they coexisted with a robust and highly diverse public school system.

Then, under sustained pressure from the Catholic church – the State Aid campaign of the 1950s and early '60s – everything changed. In 1962, prime minister Robert Menzies, deciding that the Catholic schools system actually took potential pressure off the state system, made state aid for non-government schools part of Liberal Party policy. Money began trickling, and then flowing, into the coffers of the private schools.

Until the early 1980s, most recurrent federal education spending still went to public schools but by 1996, 55 percent was being allocated to private schools. That figure had ballooned to 74 percent by 2006, even though only 32 percent of pupils were attending private schools.

Almost all education funding comes from the federal government – some dished out directly and some distributed via the states by a system so complex and opaque that even experts in the field have difficulty explaining how it works.

Of the $31 billion allocated to school operations (as opposed to capital works) in 2005–6, $7 billion was spent directly by the Commonwealth and $24 billion by the states and territories. Seven percent ($1.7 billion) of state and territory budgets went to non-government schools. Add that to the $5.2 billion allocated to non-government schools by the federal government, and total recurrent government spending on private schools amounted to about $6.9 billion.

That means about 22 percent of government funding is spent on the 32 percent of pupils in private schools whose parents are, of course, paying fees as well – around $20 000 per annum for top private schools.

Under the headline 'Private schools awash in cash', *The Sydney Morning Herald* reported on 6 October 2006 that a leading private boys' school with an operating surplus of $4.1 million for the year had received $3.3 million in government funding, while a girls' school that had received $2.5 million in government funding had reported a net surplus of $2 million for the year. Meanwhile, 70 percent of public school principals surveyed by the Australian Education Union say their schools are in need of a serious maintenance overhaul.

On 23 May 2007, the *Herald* economics editor, Ross Gittins, wrote: 'In the case of schools, Howard's greatest achievement has been to bias federal grants heavily in favour of private schools – particularly the least needy.'

Demand for private school places has never been stronger, the rate of creation of new private schools has never been higher, nor esteem for public schools lower, though some state high schools are esteemed for the very things private schools are supposed to excel at, including academic performance, the arts, sport and 'school spirit'. In some states, the top high schools outperform most private schools academically (the New South Wales Higher School Certificate results being a particularly clear example), and students from state high schools apparently do better at university, overall, than their private-school counterparts, though there are many exceptions, of course, and wide variations between individual schools.

Still, the trend in favour of private schools is now so marked, leading educationist Professor Barry McGaw has warned of the danger that the state secondary system might become a residual service for those unable to afford the alternative.

In the present climate of opinion, few would begrudge non-government schools their government funding unless it could be shown that the private sector was prospering at the expense of public schools. In a 2007 report commissioned by the New South Wales Public Education Alliance, *Making Federalism Work for Schools*, the former chair of the New South Wales Public Education Council, Lyndsay Connors, says the national system of funding schools is helping entrench social disadvantage in rural and suburban Australia, and that a funding system originally devised to favour disadvantaged Catholic schools was now advantaging the richest private schools.

The government argues that its generous support for private schools is all about promoting freedom of choice, but it's an increasingly lopsided choice: parents who want a private education for their children would presumably squeal if they had to pay the true market price for it – which is ironic, given that many of them are free-market advocates. What they actually want, presumably, is the freedom to send their children to a private school heavily subsidised by taxpayers.

The appeal of private schools in the present climate is hardly mysterious: top teachers, superb facilities, plus, being private, a freer hand in the administration of discipline and, in most cases, an emphasis on religion. They also operate with the huge advantage of being self-contained administrative units, with decision-making entirely localised in their own boards and councils, whereas public schools are burdened by the weight and inflexibility of huge state and federal bureaucracies and by restrictions on the freedom of the individual school's leaders – for example in hiring and firing staff. Private schools also tend to generate a higher level of parental involvement (partly because they are paying customers) and to be more successful at creating the sense of a school community to which whole families belong.

Those are some of the reasons why parents say they choose the private alternative, but an additional motivation is often at work: the consumer mentality that says 'If I pay for it, I can have more of a say in what I'm getting, and the more I pay, the more I am entitled to expect for my money.'

When parents of private-school pupils eulogise their children's schools, the subtext is often a bit more commercial than it sounds. As well as wanting to civilise their children via 'traditional values', many parents are also thinking of the opportunities they are buying for their children through better marks, better networks and, ultimately, better jobs.

Whatever happened to the idea that a world-class public education system – free, universal, compulsory – was the brightest symbol of

Australia's commitment to egalitarianism? The egalitarian ideal was never about equality of outcome, but it was certainly about equality of opportunity and the current school funding arrangements look like a threat to that ideal. In education, equal opportunity doesn't simply mean 'everyone can go to school'; it means there's a uniformly high standard of teaching and resources available to all school pupils – public and private.

The growing demand – and funding support – for private education may be a sign that we are institutionalising inequality on a scale that would once have seemed alien to us. If that's our intention, so be it; but we need to be clear about what we're doing, because there are alternatives. Even strongly bonded school communities can have an unintentionally divisive effect on broader neighbourhoods and communities by appearing to be bastions of privilege.

Assuming we're not about to abandon state aid for non-government schools, it's still reasonable to ask whether public schools are getting their fair share of the available public funds, and whether they could be differently managed and governed (perhaps with devolution of greater responsibility to principals and more local community involvement).

It's also worth investigating whether society receives the appropriate benefit from the money taxpayers spend on private schools. If any publicly funded private schools were to act in ways that were divisive, exclusivist and elitist, for example, we would be entitled to ask whether they should receive government support. To take one case, how does the community benefit from the $5 million per year of public money paid to the Exclusive Brethren sect's schools which, as noted in Chapter 2, are specifically designed to keep their pupils apart from

Australian society? Would we grant that kind of money to a Muslim school that had declared such an exclusivist goal?

Given the costs of education infrastructure, perhaps it's time to think more creatively about the public/private divide. In new housing developments at Melbourne's Caroline Springs and Adelaide's Golden Grove, the Delfin Lend Lease organisation has been piloting ways of encouraging public and private schools to share facilities like sporting fields, libraries, science labs, gymnasiums and auditoriums that place a heavy burden on state and private finances when they are unnecessarily duplicated.

The various school authorities in these locations have found ways of co-operating so the costs of major infrastructure can be shared without compromising the identities of each of the institutions involved.

Let's have more of that. And let's ask more schools – both public and private – to open themselves to the community. An ageing population with an increasing emphasis on lifelong learning will be expecting schools that accept public money to make their facilities more accessible to the public. Libraries, sporting facilities, theatres, gymnasiums – as well as more specific educational facilities – could well become a focus for adult education and other community-based activities.

Why shouldn't retired people who've always wanted to learn a musical instrument – or French, or History – sit in on classes or join a choir at a local school? And, while they're there, why not help out with coaching for slow readers, or career counselling for senior pupils? In schools of the future, the distinction between adults and children is likely to be blurred, with great benefits to both. As a starting point, many schools already conduct educational programs for parents – some on the subject of parenting itself.

Why shouldn't wealthy private schools occasionally make their facilities available to disadvantaged pupils from remote rural areas for music or language workshops, for example, or summer schools in mathematics, science or literature? Why not more co-operation between public and private schools, in everything from music to sport and, over time, more emphasis on shared facilities?

Eventually, we'll have to rethink the funding of public education. In the meantime, we need to find creative ways of broadening the benefits that flow from the present funding arrangements.

21

Poverty: A fact of life, or a problem to be solved?

Poverty is an unwelcome word in contemporary Australia. We're having an economic boom, after all, and we cling to the idea that ours is a land of equal opportunity; a middle-class society; a place where anyone can succeed with a decent education, hard work and a bit of luck.

'Sure,' we say, 'some Australians are richer than others, but there's no such thing as *real* poverty in Australia – not like parts of Asia or Africa. You can't live in a house and drive a car and call yourself poor.'

Yes, poverty is a relative term and we could argue all day about the definition, but when we know that 20 percent of Australian *households* have an average annual income of $22 500, mightn't that mean a lot of people are doing it tough?

In our context, 'poverty' refers to people who can't participate fully in the life of their community – feed and clothe themselves and their children to a conventional standard, have secure and comfortable accommodation, be able to afford the costs of education, transport, regular holidays, recreational activities and occasional treats, such as going to the movies or eating out.

On that definition, somewhere between one and two million Australians are poor. Why?

The high cost of housing has led to the new phenomenon of 'after-housing poverty', where low-income earners spend so much of their income on housing, via either mortgage payments or rent, that although they may be decently housed, they live in virtual poverty.

The steady drift from full-time and permanent work to part-time and temporary work has increased underemployment and created *the working poor* – an estimated one million people – who have jobs, but with fewer hours and/or less pay than they need. Many are on the minimum wage of $13.47 per hour.

People with *disabilities* typically experience reduced employment opportunities, reduced access to community services and, in many cases, are socially marginalised as well. Those problems often extend to their carers – mostly unpaid family members who carry a heavy burden of responsibility and have neither time nor energy for paid work.

And there's a factor we're reluctant to talk about: *low intelligence*. At its extreme, intellectual impairment counts as a disability but there are many people with limited intellectual fire-power who are far from disabled but who nevertheless struggle to make sense of what's happening to them and are bewildered by life's demands. They get themselves into trouble through reckless spending, unwise borrowing, relationship problems, or inappropriate decisions about housing, work, drugs or gambling.

The family you were born into and *the place where you live* can affect your access to education and employment opportunities, but can also shape your attitudes. About 700 000 Australian children are currently being raised in homes where no income is earned: they simply have no example of a working parent.

The strong correlation between *Aboriginality* and poverty is dispiriting. We look to Aboriginal leaders to propose strategies designed to break the cycles of poverty, poor health and reduced life expectancy, but no bold solutions are likely to be implemented until politicians sense that the community has the heart for serious and sustained reform.

Young people are still more likely to be unemployed and underemployed than older people, and they are also over-represented in mental illness statistics, leading to alarming social problems of youth homelessness and poverty.

Ironically, some of the social changes arising from *the gender revolution* – the high divorce rate and the increasing incidence of one-parent families – have financially disadvantaged women more than men, so it's fair to say that being a woman increases your chances of being poor, especially if you are a single mother. Older women are also at risk: in the over-60 age group, divorcees now outnumber widows and many of those women are inadequately catered for by superannuation but are not yet eligible for pension support.

Protracted *illness* can suck you down into the poverty trap, as can *addictions* of every kind, especially gambling but also including shopping.

Many explanations, but still the nagging question: in an affluent society like ours, why are so many Australians poor?

Perhaps we are asking the wrong question. If inequality is the real issue, perhaps we should be asking this one: why are so many Australians rich?

People become rich by a combination of *hard work, astuteness and good luck*. They may succeed because they manage to create a product or service that catches a wave of perfect timing and meets an unsatisfied demand.

Then, precisely as for poverty, there are *accidents of birth*. Just as some genetic and environmental influences will predispose you to struggle with life's challenges, a different set may equip you with high intelligence and strong motivation. No guarantee of success, of course, but not a bad asset to begin with.

There are also *the many faces of greed*. When wealth is accumulated for the purpose of accumulating wealth, there comes a point where it's appropriate to ask: 'How much is enough?' When no amount is ever enough, greed has taken over.

Desire for power drives some people to accumulate wealth, even if that involves the exploitation of others in order to achieve their goal.

Overestimating your value to the organisation can make you very rich. The new managerial elite – not entrepreneurs and capitalists but the managers who run their businesses for them – are now being paid at a level described by some commentators as 'executive plunder'. Writing in *The Sydney Morning Herald* of 23 May 2006, John Garnaut quoted a study by John Shields of the University of Sydney's School of Business, showing that CEOs of the 51 public companies that are members of the Business Council of Australia have received a 564 percent pay rise since 1989–90.

Hugh Stretton, the former head of the South Australian Housing Trust and author of the seminal *Ideas for Australian Cities*, has proposed that no one should earn more than three times as much as the lowest-paid person. I'd be more conservative than that: I'd suggest a factor of ten. If the lowest-paid full-time worker in an organisation earns

$40 000, then $400 000 would be the upper limit for the CEO of that organisation (whereas many senior executives currently judge themselves to be worth 100 times more than their lowest-paid employees).

In a 2005 conversation with Hugh Stretton on ABC Radio National's *The National Interest*, Terry Lane summarised the argument in Stretton's latest book, *Australia Fair*: 'Surveys show that above a certain income level, we don't get happier as we get richer, but below a certain income level, we can be very miserable indeed. That being the case, if the people above the income-equals-happiness level could be persuaded to give up some of their wealth for redistribution to the poor, then the nation's gross happiness index would rise ... There is enough wealth in this country for everyone to live free of the anxieties inherent in poverty. It just needs inspiring leadership ...' (It also needs a higher marginal tax rate than any contemporary government has the stomach for.)

By seeking an ever-larger share of the available economic pie, the rich promote inequality – often without consciously appreciating what they are doing. Perhaps some of them believe in the infamous 'trickle-down effect' the US economist John Kenneth Galbraith once described as 'the less-than-elegant metaphor that if one feeds the horse enough oats, some will pass through to the road for the sparrows'.

The trickle-down effect has been disproved by Australia's experience, and Garnaut's 2006 *Herald* article also quotes US figures showing that half of all America's productivity gains since 1996 had found their way into the pay packets of the top ten percent of income-earners.

Perhaps it's time to confront a painful possibility: are we, by our own actions, helping to institutionalise inequality?

We promote inequality whenever, as employers, we expect people to work longer than normal hours, thereby limiting the distribution of work, or whenever, as employees, we hog the available work by working overtime that could go to someone who needs more work than they currently have.

We do it whenever, as governments, we offer incentives to property investors (such as negative gearing) that push housing prices up and squeeze the poor out of the market, or introduce regressive taxes like the GST, that fall more heavily on the poor than the rich, or create disincentives to employment like payroll tax.

We do it whenever, as taxpayers, we try to avoid paying the tax appropriate to our income, which is, after all, the most efficient way of redistributing wealth to meet the needs of the poor. (And, by the way, 'the needs of the poor' have nothing to do with what we think the poor might *deserve*. In a truly civil society, we have only to establish that a need exists to have defined an entitlement. The poor are entitled to our support simply because they are poor.)

We help to institutionalise inequality whenever we encourage governments to put more money into the coffers of already wealthy private schools at the expense of public schools.

We do it whenever we think we are entitled to our prosperity – either by right or by good fortune – and that the relative poverty of those at the bottom of the heap is inevitable, unavoidable . . . and nothing to do with us.

Of course, there's nothing wrong with wealth (unless you think it's the measure of your worth). But everything is wrong with greed.

There's nothing wrong with a big pay packet, but everything is wrong with a preoccupation with possessions. As British philosopher

Bertrand Russell put it: 'A preoccupation with possession, more than anything else, prevents men from living freely and nobly.'

If we are even half-serious about reducing inequality, we must find more creative and equitable ways of distributing the available work, narrowing the chasm between high- and low-income earners, and compensating those who can't find any, or enough, paid work. (Tax cuts resulting from the 2007 federal budget, for instance, will give an extra $53 per week to those earning $200 000 a year, but only $3 a week to those earning $20 000 a year. Couldn't we have considered a strategy, just this once, to achieve precisely the opposite effect?) We must also find a way of dealing more generously with those who lack the capacity to earn an income, whether through disability, disadvantage, misfortune or incompetence.

Do we want to make them feel ashamed of themselves? Do we want to humiliate them? Or are we prepared to say: 'They are part of us; we must bring them with us, regardless of the cost.'

22

Arts funding: Are we missing a golden opportunity?

Australian governments – federal, state and territory – pour about $4 billion into the arts each year, and who's going to argue with that? You might even say it's one mark of a civilised society – rather like the provision of health, education, transport and communication services, leisure and recreation facilities, libraries and museums.

But we're entitled to raise a couple of questions, if only to reassure ourselves that our money is being spent wisely: *Who is supposed to benefit from government arts funding? And what is the nature of the benefit?*

Since it's public money we're talking about, the logical answer to the first question must be: the public. The assumption underlying public funding of the arts is that we all benefit from a thriving arts industry, because our lives are so profoundly affected by exposure to art in all its forms.

They are certainly affected, for good and ill, by architecture and industrial design, but because they are created in a commercial context, we don't need to fund them as 'art'. What about pop songs, crime drama, romantic comedies, TV soaps, political cartoons, blockbuster movies and pulp fiction? They all add to the creative ambience, but they don't need government handouts either, because they feed off their commercial success – no need to subsidise the work of Andrew Lloyd Webber, Frank Sinatra, the Rolling Stones, George Lucas or Dan Brown. Or Barry Manilow.

Ah, Manilow. The story might be apocryphal, but a 2006 news item reported that his music had been used by the British police to drive gangs out of trouble spots: amplifying the music of Manilow is evidently enough to send thugs running, hands clapped over their ears. But is Manilow's work uniquely suitable for crime prevention? Would Mahler, equally, repel miscreants? Might any kind of amplified music deter acts of violence and other crime? Is this why music is played in lifts – to calm the savage breasts of would-be assailants? Should public money be used to create 'musical neighbourhoods'? (Possibly not.)

So when should public money be applied to the arts? It's easy to defend public funding of initiatives for bringing entertaining, inspiring and educational art, music and theatre to small regional and rural communities who would otherwise not experience them. And public money is necessary to fund the creation of public art like statues, sculpture and other artworks designed to enrich public spaces. We should also support artists, writers, composers, actors, singers, directors who need time to undertake groundbreaking work with the potential to deepen our understanding and appreciation of our identity. (Throughout history, many creative artists have relied on the patronage of benefactors to support them – the church, monarchs and their aristocracies, wealthy traders and, more recently, the state.)

And we should support producers and performers committed to maintaining and reinterpreting the musical and theatrical canon that has shaped our culture, just as the literary canon must always be available to us in public libraries.

The heavy emphasis in government arts funding is, obviously, on art forms, artists and activities that aren't likely to be commercially viable. (Even charging seat prices of up to $220, Opera Australia must rely on commercial sponsorships and government grants to survive.) But there's also an implicit assumption in the arts world that the funding of 'highbrow'/elite arts (*The Ring Cycle*) is inherently worthwhile, or even virtuous, because exposure to it can make us better people in a way that 'lowbrow'/popular arts (*We Will Rock You*) can't – not just by giving its patrons pleasure, but by actually *improving* them in some moral or spiritual or even mystical way. Is that assumption justified?

In a remarkable book called *Everyday Ecstasy* (1985), the British writer Marghanita Laski examined whether the ecstatic response to art is normally – or ever – translated into enthusiasm for, say, charitable works designed to alleviate the suffering of those who may never experience such ecstasy. Is that how it benefits society, she wondered, by making us better, more compassionate, more sensitive people? Her reluctant answer was 'no' (and she didn't even quote the infamous example of that great art lover, Adolf Hitler).

In his 2006 book, *What Good are the Arts?*, the Oxford scholar and critic John Carey mused upon the strangeness of the fact that 'this farrago of superstition and unsubstantiated assertion [about the value of the arts] should have achieved a position of dominance in Western thought'. Carey, like Laski, contends that the arts do not 'improve' us any differently or any more than other forms of entertainment or recreation – including exposure to nature – that give us pleasure.

But we don't have to believe in the moral superiority of the arts to decide they are worth funding. We could simply say that audiences who like that kind of stuff are as entitled to their pleasure as those who like going to movies or football. There's nothing wrong with subsidising art, music or drama that will only ever appeal to audiences too small for commercial viability, as long as the wider community is happy to help foot the bill.

Or perhaps we believe that if we put enough money into the promotion of 'high' art it would become more accessible to people at large, who might then find they enjoyed it. Some arts funding does seem to encourage the process of bringing highbrow music, opera, paintings, theatre to people who might not otherwise think of 'the arts' as being intended for them and who discover a new source of pleasure.

In deciding which artists and organisations should receive government funding, we are in danger of overlooking a crucial point. The greatest *public* value of the arts is through participation in them, rather than merely being exposed to them as spectators. The most intense benefits of the arts flow from creating and performing, so why aren't we using public money to extend those benefits more widely?

There are lessons to be learned from sport. The way to build a sporting culture is not only to pay top players a fortune and give promising youngsters special attention, but also to foster grassroots participation across the nation. Personal participation, whether in sport or art, is also likely to enhance our interest as spectators, though that isn't the main point.

The more you look at the ills of contemporary society – alienation, fragmentation, isolation, depression – the more compelling the need for community participation in the arts seems. What better way of fostering a sense of community, promoting mental health and wellbeing, and reducing the pressures of a competitive, materialistic society than by encouraging widespread participation in the arts?

Learning to paint or write (in a class that creates its own sense of belonging), putting on plays and musicals, organising festivals, making movies, taking up photography, puppetry or tapestry, singing in choirs, dancing, playing in bands . . . these are pathways to mental health for people whose daily lives are mostly spent in non-creative pursuits.

We talk endlessly about the need for 'balance', by which we usually mean the balance between work, family and leisure. But there's another quite magical possibility: balancing the stresses, disappointments and tedium of life with the therapeutic release of tension through some form of regular creative outlet.

Many people recall with intense pleasure their participation in school plays, orchestras, choirs and art classes. Sometimes they look back wistfully and wonder where all that pleasure (and all that talent) went. Why did it stop when they left school? And why couldn't it be recaptured?

At the turn of the century, the prime minister dreamed of a nation of shareholders, enriched by their participation in the adventure of capitalism. A parallel goal of governments could be to create a nation of individuals and communities enriched through their participation in the arts adventure. Perhaps it's time to dust off all those abandoned Schools of Arts across the nation, and put them to the use for which they were originally intended.

One small step: What can an individual do?

I used to think 'there is no such thing as society' was one of the silliest things ever said by the former British prime minister, Margaret Thatcher. But now I wonder if there's a deep wisdom in it. What Thatcher so famously said in a 1987 interview for *Women's Own* magazine was this: 'There is no such thing as society. There are individual men and women, and there are families. And no government can do anything except through people, and people must look to themselves first. It's our duty to look after ourselves first and then also to look after our neighbour. People have got the entitlements too much in mind, without the obligations.'

Of course, there *is* such a thing as society; like 'the community', it's a bit hard to see, because we're all in it. It's our sense of society that produces our moral sense: we act out of altruism, courage, heroism or compassion precisely because we feel part of a larger whole. But it's true, as Thatcher implied, that if we are to enrich this thing called society, we must examine how we are acting *towards each other*, rather than on a large stage called 'society'.

Our relationships with each other are the source of our life's meaning. Our sense of personal identity only exists in the context of those relationships. Communication is not only our currency, but our life force. Society is like an electricity grid, humming with energy and potential power, and we must tap into it if we are to share that power – not in a grandiose bid to change the world or solve the problems of society, but through local, individual, personal influence.

We are born to communicate, to join, to connect and to share. When we deny those natural impulses, we diminish ourselves. When we cling to our infantile narcissism or give ourselves up to enmity based on religious, social, ethnic, political or other prejudice, we inhibit the full flowering of the noblest and richest human possibilities within us. When we embrace materialism and enshrine it as our core value – as Australia is in danger of doing – we not only let 'the economy' obscure our view of society, but we nurture the crazy idea that our wealth defines our worth. (If that's true, more is bound to be better, so get back on the treadmill right now.)

Given the many challenges facing us, what can an individual hope to achieve? Every step we take, every move we make, helps shape the kind of society we will become. Example counts. Every ripple travels . . .

You'd like to see a more peaceful world? Join a protest march, by all means, but first make peace with your family, your friends, your neighbours, your colleagues. You're appalled by the idea that lonely people can die in their homes, undetected for days? Make sure there's no one in your street suffering that kind of isolation. You think we're becoming media-saturated at the expense of personal relationships? Watch less; talk more.

You're worried about the rise of fundamentalism – in religion, economics, politics and elsewhere? Reject facile answers and resist the tug of simple certainty. Hold on to your scepticism about *everything* (everything but love, that is: abandon yourself to that).

You're appalled by bullying? Speak up, every time. You weep over homelessness, disadvantage and poverty? Ring up any of the charities responding to these problems and ask what you can do. (They might need you to drive a minibus, peel spuds, sort clothes or serve meals for a few hours a week.) You think society is suffering from too much busyness, too little courtesy, too little eye contact? Or that loyalty and honesty are things of the past? You think it's outrageous that people don't even know their neighbours' names?

There's no magic wand. You exist in a circle. Join the dots.

Acknowledgments

The book draws heavily on material from *The Ipsos Mackay Report*, and I am grateful to Ipsos Australia for permission to quote from the reports.

Tony Sernack and Diana Rickard of The Donington Group commissioned me to write a series of articles about social trends for their corporate newsletter and have graciously allowed me to use edited extracts from several of those articles.

Sections of several chapters began life as newspaper columns for *The Sydney Morning Herald, The Age, The West Australian* and the *Sun-Herald* and appear here in edited and extended form.

The proposal to tackle another book about social change came from my publisher at Hachette Livre, Bernadette Foley, and she has been generous and assiduous in her support and encouragement. My editor at Hachette, Deonie Fiford, has worked on the project with her characteristic skill, perspicacity, sensitivity and grace.

Max Suich and David Dale, who provided the impetus for me to write my first book, *Reinventing Australia,* were similarly enthusiastic about this project and have offered characteristically astute suggestions and insights.

My wife, Sheila, has been muse, sounding-board and a relentless hunter-gatherer of data, all with unflagging patience and good cheer.

Elizabeth Turnock, Margie Beaumont and Prue Parkhill have worked with me on *The Mackay Report* (which became *The Ipsos Mackay Report* in 2003) for most of its 29-year history, and have been dream colleagues, ever since we began working together on other projects in the 1960s. Rebecca Huntley and Fiona Collis, newest members of the *Ipsos Mackay Report* team, have made significant contributions to the project.

Friends and colleagues have been generous in discussing the themes of the book, and in providing material to assist in the writing. In particular, I want to acknowledge the contributions and support of Julian Wood, Kerrie Collings-Silvey, John Shepherd, Margaret Sanders, Bruce Kaye, Keith Mason, Betty Byrne Henderson, Nina Walker, Peter Bruce and Lauren Hendry Parsons.

Finally...my respondents. As a 'hands-on' social researcher, I have always been impressed by the willingness of people to spend time talking about their lives to a total stranger they have admitted to their homes. Their participation makes such intensive research possible; their frankness gives it its integrity. All I really have to do is listen.

Index

ABC 13, 66, 124, 194, 315, 346, 358

Aboriginal and Torres Strait Islander Commission (ATSIC) 246

Aboriginal and Torres Strait Islander peoples 18, 154–5, 246, 260, 303, 356
  apology to Stolen Generations 309, 310, 312–15, 320
  reducing gap in life expectancy 19–20
  taskforce on health and welfare 320–1

Abu Ghraib 249

activism, plea for 369

Adams, Phillip
  Australian, The 267, 306

addictions 356

advertising 248, 326

affluence 8, 326–7

Age, The 42, 109

ageing society 87–8, 206–9

ageism 90

al-Qaeda 13, 308

alcohol 11, 19, 240, 273

anger 10

anti-terrorism legislation 250, 272, 303

anticipatory fear 271

antidepressants 4, 239

anxiety 7, 14, 85, 261, 275, 279

Anzac Day 11

Anzac tradition 156

ANZUS treaty 141

apology to Stolen Generations 309, 310, 312–15, 320

arts funding 361–5

Ascherson, Neal
  The London Review of Books 138

assault 22

Assemblies of God 12, 275

assertiveness 194

assimilation 152

asylum-seekers 149–50, 158, 249, 257, 260, 303, 307, 308

atheism 13

Australian, The 77, 124, 267, 305, 306
Australian Council for Educational Research 82
Australian Council of Trade Unions 48
Australian Education Union 348
Australian identity *see* national identity
Australian Institute of Family Studies 82, 204
Australian Social Trends 211
Australian values *see* values
Australian Wheat Board *see* AWB
Australian Workplace Agreements (AWAs) 298–9, 307
AWB 251–2, 303, 308

baby bonus 185
Baby Boomers 88, 89, 90, 97, 191, 208, 209
backyards 266
banking technology 120
Bashir, Professor Marie 260
Beaconsfield mine disaster 157
Beazley, Kim 252
belief 283
bereavement 213–14, 215, 220, 229
bin Laden, Osama 13
biotechnology 186–7, 219
Birkets, Sven
    Gutenberg Elegies, The 114
birthrate 5, 6, 38, 46, 48, 88, 184–90, 197, 219
Bittman, Michael 201
Blair, Tony 249
Bligh, Anna 321

Blix, Dr Hans 308
blogging 124, 129
body images 10
'boomerang' generation 233
Bouma, Professor Gary 11–12
    Australian Soul 11, 154
Brenchley, Fred
    Sydney Morning Herald 323
Brett, Samantha
    Sydney Morning Herald 124
British Attitudes Survey 138
British identity 138
Bryce, Quentin 318
Buddhism 11, 282
bullying in the workplace 67–9
Burke, Brian 297
Burrow, Sharan 48
Bush, George W. 9, 13, 247, 249, 308
busyness 7, 230

Cadzow, Jane
    Good Weekend 204
Caldwell, J.C.
    Theory of Fertility Decline 225
capitalism 7
carbon neutral policies 333–4
careers 5, 6, 35, 61
Carey, John
    What Good are the Arts? 363
Cartwright, Susan
    The Psychologist 68
casual employment 62, 79
Cavalier, Rodney 337
celebrity, cult of 177
censorship 272–3
Cerulo, Karen

Annual Review of Sociology article 114

charities 260, 326–7

chauvinism 35, 56

childcare 32, 73
  grandparents and 39–42, 95

childlessness 197–8

children
  abuse 19, 273
  child pornography 104
  effect of divorce on 167–9
  equipment 194–5
  gifted and talented 193
  health 21–2
  hostility to 198–201
  indulgence of 191–7
  Little Emperor syndrome 191–7
  pets as substitutes 189–90
  quality time 81, 201
  raising 4, 201–6
  relationship with parents 201–6, 230
  responsibility for 34
  sexual abuse 19
  smallest generation of 190–201
  welfare 21

children overboard incident 303

Christianity 11–14

church attendance 11

citizenship 151

climate change *see* global warming

Clinton, Bill 304

coaching 193

Coalition 13
  electoral defeat 2007 302–11

collective guilt 314

Commonwealth Scientific and Industrial Research Organisation (CSIRO) 334

communication, method of 4, 111, 367
  emails 23–4, 74–5, 99–101, 111, 112, 117, 122, 135
  mobile phones 117–20, 125
  short cuts 122
  text messaging 6, 24, 111, 112, 122, 132

community, sense of 14–15, 285–92

compassion 256–62

connectedness 111–16
  lack of 10
  mobile phones 119–20
  tribal generation 288–92

Connors, Lyndsay
  Making Federalism Work for Schools 349

consumerism 7, 107–8, 279

consumers, re-engagement of 325–7

contraception 187, 225

control 10, 245–54
  bodies 253
  workplace 71–7

cooking 228

Cooper, Cary
  The Psychologist 68

corporate culture 36, 38

Costello, Peter 21, 87, 90, 185, 252, 297, 304, 309–10

courtship rituals 131–2

Crabb, Annabel
  Sydney Morning Herald 316–17

credit revolution 7, 120–1

crime 22, 258
  economic 68

Cronulla beach riots 148, 295

Dale, David 254
  Sydney Morning Herald 125
  Who We Are 125
Dawkins, Richard
  God Delusion, The 13
  Selfish Gene, The 13
Day, David
  Claiming a Continent 133
de Beauvoir, Simone
  Second Sex, The 45
de Botton, Alain 75
debt 7, 14, 89, 98
  credit revolution 120–1
Denton, Andrew 13
depersonalisation of society 10, 108
depression 7, 85, 288
detention centres for refugees 150,
  257, 307, 308
  inhumane treatment 307
disabilities, people with 355
disengagement 241–52, 264, 278,
  301
divorce 5, 6, 48, 51, 63, 95, 163–9,
  173, 174, 178, 214, 217, 220, 229
domesticity 264–8
Donnelly, Kevin
  Dumbing Down 267
doubts and yearnings 8–11
Downer, Alexander 251
downshifting 86
downsizing 232, 233
drug abuse 11, 57, 240, 258
dumbing down 267

eating 4, 21–2, 23, 227–8

Eckersley, Richard
  Well & Good 87
economic rationalism 275–6
Economist, The 22
economy 7, 63, 247, 318–19
  federal election campaign 2007
    304–9
  petrol prices *see* petrol prices
  restructure 7
  US sub-prime mortgage market
    collapse 318
education 18, 96, 192–3
  birthrate and 187–8
  funding 20–22, 346–53
  public 346–53
egalitarian society 6, 85, 157, 351
elitism 158, 363
emails 24, 74–5, 99–101, 111, 112,
  117, 122, 135
Emerson, Dr Craig 320
employment 4
  erosion of permanent full-time
    work 62
  service industries 70
employment patterns 62
empty nests 229–34
energy sources 336
entertainment 4, 126
environment 294, 312, 324
equality
  gender 27–31
  New Bloke and 57, 59
  workforce 34–6
escapism 268
Eureka Stockade 156
Exclusive Brethren 12, 351
'executive plunder' 357

Facebook 129, 130
Faiola, Anthony
  Washington Post 94
'fair go' 157, 158, 279
families 73
  long working hours and 80–2, 86
  one-parent 211
  surrogate extended 289–92
Family First 12
Family Law Act 1975 51, 165
fast food 122
fatigue 10
Faulkner, John 307
fear 9, 269–71
federal election 1996 242
federal election 2007 302–11
Fels, Alan
  Sydney Morning Herald 323
feminism 12, 27–31, 42–9
Ferguson, Martin 321, 322
fertility 185–7
'flaming' 104
Flannery, Tim
  Weather Makers, The 331
flexibility 16
  working arrangements 38, 71–7
food 21–2, 144
Ford, Richard
  New York Times article 134
free market beliefs 275–7
freedom 7, 221
Freedom of Information laws 321
Friedan, Betty
  Feminine Mystique, The 45
Friendster 130
Fryer, David

Australian Journal of Social Research
  82
Fukuyama, Francis
  Journal of Democracy article 146
fundamentalism 12, 13, 274, 275,
  282, 368

gambling 11, 278
gardens 266
Gare, Shelley
  *The Triumph of the Airheads and
    the Retreat from Commonsense*
  127, 267
Garnaut, John
  Sydney Morning Herald 357, 358
Garrett, Peter 321
Gates, Bill 99, 112
gender differences 59
gender revolution 7, 27–60, 219, 356
  background to women's movement
    42–9
  men and 49–55
generational attitudes 6, 16
  marriage 170–6
  privacy 128–31
  under-thirties and employment
    96–8
  women and feminism/liberation
    27–31
GetUp 296–7, 328
Gittins, Ross 79, 306, 348
glass ceiling 35, 36
global inflation 323
global warming 14, 151, 239, 277,
  294, 297, 300, 309, 331–6
globalisation 62, 245, 247
Glover, Richard 195

Sydney Morning Herald Spectrum 199–200
Gore, Al
  Inconvenient Truth, An 331
governor-general 318, 343
grandparents 39–42, 95, 165–6
Great Australian Dream 15–17
greed 357, 359
Greenpeace 321
Greer, Germaine
  Female Eunuch, The 42, 45, 49
Greig, Alastair
  Inequality in Australia 21
grey power 206
GST 244, 246, 259, 311, 359
guilt and shame 313–14

Habib, Mamdouh 303
Hamilton, Clive
  Affluenza 87
Hand, Jenna
  Sydney Morning Herald article 129, 130
Haneef, Mohammed 303
Hanson, Pauline 146, 244
Harding, Professor Ann 85
Harris, Sam
  Letter to a Christian Nation 14
Hartcher, Peter 323
  Quarterly Essay 25 241
Hawke, Bob 242
head of state debate 343–5
health 82, 246
health care 9
  Indigenous people 18, 19–20, 246
helicopter parenting 196
herd instinct 224–9

Hicks, David 296, 303
'highbrow'/elite arts 363, 364
HILDA survey 82, 253
Hillsong Church 12, 275
hip-hop activism 297
Hitchens, Christopher
  God is Not Great 14
HIV/AIDS 288
holidays 240
home ownership 15, 16, 89
home renovation craze 3, 253, 264–5, 300
home security industry 253–4
hope 311, 328
Horin, Adele
  Sydney Morning Herald article 168
Horne, Donald 63
hospitals, public 9–10
Household, Income and Labour Dynamics in Australia (HILDA) *see* HILDA
households
  group 6
  shrinking 6, 210–36
  young people staying at home 7, 229–31
houses
  buyers 6
  prices 14, 355
  renters 6, 15, 16–17
  size of 222–4
housework 32, 37, 51
Howard, John 9, 77, 147, 150, 243–4, 248, 249, 252, 255, 260, 300, 301, 302, 304, 306, 308, 309–11, 314, 319, 320, 346

Human Rights and Equal
  Opportunities Commission
  *It's About Time – Women, Work,
    Men and Family* 73
  treatment of asylum-seekers
    evidence 307
Huntley, Rebecca
  World According to Y, The 96,
    180–1
Hussein, Saddam 251, 308

IBIS*World* 22, 84
illness 356
immigrants 9, 145, 257, 258–9
incomes 83–4, 357–8
Indigenous people 18, 19–20,
  154–5, 246, 260, 356
  apology to Stolen Generations
    312–15, 320
industrial relations laws 64, 65 *see
  also* Work Choices
inequality 358–60
infidelity 104
informality 22–4
information technology revolution 6,
  7, 74, 99–136
  consumerism 107–8
  courtship rituals 131–2
  dependence on 108
  depersonalisation of society 108
  divisive influence 110–11
  effects 101–7
  employment and 108
  moral dangers of 134–6
  obsolescence 109, 110
  personal interaction 111–16

privacy 6, 33, 108, 114, 128–31
  security 108, 128
inhibitory fear 269–70
inner-city communities 15, 228–9
insecurity 15
Insight 315
integration 152
interest rates 14, 319, 325
International Whaling Commission
  (IWC) 321
internet 103–7, 115, 117, 234
  democracy and 132–4
  privacy 128–31
  romance on 131–2
  sleep deprivation 106–7
  surveys online 133
  virtual worlds 115–16
intimacy 114
Ipsos Mackay Report 16, 33, 65, 74,
  85, 96, 105, 120, 125, 223, 235,
  251, 257, 260
  Australians at Home 223, 232
  Australians at Work 65, 66, 74, 78,
    85, 96, 97, 251
  Home Alone 215, 218
  Living with Debt 16, 120, 121
  Mothers & Daughters 33
  What We Do with Television 125,
    235
Iraq war 142, 151, 241, 247–9, 263,
  265, 296, 303, 308
Islam, militant 14

job insecurity 6, 61, 62, 63–4, 98
Jones, Barry 13
Jones, Tony 298
Joyce, Barnaby 340

Karpf, Anna
  Sydney Morning Herald 129
Keating, Paul 242–3, 297–8, 301,
  302
Keig, David 125
Kelly, Paul
  Weekend Australian 309
Knowles, David
  Australian Financial Review 326
Kyoto Protocol 310, 412

Labor Party 9, 12, 15, 298, 303,
  304–9
Lane, Terry 358
language 23–4
  gender neutral 52
  illegals 257, 260
  information technology and
    99–101
  unAustralian, meaning of 141–4
Laski, Marghanita
  Everyday Ecstasy 363
Lateline 298
Latham, Mark 12
Lawrie, Ross 155
leadership 324
learning difficulties 93
Lebovic, Sol 241
Lewis, Shari
  One-minute Bedtime Stories 123
Liberal Party 243
life expectancy 88
  Indigenous people 18, 19–20
lifestyle 15, 16, 30
lifestyle programs 2–4, 293, 327
Little Emperor syndrome 191–7

living alone 212–22
  changing attitudes to 218–19
loneliness 213, 215–16
longevity 6, 220
Lovelock, James
  Revenge of Gaia, The 331
'lowbrow'/popular arts 363
'lucky country' 63

McCallum, Professor Ron 66
Macfarlane, Ian 97
McGaw, Professor Barry 349
  New Matilda 20
Mackay, Hugh
  Generations 171–2
  Media Mania 132
  Reinventing Australia 51, 110,
    121, 164, 271
Mackay Report 102, 107, 148, 186,
  243, 244, 248
  Computers, Technology & the Future
    102
  Living with Technology 107
  Turning 30 186
McKinsey Quarterly, The 132
McMansion phenomenon 224
Mann, Sandi
  The Psychologist 75
market democrats 320
Marr, David 12
  Dark Victory 259
marriage 4, 5, 16, 29, 35, 48, 49, 51,
  61, 81, 163–4, 225
  cult of perfectionism 176–80
  institutional versus instrumental
    view of 173–6

legalised and de facto, blurring of distinction 175
postponement 169–73, 180–1
Marriage Guidance Council of Australia 175
masculinity, authentic 60
mass media, role of 234–6, 280, 327
materialism 7, 10, 14, 57, 86, 108, 230, 240, 258, 280, 295, 325, 367
maternity leave 73, 74
mateship 55, 157, 279
Medicare 9
Meet the Street program 287
Megalogenis, George
  Weekend Australian 83
Melbourne Institute of Applied and Social Research 82
men
  care of children 34–5, 50
  effect of women's movement on 49–55
  retired husband syndrome (RHS) 91–6
  sensitivity 53
  SNAGs 53–4
  work/family/leisure balance 38–9
mental health 107
Menzies, Robert 347
metrosexuals 54–5
Millett, Kate
  Sexual Politics 45
Mind & Mood reports 8, 55, 56, 148, 243, 244, 248, 257, 258, 260, 263, 265, 266
ministerial impropriety 340–1
mobile phones 117–20, 135, 168
Modjeska, Drusilla 313–14

monarchy 342–5
Moore, Matthew
  Sydney Morning Herald 321
Moorhouse, Frank 272
  Griffith Review, The 250
moral dilemmas 14
mortgages 5
mothers 31–9, 46
  paid employment 34–9, 73, 86
multiculturalism 144–53, 295
music 362
Muslims in Australia 13, 145–7, 260, 295
MySpace 129, 130, 135

narcissism 278, 367
National Centre for Social and Economic Modelling 83, 89
National Health Survey 87
national identity
  Asia Pacific region and 140
  attitudes to Muslims 145–7
  Australian values 154–8
  Britishness 138–9
  citizenship tests 151
  diversity 137, 159
  multiculturalism 144–53
  unAustralian, meaning of 141–4
  US ties 140–1
National Interest, The 358
National Multicultural Advisory Board 147
neighbourhoods 285–8
Nelson, Brendan 310, 321, 323
New Bloke 55–60, 174
New South Wales Premier's Literary Awards 313

New South Wales Public Education
  Alliance 349
New Yorker 99, 100
Newman, Dr Louise 307
Newman, Professor Peter
  West Australian, The 333
Newspoll 241, 248, 296, 300, 303,
  322
nuclear debate 294–5, 334–5
nutrition 18

Oakley, Barry 124
obesity 21–2, 199, 200, 278
oil-for-food program 251
oil prices 319, 321–2 *see also* petrol
  prices
One Nation 146, 244
online dating 132
open-plan living 223
openness in communication 33
optimism 327–8
Opus Dei 12
Organisation for Economic Co-
  operation and Development
  (OECD) 20, 73, 83
overgovernment 341
overregulation 271–4
overwork 62, 68, 79–85
Oxfam 18

Pacific Solution 249–50
parenthood 30, 56
  cultural status 198–9
  Little Emperor syndrome 191–7
  overprotective 192, 196–7
  postponement of 5, 16, 184
parenting 201–6

parenting books 204
parliamentary process 338
part-time work 38, 79
participation in sport and arts 364–5
passive welfare 19
Peacock, Andrew 243
Pearson, Noel 19
perfectionism 176–80
permanence 16
personal relationships 81
personal responsibility 272–3
personality politics 337–8
Petrie, Daniel 326
petrol prices 322–4 *see also* oil prices
pets 189–90, 216, 266
Peyton, P.R.
  Dignity at Work 69
philanthropy 326
plagiarism 106
planning 6
political pressure groups 12
political stability 9
politics
  change of federal government
    2007 302–11
  conscience votes 340
  disengagement from 7, 241–52
  government incumbency 255–6, 293
  improving the system 337–41
  lies and deception 251–2
  personality politics 337–8
  post-election euphoria 319–22
  re-engagement with 302–28
  religion and 12–13
  two-party system 339
  voting behaviour 255–6, 293–4,
    302–11

politics of fear 269, 310

pornography 19, 31, 103, 273

Postman, Neil
Age, The 109
Amusing Ourselves to Death 109

poverty 18, 85, 354–60, 368
causes 355–6
definition 354

powerlessness 246, 248, 256, 275

practical reconciliation 246

Prechter, Robert
The Wave Principle of Human Social Behaviour and the New Science of Socionomics 300

prejudice 149, 256–62, 313, 367

pressure 10

PricewaterhouseCoopers 68

privacy 6, 33, 114
redefining 128–31

productivity 20

profit motive 65, 67

prohibition 273

prosperity 8, 83, 241, 359

Protestant fundamentalism 12, 275

Pryor, Lisa
Sydney Morning Herald 229

public education 346–53

public funding of the arts 361–5

Question Time 338–9

racism 150, 261–2, 295

radio 234–5

Rau, Cornelia 303

raunch culture 12, 31

reactions to societal changes 239–40

recession 63, 64, 97, 243

reconciliation movement 246, 303, 309
apology to Stolen Generations 312–15, 320

recreational drugs 57, 282

Reduced Social Interaction syndrome 113

referendum 1999 245

refocusing 90, 91

refugees 9, 150–1

relationships 367
breakdown of 165–9
cult of perfectionism 176–80
marriage 163–76
parent/child 201–6, 230

Relationships Australia 175

Relationships Forum Australia 82
Unexpected Tragedy, An 80, 295

religion 11–15, 154–5, 274–5, 283–4, 286

religious conflicts 13

renovation obsession 3, 253, 264–5, 300

reproduction, assisted 186–7

republicanism 318, 342–5

resources boom 63, 66, 241, 305

retail therapy 266–7, 325

retired husband syndrome (RHS) 91–6

retirement 87–91
men 91–6

rich and poor, gap 8, 82–5, 157–8, 357

Riemer, Andrew 156
Where to Now?: Australia's Identity in the Nineties 137

Rudd, Kevin 9, 12–13, 19, 20, 251, 297, 298, 300, 302, 304, 305, 306, 308, 309, 311, 318, 319, 320, 323

schools 12, 192, 201–2 *see also* education; public education
  attendance 19
  Catholic systemic 346, 347
  church-based private 14
  private 41, 346–7
  sharing facilities 352–3
sea change 233
Second Life 115–16
Secret, The 274
self-employment 77–9
self-esteem 194
self-help books 274
self-indulgence 278
selfishness 10
Sensis 74
sexual abuse 19
sexual permissiveness 11, 14
Smith, Adam
  Theory of Moral Sentiments 276
  Wealth of Nations, The 276
SNAGs 53–4
Snow, Deborah 152
societal change 5–7, 239–40, 264
society, sense of 367
solar power 334
Sorry Day 246
South Australian Housing Trust 351
speed 121–8, 258
  attention spans 124–6
  boredom thresholds 126
  communications 122
  dating 123–4

fast food 122
  short breaks 123
Speed Cleaning 123
spin doctors 248
spirituality 11, 14, 282
sport 158, 194, 266, 364
Spotless 123, 266
stability 16
  paid work 61
Stateline 346
Stern, Nicholas
  Economics of Climate Change, The 331
Stolen Generations 310, 312–15, 320
stress 8, 23, 72, 75, 258
Stretton, Hugh
  Australia Fair 358
  Ideas for Australian Cities 357
substance abuse 19
Summers, Anne
  End of Equality, The 47
Supermum, life and death of 31–4
  granny backlash 39–42
Swan, Wayne 304, 305
Sweeney Research
  Eye on Australia 111
Sydney Institute 320
Sydney Morning Herald 12, 79, 124, 125, 129, 152, 168, 200, 229, 298, 306, 316–17, 321, 322, 348, 357
symbolism 314, 317

Talent2 37
talkback radio 234–5
Tampa 150, 259, 303
tax cuts 304–6

taxation burden 88
Taysom, A.R. 43–4
technology
    effect of 10
    resistance to 135
    teleworking 74
television 124–5, 202, 234, 235–6, 254–5
terrorism 14, 239, 241, 248, 264
Thatcher, Margaret 367
Thorpe, Ian 55
Throsby, Margaret 66
tolerance 9, 145, 150, 159, 256–62
trade unions 66–7
tranquillisers 4, 239
transience 16, 71
travel 240
tree change 233
trends 6
    cultural 87
    demographic 87, 207, 212
    marriage and divorce 163–4
tribal generation 288–92
Trujillo, Sol 74, 113, 132
trustworthiness 258, 274
2020 Summit 312, 315–17
2000 Olympics 245
2001 terrorism attacks 247
Turnbull, Malcolm 133, 310

UK-born residents, proportion of 139
unAustralian, meaning of 141–4
underemployment 79–85
unemployment 63–4, 79, 191, 245, 319
UNICEF 21

universities 20–1
uranium 334
urban planning 287
USA, attitudes to 140–1

Vaile, Mark 251
values 11, 16, 258, 279–83, 295
    Australian 154–8
    religion and 14
viewing habits 254–5
violence 10, 147
    domestic 47
virtual worlds 115–16
voting 255–6, 293–4, 302–11

water conservation 324, 335
Watson, Don
    Death Sentence 267
wealth, redistribution of 82–5
weddings 178–80
Welch, Dylan 152
Wikipedia 105
Wilkinson, Marian
    Dark Victory 259
Williams, Pamela
    Australian Financial Review 310
Winefield, Anthony
    Australian Journal of Social Research 82
Wise, Sarah 204
women
    average earnings 47–8
    feminism and 27–31
    fertility 185–7
    oppression 46
    representation in Rudd government 317

retirement and 92
subserviant roles 12
workforce participation 5, 32–9,
     34, 35, 62–3
women's magazines 127
Women's Own 367
work, attitudes to 85–7
Work Choices 65–7, 250–1, 293,
     298–9, 303, 307, 3 0, 311, 328
work/leisure balance 37, 280–1, 365
work, redistribution of 79–85
working poor 355
workplace environment 64–9
  boredom 75
  bullying 67–9
  casual Friday concept 72
  email stress 75

feminisation of 37, 69–71
'hotdesk' 76
workplace revolution 7, 61–98
  gender 34–9

xenophobia 147

Year Book 79
young people 6
  appeal of conservative religious
     groups 12
  attitudes to work 61–2, 72, 96–8
  poverty and 356
  renting 15
youth suicide 288
Youth Summit 316
YouTube 135